# BE A REVOLUTION

# BE A REVOLUTION

## HOW EVERYDAY PEOPLE ARE FIGHTING OPPRESSION

## AND CHANGING THE WORLD—AND HOW YOU CAN, TOO

# IJEOMA OLUO

**HarperOne**

*An Imprint of HarperCollinsPublishers*

HarperCollins books may be purchased for educational, business, or sales promotional use. For information, please email the Special Markets Department at SPsales@harpercollins.com.

FIRST EDITION

Library of Congress Cataloging-in-Publication Data has been applied for.

ISBN 978-0-06-314018-9

23 24 25 26 27 LBC 5 4 3 2 1

*To my mom: thank you for teaching me that love is an action.*

# CONTENTS

IF YOU WRITE OR speak on issues of race and racism, you'll often hear statements and questions like these:

"Racism is horrible. I wish there was something I could do."

"Racism is horrible. But it's too big of a problem to know where to start."

"We won't be able to fix racism until we get a new great leader like Martin Luther King Jr."

"When is somebody going to do something about racism?"

"I wish I could do something about racism, but I'm not an activist."

Often, if I don't have a quick, clear response to these questions and statements, people become frustrated. Am I actually an expert on racism if I can't *solve* racism? Others don't come to a talk or read a book for solutions. The simple act of engaging with the work of anti-racist scholars is enough. Feeling bad about racism is the same thing as doing something about racism, right?

But in all seriousness, systemic racism is a very complex and vast issue with no one solution. And many people with the sincerest of intentions to make a difference don't know where to start. We know something needs to be done—in fact, it seems like *everything* needs to be done. So where do we find our part? Is there a part in this work for us at all?

When we're overwhelmed by the scope of the problem, or the lack of clear guidance on next steps, we may default to sharing a status on social media, signing a petition, hoping somebody will announce a protest online in our neighborhood that we can join, or sending a few dollars to one of the more well-known anti-racist organizations we've heard of.

I've spent most of my writing career trying to explain these complex issues in an accessible way, so people will have a better chance of putting that understanding to work. But I'm not a movement organizer. It's not a fit for my personality or my skill set. One thing I hope will be clear in this book is that we all have different work to do in the fight for liberation, and writing is my space right now.

I cannot give people their own personal path through movement work. I cannot mentor frontline movement workers. I cannot organize the protests for you to join. (I can't organize anything at all, actually—as evidenced by the *51,000* unread emails currently sitting in my inbox that will never be sorted, replied to, or deleted. They just...live there now.) But I can show you some of the paths that others have taken in their revolutionary journeys. I can show you how people with vastly different skills, abilities, privileges, experiences, and more have found their own place in movement work, and have been creating vital change within those spaces. I can show you that no matter who you are, if you want to be involved in this revolution, there is a space for you.

I didn't write this book only for what it might give others. In fact, one of my greatest motivations was what I hoped the book might give me.

By the time I sat down to figure out what my next project would be, I had been writing books on racism in America for five years straight. My first book, *So You Want to Talk About Race*, had me neck-deep in my own personal history with racism. My second book, *Mediocre: The Dangerous Legacy of White Male America*, had me neck-deep in the history of violent white male supremacy in the US.

After five years on these projects, I was done. My heart and soul as a Black woman were so hurt. I had spent years of my time and talent in places of pain and horror—and yes, I'm very proud of what I was able to create from those places. But whatever limits I had set, I'd long since worked past them and I felt wrung dry. In some of my most difficult moments, it was the support of my family and the support of others in the anti-racist movement community—especially Black women—who cared for me, and gave me the safety and space to continue to move forward.

My initial plan, after finishing my last book tour, was to just spend time in community. Spend time with people who were proving every single day that all was not lost, that every day there was vital work to do, work that was providing important victories for the people we love.

But as I spent more time planning the beginning of my healing journey, I realized I wanted my words and work to go toward sharing the stories and insights of these amazing people who give me hope every single day.

Once I decided this would be my next book, I was excited to begin. I knew it would likely be an enriching and challenging project for me.

But I was not prepared for how changed I would be by this book.

The hours upon hours of conversations I have been able to have with movement workers have fundamentally changed the way I see this work, and my place in it. I feel opened up to possibility in a way I never have before. I feel more hopeful of what we can accomplish than I ever have.

This project has not been easy. I've never felt so challenged as a writer or a movement worker in my life. And every step of the way I have felt blessed.

The generosity of each person who sat down to talk with me, who shared their wisdom and experience, is of such a magnitude that I will be forever grateful for it. And I hope I have been able to honor that generosity, in whatever way I can, in these pages.

This has been the most beautiful and transformative writing experience of my life. I have seen what revolution looks like in the everyday. It looks a lot like love. And I hope, as you read these testimonies of these amazing people, that you will find your own revolution as well.

## AUTHOR'S NOTE

WHEN WE TRY TO write with care, we're faced with dozens of decisions on every page about what words we'll choose and what impact those words may have on readers. In writing about the politics of race and ethnicity, disability, gender, sexuality, and other social issues, those choices are of vital importance, and impossible to get perfectly right.

I have, in this book, tried to balance readability, understandability, respect, and care. I have tried to remove as many ableist phrases and words from my writing as I could. I have tried to stay away from cisnormativity and heteronormativity as much as possible. And yet I know that all of this and more will surely be found to some extent in these pages.

Where the people profiled in this book have referred to themselves and their peers in terms that others may not be comfortable with, I have left those descriptions as they said them to me. Most of the people in this book prefer identity-first language (e.g., "disabled" instead of "person with a disability"). This is, I have found, preferred in the majority of social justice spaces, and so I have used identity-first language throughout this book. But I'm aware there is a generational gap with regards to this language, and there are plenty of people in the disability community and other communities who prefer person-first language. If you are in one of these marginalized groups and prefer to refer to yourself differently than how people have referred to themselves in this book, that is your prerogative, and I respect that as much as I respect how the people in this book have referred to themselves. If you are outside of one of these groups and are uncomfortable with how people in these pages have referred to themselves, this is a good opportunity to sit with discomfort for a moment and try to investigate its root causes. We have the right to define ourselves, and the removal of that right is one of the strongest tools of oppression.

For the most part, when writing about women, I am referring to all women—inclusive of trans women. When writing about trans people specifically, I have tried to say trans people. When writing about people of color, I am writing about all people who are not white. I alternate between "people of color" and "BIPOC" (Black, Indigenous, and other people of color) as more of a stylistic choice. I know that some prefer BIPOC over POC, because many white people use POC to avoid addressing issues facing Black and Indigenous communities. But I've found that white people just as easily do the same with BIPOC, and I'm tired of changing my vocabulary to avoid the unavoidable. At the end of the day, we know when people are being genuine, and we know when people are being anti-Black or anti-Indigenous, regardless of what words they use. When I'm talking about Black people, Indigenous people, Asian people, or Latine people specifically, I will say "Black" or "Indigenous" or "Asian" or "Latine."

Queer and trans BIPOC have long been at the forefront of revolutionary liberation work. So it should be no surprise that you will see a variety of pronouns used in these pages, and some people prefer no pronouns at all. This does have a stylistic impact on some of the sentence construction in this book that may feel unfamiliar to the reader at first, but these sorts of adjustments are the bare minimum we can do to respect people and their identities.

Finally, I hope you will see in these pages the love and care with which I have chosen my words. Everything I have written has been written with deep respect for the people I've spoken with and the communities they are from. But there will likely be places where my language choice is not optimal, where I may not be aware of harm in my choices, or where harm cannot be reasonably avoided. Over the years, our language continues to shift to address terms and phrases that are harmful, so some of my word choices may be seen as out-of-date or insensitive. For that, I apologize for any harm caused and hope that we can have a continued dialogue about the power of our words, how to address the biases and oppressions built into our language, and find ways to communicate and connect with one another that are less harmful and more healing.

## PUNISHMENT, ACCOUNTABILITY, AND ABOLITION

WHEN I FIRST STARTED my activist work, I spoke the language of reform. I knew all the stats. I knew the history of our carceral systems. I knew how bloody and deeply broken they were. My writing started with the brutal killing of a Black child, Trayvon Martin, and with the refusal of our criminal justice system to see that Black child's life as worthy of justice.

I had friends and family who had been beaten by police officers. They had bones broken. They needed stitches. In my first-ever interaction with a police officer as a teen driver, he reached for his gun because I bent over to get my registration out of the glove box without assuring him that I wasn't reaching for a weapon first.

My heart would race every time a police car pulled up behind me on the road. I would frantically check my speed, hope my taillights and blinkers were working, try to remember if my registration tags had expired. I would wonder if I should call someone, just in case.

When I was gardening in my yard and cops responded to a call next door, I nervously dropped my pruning shears to the ground, lest they think I was carrying a weapon.

And still, I talked of reform.

I talked of reform not because I didn't believe in or want abolition but because I didn't believe it was possible. Because the people who spoke openly or loudly about it were told they were too radical, were often pushed out of the room. And when it came to policing, I desperately wanted change, some sort of change.

So I talked about reform. I talked about oversight. I talked about more Black and brown officers. I talked about more accountability. I talked about training.

I didn't talk about the thing I wanted most of all: for it not to exist.

Not any of it. The cops, the courts, the cells. I didn't want any of it to exist anymore.

And that's because while I dreamed of abolition, I didn't really understand it. I didn't understand the work of it. I didn't get that the same people being kicked out of rooms for talking about a world without cops were also building new rooms of their own. I didn't get that when they were told they were asking for too much, they were showing us that we were asking for too little.

Then suddenly people were saying, "Defund the police." Yes, some people had always been saying it. But more people were, and yes, people were still saying it was an unreasonable ask, an impossible one. And yet others were asking, "What do you mean by that?"

And suddenly conversations that had been pushed to the fringe for decades were everywhere. "What is abolition?" "What does it mean to defund the police?" "Do you really mean defund the police?" "Do you really mean no cops?"

And I realized that I had fallen victim to one of white supremacy's greatest weapons: the war on imagination.

In our heavily carceral systems, abolition requires strength and resilience. But it also requires the audacity of unapologetic imagination. It requires that we cast aside what we've been told is possible, what we've been told is the best we have to hope for, and try to build from our wildest dreams.

We're discouraged from even daring to imagine the possibility of such a future. We're told that this is the best system we can get. We're told that the alternatives are much worse. We're fed fear of the unknown. We're made to doubt ourselves and our capabilities. If we don't set our imaginations aside to settle for incremental change, we're punished. We're disinvited from the table altogether. We're the reason why nobody gets *anything* now.

But please believe me when I say this: we're already living the worst-case scenario. Set aside the fear that has been pumped into us all each and every day and take an honest look at where we are right now.

We live in a country that has the highest incarceration rate in the world. A country where one in eighty-one Black adults is currently behind bars. Where Black people make up over half of the prison population in twelve states. Where police kill hundreds of people a year, and yet only a handful ever even see a trial for those killings. We live in a country with all of this incarceration, all of this police brutality, and yet only 3 percent of rapists ever see jail time for rape. Women trying to leave abusive partners are regularly denied effective protection. In fact, people married to police officers are at an increased risk of abuse in their marriages. Studies have shown that between 28 and 40 percent of officers abuse or have abused their intimate partners or children (Nellis 2021; Blumenstein 2009; Klugman 2020).

We give up a large percentage of our population—millions

of people—to the violence and isolation of prison. We routinely subject disabled people and people of color to violence and even death at routine traffic stops and wellness checks. We live with the reality that one in five women will be sexually assaulted and the overwhelming chances that the person who assaulted us will never face any accountability, nor will anything be done to ensure they won't offend again. We let our children get dragged off to jail cells from their schools for arguing with teachers or fighting in the halls.

All of that because we're told it would be so much worse if we didn't have this system, if we didn't know we could call a number and someone trained to kill—someone who sees people of color and anyone with a disability as a potential threat—would arrive at our doors.

How much worse do you really think it could get?

If we're not living the worst-case scenario right now, I argue that the worst case lies in the direction of *more* cops, not fewer. With more and more people targeted by a system that sees people as irredeemable, that sees a human being in crisis as a mortal threat. As the system sucks up the resources we could use to address the root causes of crime and violence, and uses it to further empower officers who can arrive only after the violence has occurred, and who regularly add their own devastating violence to the situation.

How many more people will be lost to this system of punishment if we don't choose a different course? How many more of our resources will be stolen from our communities? How many more rights will we lose? Those are the what-ifs that keep me up at night, and yet we're told that the real nightmare is what could happen if we said, "No more," turned away from what has always harmed us, and turned toward our belief in ourselves and one another, our ability to build something new and better.

There are people who have been living in their faith in humanity for a long time now, who have been working to build something new and better. And they really, really hope you—and I—will join them.

## RICHIE RESEDA AND MANNIE THOMAS

The first time I was arrested, I was eleven. For playing too rough," Richie Reseda says to me, matter-of-factly.

I know this happens to Black kids. I know it happens far more often than many people would think. I've heard the stories; I've read and even written about the statistics. It's my job to know this. And yet this sentence still hits me in the gut as a mother, as a Black woman.

Eleven.

"The first time I had a negative interaction with the police, I was four. The first time I was kicked out of a class, I was—I don't know—maybe eight," Reseda continues at a clipped pace. "I just experienced a lot of suffering as a child at the hands of the police state and the education system, which, in many places—but especially in Los Angeles—are the same."

Like many other Black men, Richie Reseda was criminalized by the prison-industrial complex as a young child. Years that were supposed to be safe, that were supposed to be defined by play and discovery and adventure, were instead defined by violence and incarceration. Black students are almost four times as likely as white students to be suspended from school, and 2.3 times as likely as white students to be referred to law enforcement by their schools (UNCF, n.d.).

By the time Reseda was fourteen, he had been arrested numerous times. He was failing school and selling drugs. And it was at this time—as a young teen trapped in systems of poverty, racism, toxic masculinity, and violence—that he met his political mentors:

Patrisse Cullors and Mark Anthony. Reseda was not a "reformed" kid when he met them, and he wasn't "reformed" after working with them. He was politicized. He was met where he was at, without shame, and given systemic explanations for why his world was the way it was. Reseda was empowered to change it without being excluded or devalued.

Reseda began working with Cullors and Anthony on local organizing campaigns. His first campaigns were to stop fare hikes on Los Angeles buses, and to decriminalize truancy and remove police officers from Los Angeles schools.

This organizing helped give Reseda focus and healthy examples of community, but he was still trapped in unhealthy cycles of poverty and violence, which led to his imprisonment for armed robbery at the age of nineteen, sentenced to ten years.

For many people, that is the end of their story—or at least many others in society would like to think it is. A bad person gets locked away where they belong. They're gone and no longer our problem. Even a nineteen-year-old child (yes, as a mother of a twenty-two-year-old and a sixteen-year-old, I will say with confidence he was still a child) is labeled irredeemable by our carceral systems, and our carceral society. This does immense damage in our communities, particularly Black communities, where our loved ones—our children, our partners, our parents—are routinely locked away for the ways in which systemic oppression, intergenerational trauma, and forced white supremacist patriarchy manifest themselves.

Our prisons don't reform people. Our prisons don't heal people. If Reseda was going to be able to one day build a life for himself out of prison, he was going to have to create his own healing space within one of the most harmful systems in our society.

It was in prison that Reseda deepened his organizing work. He found Black feminist theory and, in it, the first real, accurate descriptions of the violent patriarchy that had shaped and harmed him so much. Even while incarcerated and working to get out of prison, Reseda saw that his freedom also lay in breaking away from harmful beliefs and behavioral patterns. He looked around and saw similar internalized harm in those incarcerated with him. So Reseda co-founded his first cultural organization: Success Stories.

"It's a transformative justice organization," Reseda explains. "It's a place for people to transform their beliefs, and therefore their behaviors, by learning Black feminism and engaging with it, and healing from patriarchy together. Cuz I knew patriarchy was central to how I was harming myself, and my community."

Success Stories is more than just talk. It's a thirteen-week workshop series that aims to help incarcerated men heal from violent patriarchy and learn how to handle fear, pain, and conflict in healthier ways based in Black feminist theory. It also helps alumni of the program to connect with job postings, small-business resources, professional wardrobes, and more.

Reseda simultaneously co-founded another organization, Initiate Justice. This organization focuses on getting together people who have been directly affected by our prison–industrial complex to change and pass laws with the goal of ending incarceration. They work to get people released, reduce and commute sentences, change sentencing laws, and much more. Initiate Justice has helped people get free, literally. Reseda included. He was able to go home two years early due to legislation that his organization helped pass.

While he was able to finally leave the California prison system, Reseda's legacy and his work has remained and continues to make a difference in the lives of incarcerated people in California and across the country.

*    *    *

"There was a point in my life where I used to say I didn't care about nobody but myself. But the truth is, I didn't even care about myself."

Mannie Thomas is reflecting on who he was before he spent fourteen years in prison. Who he was before he set aside everything he thought he knew about himself and started over. Before he met Richie Reseda.

While Thomas can see his old self and his old self-destructive ways more clearly now, he didn't know at the time how much self-harm he was engaging in—self-harm that led him to harm others as well.

There are a lot of harmful and racist narratives about the families and communities of people who get caught up in our prison system, especially those of the Black people who end up behind bars. Thomas's upbringing was different from what many would expect for a Black man in prison. He grew up with both of his parents. His dad was a workingman, he says, who wasn't very affectionate but provided for his family. Thomas was a good student and athlete. He could see how he had more opportunities in his upbringing than many of his peers had, and he felt that set him apart from his cellmates. "The narrative that I was giving myself was that I was a good kid. So when I got arrested, I was this 'good guy that got caught up in a bad situation,'" he tells me.

This narrative kept Thomas from recognizing what he had in common with the men incarcerated with him. "I would look at folks that I was surrounded by and see myself as different. I was arrogant. The truth is, I saw myself as 'better than,'" he admits.

But over the years, Thomas started to see similarities between himself and those locked up with him, especially around how he handled conflict or difficulty.

"I was noticing that their responses to things was the same as my response would be. And when I started to realize that, I was like, *Okay, I'm not different*," he recalls with a chuckle.

This realization led Thomas down a path of self-discovery. He started to set aside the idea that he was better than his cellmates and started trying to figure out how he had ended up on a path that led to prison. In the years that followed, he did a lot of work on his own. He read, he studied, he completed degrees. He was a model prisoner—a prison success story by many people's measurement, including his own.

"I was arrogant again. *Oh, I got my shit together. I've changed.*"

Thomas's definitions of transformation and success were all external. They were all about how he looked to others and how well he was appearing to live up to society's definition of reformation.

But one chance conversation sent Thomas on a whole new path of self-discovery, a path that led to the work he's doing today.

"Me and Richie were working out in the yard, and I made a comment about one of his tattoos." Thomas pauses a second and then says with an embarrassed smile, "I told him his tattoo was gay."

These sorts of homophobic "insults" that many of us grew up hearing on school playgrounds can cause serious conflict in prisons, but Richie Reseda's reaction surprised Thomas.

"In this very Richie way, and I'm still surprised at how he did it, he just literally hit me with a question. He was like, 'Have you ever thought about how you use language that furthers the oppression of other people?'"

Even hearing this story years after the fact, I'm struck by the directness, honesty, and audacity of Reseda's question, especially in a place so ruled by violent patriarchy.

"I don't think anybody had asked me a question like that before," Thomas says. "Nobody in prison had asked me a question clearly— nowhere even near that."

As powerful as the question was, his first impulse was to brush it off. But Thomas is a curious person, and Reseda's question was intriguing. So he kept talking with Reseda, and then Reseda invited Thomas to join Success Stories.

Reseda continued to challenge Thomas on how he saw himself and the impact that his self-image had on him and those around him.

Thomas remembers: "We had another conversation, and he was like, 'Hey, bro, have you ever thought about how [the way] you define masculinity may be keeping you from being the best version of yourself?' And I was like, 'What? Bro. I'm good. I haven't been in trouble for years. I've started groups, done college. What do you mean being-the-best-person shit? In terms of prison, I'm a prison superstar. Like, what are you talking about?'"

As incredulous as Thomas was, Reseda's words stuck with him. He started challenging himself, wondering what his answers to Reseda's questions might tell him about his own life.

Thomas joined Success Stories, and quickly the rest of his resistance was blown away.

"I would say by week three I was just like, *Oh, I got more work to do.*"

In Success Stories Thomas started to learn about patriarchy and how it had negatively affected his life as a Black man. It was the first time he had a real understanding of the personal impact of patriarchy and of patriarchy as a social construct.

"When we were in prison having this conversation," Thomas recalls, "and you said 'patriarchy' to somebody, their only understanding of patriarchy was male leadership. We had never heard of it as a systemic way of oppression. We didn't know about systems that were put in place to keep the most vulnerable of our society down."

When we talk about social issues, especially social theories, we often talk in abstract or overly academic ways. This can not only alienate people in terms of language and vocabulary but also make people feel like they have no real connection to the issues being discussed. I've seen many a misogynist wax eloquent about the evils of patriarchy, because he's been able to "educate" himself on everything about it, except for his participation in it and its effect on his life.

But Reseda had Thomas first look at patriarchy and how it had structured his relationship with his father. This really opened up the concept for Thomas. He knew that his father had done his best by Thomas, and had been the type of father our patriarchal society had told him to be.

"I realized that my dad at the time was living by the three p's of manhood: His job was to protect, provide, and punish. That was it," Thomas says.

Thomas had needed more than what his father knew how to offer. He needed love that showed care for his emotional well-being, not just his physical well-being. Thomas was able to see how he internalized this lack of warmth as a child, making him feel like a burden instead of a child who was wanted.

These relationship dynamics were found in more than just Thomas's relationship with his father.

"I couldn't figure out why things were the way they were. I had already gotten to the conclusion that a lot of male-to-male partnerships are really transactional, and that there was really no depth to them. But I didn't understand why. In Success Stories, when we got to talking about masculinity and patriarchy, I started to discover the why."

After Thomas finished his first season in Success Stories, he became a facilitator. Now, out of prison, married, and with a young daughter, he is the co-executive director of Success Stories. As such, he gets to help other incarcerated men understand how patriarchy is affecting their lives and their communities.

Like Reseda before him, Thomas doesn't try to shame or bully people into change, and he doesn't try to lecture. He tries to meet people where they are and build from there.

"If you start talking to people about the history of feminism, white feminism, Black feminism, they get lost. It's a lot for them to learn. But when I'm like, 'Okay, let's talk about this set of rules that you were given as a man,' and watch how they played out in everybody's household, then people start going, 'Oh, okay. I get it.'"

So often in these discussions, I'm talking with people who are, frankly, exhausted and traumatized from the nature of the revolutionary work they're doing. And often it's the most brutal of liberation work that gets the most attention. But I'm also often talking with people who get great joy from their work. Thomas is one of these people. He clearly really loves and personally benefits from the work he's doing.

"We're really becoming interrupters of this perpetual harm," he tells me with a smile. "Not only giving folks a new template of how to be in their most authentic selves, but to be the interrupters of gender harm and all these other things. It's a wonderful thing to do, just by having these series of discussions, right? It's very fulfilling for those of us who get to do the work."

Thomas is now turning some of his attention to young people, especially young Black people. He wants to focus on what happens to young people before they end up in his program in prison. He wants to address the violence and trauma that can make their futures seem predetermined for them.

"If you talk to young Black folks, regardless of how they grew up, regardless of their socioeconomic background, regardless of geographics or anything like that, most of them will tell you for reasons unbeknownst to them that they don't really think they are gonna live past sixteen."

As Thomas says this to me, I remember my partner saying something similar a few years earlier. He grew up thinking that, as his friends and peers were dying even in middle school, he wouldn't make it past eighteen.

The implications of this are terrifying on many levels.

"You have a whole generation of people that is like, 'I don't think I'm gonna live past sixteen.' And then they get to sixteen, and then to eighteen, and then to twenty-one . . . But think about what happens then. If you didn't think you were gonna get there, and then you get there, it's like, *Okay, well, what now? What next?*" Thomas adds, "I think that comes from this white supremacist system that we live in, that we could kind of tell that the system is geared against us. So it creates this impending doom to like, *I'm living on borrowed time.* We must ask ourselves: What happens to people if they're living that way?"

How do you build for a future that you don't think you'll live long enough to see?

Thomas wants to reach young people who may be living like they won't see sixteen or eighteen or twenty-one. He wants to open them up to the possibility of a different life while it might be a little easier for them to hear. When they haven't yet made life decisions that are much harder to come back from. When they aren't yet hardened adults locked behind bars. Thomas sees Success Stories' founder, Richie Reseda, as an example of how important it can be to start learning these concepts earlier in life.

"You know, Richie was in this work very young. So it was very easy for him to grasp on to certain concepts and change relatively quickly," Thomas explains. He can see how much more difficult this understanding and change was for himself and others who weren't introduced to these feminist concepts at a young age.

One thing that really strikes me about both Reseda's and Thomas's stories is that someone reached out to and invested in both of them at a time when so many people had written them off—perhaps at a time when they had even written themselves off.

Reseda was a teenager in and out of jail already when Patrisse Cullors and Mark Anthony started mentoring him. And when he ended up in prison as a young adult, they didn't abandon him. They continued to put time and effort into helping him heal and become more of his true self. In turn, Reseda found promise and potential in Thomas and so many others in prison while he held on to his belief in himself. He started challenging those around him to invest in their own personal growth and healing while they all were still behind bars.

And now, out of prison, Thomas gets to do the same for more men. Men who, like him, were seen by many in society as beyond redemption. And his work is paying off. It's helping these men and continuing to help Thomas become his best self. Those closest to Thomas have also benefited.

"It's made me a better husband and a better father," he says. "It really shifted things into perspective when my daughter was born." Thomas is now able to be the father he himself had so desperately needed as a child.

The idea that Thomas could be someone not only worthy of a second chance, not only worthy of love and care, but also worthy of respect and even admiration has been a revelation for him, and in it lies a revelation for the rest of us, if we're willing to see it.

"My sense of self-worth is different now because I'm believed when I walk into spaces," he says. "That has been powerful. Because I'm seeing and I'm experiencing in real time that folks are realizing that it takes many different people within our communities to create these futures that we're trying to create. That's revolutionary in and of itself."

But in order for us to be able to create these futures, we need to build space for people to heal, and we need to work to battle the systems that are harming the people who are so necessary to our movements—even if we don't know it yet. Without that, we will be forever playing catch-up with white supremacy and patriarchy.

Thomas is proof that we can do both. We can heal and we can fight at the same time. He is an example of the power of caring about an individual person, seeing their humanity, and investing in their healing. But while Thomas is investing in individuals who had long been discarded by society, he's also regularly engaging with systemic change. In doing so, he has become a respected leader.

"Today, professionally, I am in spaces where I'm continually pinching myself and asking myself, 'How did I get here?'" he says. "I'm always surprised that people want to hear my perspective. I think for a large part of my life I questioned my own value. This feels good."

Thomas remembers when he first started talking with people and organizations about the connection between patriarchy and prisons. He says that nobody wanted to hear him. But now when he talks with school administrators, or even with corrections officials, he says, "They do not want to admit it, but they get it. And it's not as much of an uphill battle as I once thought it was going to be."

Thomas hopes that more of us will "get it" so we can start addressing harm at its root cause, so we can free those harmed by patriarchy and white supremacy, and so we can prevent future harm. He's living proof that it can be done.

## Race, Patriarchy, and Punishment Culture

When giving talks or interviews, I'm often presented with a variation of the same question:

"Is this a feminist issue?"
"Is this a racial issue?"
"What about class?"

All of these questions are asking the same thing: "What box can I fit this oppression into?"

As if we are lined up by privilege and handed out rules of behavior. *Here is patriarchy for you… Here is white supremacy for you… Here is classism for you…*

But oppression doesn't fit neatly into boxes. And if you think it does, that's likely your privilege talking. Privilege is meant to be invisible to those who have it. Often when systems that are difficult or oppressive for others seem to be working just fine for us, they are working for us because they were designed for us—at the expense of others. Privilege is also relative. This means that one aspect of our identity may be oppressed by a particular system, while another aspect may give us privilege over others, and we may fail to recognize the different ways in which the same system can be harming others.

When I was preparing to talk with Mahnker Dahnweih about Freedom, Inc., I spent a fair amount of time reading press coverage of their work. From how they are covered in media, you would think they are strictly an abolitionist group, focused on issues of incarceration and state violence against Black and Southeast Asian people. But when I talked with Dahnweih, she was very clear that Freedom, Inc., is a gender justice and queer justice organization. And because they work in communities of color, they have to address state violence.

Just as Success Stories has to address patriarchy in order to be effective in handling community and state violence, Freedom, Inc., has to address state and community violence in order to fight gender-based and interpersonal violence, and vice versa.

Dahnweih says, "If we can come together and use our expertise and our community, and transformative and restorative justice to move through interpersonal violence and intimate partner violence, then that will strengthen us to be able to fight the big violence, which is state violence."

Patriarchy not only contributes to state-sanctioned violence against populations of color. It also is the architect of that harm.

In seeking to understand how Mannie Thomas and his fellow cellmates ended up where they were, Thomas kept coming back to white supremacist patriarchy at the root of it all: "When we look at patriarchy...patriarchy is this idea of dominance. We live in a revenge system because of patriarchy. Patriarchy says, 'All right, if you do this, now I'm gonna equally subject you to harm.'"

Thomas sees great harm in this culture of revenge that goes far deeper than how we treat people in our criminal justice system.

"It objectifies people. Of course it's gonna objectify people, because by objectifying people, it makes it easier to do these harmful things to them, if you don't see them as a person, right?" Thomas points out that the objectification of marginalized and vulnerable people makes the violence of our carceral system easier to justify, because while a person may be redeemable, an object is not.

A lot of people confuse accountability with revenge. But accountability and revenge cannot coexist. Accountability is a relationship. It requires healing–healing of the people harmed and healing of the relationship between those who committed harm and those who have been harmed. It requires healing of the community that enabled harm. Yet our system has deliberately confused the two. We call revenge and punishment accountability, and have no tools for *actual* accountability.

And in that system, in which we measure the value of someone based on how much revenge is enacted on their behalf, we end up doubly harming those deemed "less than." People of color, disabled people, queer and trans people, are often not deemed worthy of revenge when they have been harmed by those more valued by society (like white, cis, abled men). This makes us less safe in the world, as people know they can harm us with no consequence—the only consequence made available is not going to fall upon them. Those who are deemed valuable by society are also automatically offered redemption, even if they show no desire to grow past the harm they have caused or to be held accountable in any way to those they harmed. Yet when *we* commit harm, because we are seen as of so little value, we are often subjected to punishment that has no interest in our healing or growth, because the system governing our lives does not see us as people.

Transformative justice is practiced to some extent by the state—it's just practiced with only some people. "We choose who we want to do it with," Thomas points out. "We have, you know, businessmen or wealthy people or cops who do terrible things. [Judges] don't try to sentence them to the maximum. They're like, 'Oh, well, let's get you to this program,' or 'Let's do this.' So we have found ways to deal with harmful behavior in loving ways. We're selective about who we give it to. And you know, 99 percent of the time, that's not directed at people of color. It's directed at white folks in powerful positions."

State violence, gender-based violence, community violence, and ableism are all woven into a giant tapestry of harm. It's impossible to separate it even as it's important that we see all of the individual threads that go into it. When we don't want to step back and see the complete picture, or when we don't want to see the warp and weft of intersecting oppressions, we can create even more harm.

Many mainstream gender justice movements, even when they try to see how race affects the lives of those harmed by gender-based violence (and they often fail to do even that), still rarely look at how racial and state violence contribute to and create gender-based violence.

"We know that mainstream systems of dealing with sexual assault are very much reliant on enforcement," says movement worker and professor Theryn Kigvamasud'vashti, "but we also know that enforcement violence is at the center of a lot of people's experience in our community who experience state violence, right?"

So for many movement workers like Kigvamasud'vashti, they seek to find justice, accountability, and safety outside of these existing systems. It's not just that these existing systems fail to address violence; they themselves are also often the cause of violence.

In trying to do this work to keep Black and brown women safe from violence, Kigvamasud'vashti found time and time again that punishment culture impeded her progress. "The City of Seattle sat us down one day and said, 'We're not gonna give you money to work with sex workers, because how can you guarantee they're not gonna get raped? Their job puts them at risk for getting raped.'"

It was not just sex workers who were deemed unworthy of help or protection by our carceral systems.

"It was our sex worker work and [our] working with young Black girls who are incarcerated that the city chose to defund," Kigvamasud'vashti remembers. She was told to apply for funding for each of the organization's programs separately, so that the city could pick and choose what programs it deemed worthy of funding. Programs helping sex workers, people struggling with addiction, and incarcerated girls—some of our most vulnerable Black women and girls—were unfunded.

"So, at the end of the day, they were not interested in ending violence in the lives of Black women at all," Kigvamasud'vashti says.

Systems built on punishment will prioritize compliance and control over safety and healing. Patriarchal systems of punishment will most harshly punish those it deems "less than"—as any noncompliance is seen as a threat to those systems of power.

Dahnweih tells me, "I worked on a case a couple years back where, for the first time in Wisconsin history, a woman was prosecuted by the DA for fleeing with her children and violating a custody agreement. And this was a Black woman. This woman had her own day care, had her own business, everything. Multiple streams of income, whatever—that didn't matter. She was Black."

Dahnweih spoke with the district attorney to try to advocate for the woman. "I said, 'There are complex racial implications. Patriarchy's at play here, but also, you know, white supremacy's at play here. There are so many things at play here. I'm telling you, as an advocate for gender justice, an expert, someone who works with victims and survivors every day, you cannot prosecute this woman for trying to defend her children. She did what she could to get outside of his reach of influence and power.'"

The DA, a white man, was unmoved by Dahnweih's pleas. He insisted that it was his job to make an example of this woman and come up with a punishment for her breaking the law.

This woman, who was so desperate to get away from her ex-partner that she fled her home and her business, was being charged because taking her children out of state violated a judge's order. Even though the father of her children had multiple past felonies, and was accused of sexually abusing the children, the prosecutor and the judge cared more about the woman's disobedience.

"The judge said, 'It's the same thing.... You violating my order and him being accused of sexually assaulting your children ... it's the same thing in my eyes.'" Dahnweih tells me that even after being arrested and separated from her children for ten months—her children had been placed in the custody of their father, whom this woman felt was a danger to their well-being—the judge still chastised the mother for not "taking accountability" for her actions. He told her that her explanation for why she felt that she had to take the children out of state in order to protect herself and them was simply her trying to blame others for why she broke the law.

To our patriarchal, punishment-based systems, compliance takes precedence over all else. Safety, healing, growth—none of it is as important as punishing people (especially marginalized people) for falling out of line.

"That is the very real way that patriarchy and white supremacy interact with each other," Dahnweih says. "Because it is a patriarchal white supremacy that white people used to colonize the rest of the world. Black people and the rest of the world. And that is what we live under today. It's not only 'You broke the law,' which is white supremacy, but 'I'm going to teach you, as a man, as a white man—I need to teach you a lesson.' And that [father], who has all these cases against him and all of these accusations, he still has the right to those children. And to you."

## TALILA LEWIS

I uplift the name of John Herbert Lee Wilson Jr., who was the man whose case I first came across. Black, Deaf, disabled elder. From DC, low income. Got a life sentence in the feds, and I looked at his case really quickly and was like, 'Oh! Homeboy didn't do this.' It was that obvious to me. And of course, I'm not gonna let it slide, right?"

Talila Lewis is a community organizer and abolitionist. Lewis is thirty-seven, Black, queer, neuroqueer (a term coined by Nick Walker, PhD, to describe the deliberate political and social queering of neurodiversity), and trans. When I ask how Lewis's work began, I'm told the story of John Herbert Lee Wilson Jr.

Our "criminal justice" system is cruel, unpredictable, and violently unjust for so many. News headlines are often dominated by stories of Black people who have found themselves on the receiving end of the most brutal of these injustices. But less discussed is how often disabled people find themselves the target of our criminal justice system. If you're Black and disabled and come into contact with our criminal justice system, your chance of escaping this encounter unscathed is much lower than most.

While in college, after reading about the case of a Deaf Black man facing a life sentence, Lewis became obsessed with righting what seemed to be an obvious wrong. Lewis started reaching out to organizations dedicated to getting justice for the wrongfully incarcerated, thinking that surely, once they learned about what had happened to Wilson, they'd be moved to action.

"You know, I was naïve," Lewis remembers. "This was 2006, 2007. I'm young. I don't have any sort of credentialing in anything. I'm working multiple jobs in undergrad, going to school full-time. And an internship on top of multiple jobs. Houseless part of the time. Like, just going through it. But also I'm not gonna let this man rot in prison."

Lewis put together a memo that quickly expanded to seventy pages, outlining the problems with Wilson's case.

"I'm trying to explain to people how this happened," Lewis recalls, "a finger-spelling police officer who was Black, quote, unquote, 'interpreted' for him, misinterpreted all sorts of stuff. Cross-cultural miscommunications, typical carceral system problems—but layered on top of ableism. It's a recipe for wrongful conviction—not to mention the Reid Technique."

The Reid Technique is a popular interrogation method that uses deception and rapid escalation of tactics in order to coerce confessions from suspects. It is known for confusing and terrorizing suspects into making false confessions, and those with disabilities are even more vulnerable to false confessions when officers use these tactics.

Lewis remembers how these white institutions would look at the memo outlining Wilson's case and comment on how "fascinating" the case was. And that would be it. Further requests for assistance were met with silence. Unable to get help from established organizations, Lewis decided to go to law school in order to better help Wilson. By that time Lewis had begun looking into other cases of Deaf people who had seemingly been railroaded into unjust convictions. In 2011, Lewis and Lewis's partner, Ki'tay Davidson (who passed away in 2014), started HEARD, an organization originally dedicated to helping Deaf people who had been wrongfully convicted and sentenced to prison. ("HEARD" as in the word in capital letters, not as an acronym.)

Lewis was filled with passion and a sense of urgency in this work. Lives were on the line. Through research and often emotionally painful conversations with incarcerated Deaf Black and Latine people, Lewis was able to see that HEARD's focus on the "wrongfully convicted" was too narrow. Prison was torture, especially for Deaf and disabled people of color. It was always wrong.

"I started that work as supporting Black people and Latinx Deaf people who I believed were wrongly convicted," Lewis says. "But it quickly shifted into, like, it doesn't matter if any of these folks are guilty or innocent. What's happening on the inside is absolutely appalling and unconscionable, and something has to be done."

This work, which Lewis has now done for over fifteen years, is arduous and expensive. And it's work that very few people seem willing to do.

"People started sending me other cases that looked just like his [Wilson's], and then I would pay my own money to drive to meet them because there are no video phones in prisons across the nation, for signing and Deaf folks to even communicate with anyone, much less people trying to get them out."

Many incarcerated people are sent many miles away from their families and communities, making phone communication typically the only way for them to stay connected to friends and family while inside. Incarcerated Deaf people often aren't provided accessible telecommunications services or technology, leaving them immensely isolated.

"Which is torture in and of itself," Lewis explains. "That is currently happening. . . . Most signing and Deaf people, signing Autistic people, who are incarcerated presently do not have access to telecommunication."

While some people working full-time in the social justice movement may be paid well enough to live somewhat comfortably, work with incarcerated, disabled, or Deaf Black and brown people is not usually prioritized in funding. Lewis is often not comfortable making money from this work, because of the ways in which it's tied to the oppression and abuses of Black, Indigenous, and other people of color in many circumstances—especially if those funds come from affected communities. "I don't want me asking for money to be a barrier to anyone's liberation, to education," Lewis explains.

Because abolition work doesn't often pay, and because many grant funds go to more established and white-centered organizations, Lewis sometimes has to juggle two, even three, other jobs to get by.

Passion and youth combined to allow Lewis to keep working like this: supplementing long days of dedicated advocacy and activism work with other side jobs to cover the bills. But now, after so many years, Lewis feels worn down—physically, mentally, and emotionally. Lewis says, "This sort of overwork, burnout—I don't like the word 'burnout.' I'm trying to figure out what to call it. For me, it's like a bone-spirit-heart-compassion tired."

After years of work, Lewis was able to help get Wilson out of prison. His name and record weren't cleared, as Lewis had hoped, but he was finally able to get parole. Wilson went home after twenty-five years in prison. His children had grown up without him.

He had missed out on so much, but now he was home with his family.

Lewis becomes visibly agitated explaining what happened next.

"We finally get him out on parole—not on actual innocence, but he is coming home," Lewis says. "He gets out in spring of 2019, and passes away literally six months later. There's kind of no words for that."

Lewis is right. There are no words.

"There's no way to explain that. His daughter, Fria. His grandchildren, Fray, Kyree, Andrew. Travis, his son. His other one of his sons he met in federal prison. You know what I mean?" Lewis continues: "The cruelty of these systems. To finally come home. And then to die six months later of prison-induced violences, right?"

There was no time for Lewis to process the loss of Wilson, or to even grieve, as tragedy in the community that Lewis was fighting so hard for continued to strike.

"A few months later, we lost another one. A few months later, we lost *another* one. That was Alfonso, and that was Cedric. Elliot York died the same year. And COVID. All this, COVID—so we're losing people." Lewis recalls, "I was like, 'Keep working. Cuz we don't want more people to die.' John Wilson's funeral was on the 24th. On the 25th, I'm somewhere at a workshop collecting information to help the organization do this, that, and the other."

Lewis doesn't want to do this work anymore.

When Lewis tells me this, I can see that it isn't being said in a defeatist way. Lewis doesn't want to do this work anymore because this work only exists because such horrific violence against Black and brown disabled people exists. Nobody, Lewis argues, should want to do this work—at least not for long.

"Those of us engaged in this work who are in principled struggle don't want to be doing this," Lewis explains. "I've been trying to not do this work since it began. If your goal is to keep doing this work, you're kind of not necessarily struggling in a principled way. And I think even the struggle to leave the work causes a tension in your body-mind-spirit."

I want to say that racial justice work will always be rewarding. That it will bring joy and connection. But that's not always the case. Even for those engaged in more joyful resistance work, there's no way to take on systems of oppression without being harmed in some way. And the more vulnerable to that oppression, the more personally targeted by it you and your community are, the more brutal this work can be.

"Yesterday I got a text message from a loved one that was like, 'Can cousin so-and-so call you? Cuz one of her cousins passed away in prison, and my mom wants to talk to you about it.' Those aren't the conversations that white folks doing this work are having every day." Lewis says, "I don't think people fundamentally understand, when we say we are doing this literally to save our and our children's and our family members' lives, how real that is."

---

## What Is Abolition?

When I was in grade school, abolition was talked about only in terms of slavery. Not the many ways in which slavery exists today, but the horrific chattel slavery of this country's history. Abolitionists were people who are now long dead. Who struggled to end slavery. And that struggle ended with the American Civil War, when slavery was abolished.

Of course, outside of our highly problematic public school system, abolition was still being discussed and fought for. People like Angela Davis, Frantz Fanon, Grace Lee Boggs, Mariame Kaba, and Dorothy E. Roberts, as well as the Black liberation movement and American Indian movement, have been working to define and fight for freedoms that many want to say are impossible.

Liberation workers have shown us and continue to show us that the struggle for abolition is a very current and very necessary fight.

Abolitionism today is the fight for freedom. It is the fight against slavery and exploitation in all its forms—including imprisonment and medical incarceration.

Prison abolitionism, as I'm writing about it, has deep roots in Black liberation, and it is predominantly Black writers, thinkers, and movement workers who have developed these vital understandings of what it means to be free and what systems stand in the way of our freedom.

Abolitionism in this understanding recognizes that hierarchical systems of crime and punishment seek to control and exploit people in the model of chattel slavery, and that the majority of these systems are a continuation of this slavery. Abolitionism understands that wherever these exploitative and carceral systems are left standing, all people will be at risk for enslavement and our society will be unable to adequately address issues of health and safety. Abolitionists envision a world that doesn't rely on punishment or control to address social issues. Abolitionists see the value of all people in ways that aren't defined by capitalist notions of productivity or profit. Abolitionists look to root causes of social issues and believe in collective responsibility for those issues.

Basically, prison abolitionists believe in people. We believe in relationships and social contracts. We believe in our power to heal ourselves and one another. And we believe that people have the right to decide what's best for themselves, and that communities have the right to decide the same together.

Abolitionism—the fight to dismantle systems of imprisonment, exploitation, and punishment—is one of the most beautiful, optimistic, important, and difficult social change movements existing.

It can be pretty easy to identify target systems in abolitionism. Prisons? Check. Youth detention? Check. Even if someone doesn't recognize a system as a target for abolition—like a child welfare system or forced mental health care—once a system's harmful and often deeply racist and ableist workings are pointed out, it's usually easy to understand why many abolitionists choose to focus on these targets.

When a system has its boot on your neck, it's quite easy to point to the boot and say, "Here—this boot needs to be removed." But it's even easier to say, "This boot should not exist at all."

Two questions make this work difficult: "How?" and "What next?" What if, while you're focused on that boot, someone else is busy building a cage around you? What if this whole time you've been helping to build that cage, but you were unaware because this damn boot is taking up so much of your time and energy, or perhaps you've been told that building this cage is what would remove that boot?

Richie Reseda finds dark humor in how skewed our priorities can be in this work.

"It's so funny," he says. "Like, we want this abolitionist world, so we start by talking to cops? We start by talking to the government? Like, our strategy has been, 'Let's go for the people who are most against us and, like, convince them.' But we're actually jumping over ourselves! We're jumping over our whole communities. We're jumping over all the people around us."

It's easy to target systems for abolition. It's much less easy to practice abolition in our day-to-day lives, in our communities and our families. Because even though large, oppressive, and exploitative systems are easier to spot, the same hierarchical patterns of punishment and reward, compliance or revenge, are ingrained in all of our interpersonal relationships.

While we keep our focus outside of our communities, we keep perpetuating unexamined harm against one another. The last few years, especially, have seen so many of the community members that Reseda and I know caught up in this drama, caught up in this harm that we've been enacting upon ourselves, because we didn't apply abolitionist principles to our community first.

"We're all talking shit about each other, taking from each other, da, da, da, da, da, revenge here, punishment there, violence there," Reseda says, pointing all around him in demonstration. Then he laughs. "But by all means, let's all rally up thousands deep and tell the white supremacists how they should act!"

I certainly don't think Reseda means that we cannot work to dismantle oppressive systems until we've addressed how we treat one another. Much of his work is targeted at these systems, after all. But he points to a real hard truth: Until we put abolitionist practices to work, everything we're building toward is just theory. And if we don't put those practices to work now, we will bake oppressions into our definitions of progress.

This is work that we must do at the same time as we do the incredibly important work of dismantling systems of incarceration and imprisonment.

It's also important that we learn how to talk with one another and work through conflict, instead of avoiding or punishing conflict. Learning how to relate to one another with care and integrity is the top priority in beginning to make change, according to Reseda: "That's the number one thing I would encourage people to do. When people are like, 'I want to get rid of prisons. What's the first thing? What can I do?' For real, I tell them that."

In order for us to do this important internal work, in order to be able to build the beautiful world that we want to replace prisons and punishment, we have to have the freedom to do so. And that means everyone has to do their part. White people and others with the skin tone and the systemic privileges that make them less vulnerable to these oppressive systems have to make both abolishing these systems and reducing their own contributions to carceral systems a top priority.

While many abolitionists focus on reducing harm from current systems, it's important to remember that any work that leaves these systems standing will always result in only harm reduction, never more than that. This doesn't mean the work isn't vital. These systems are large and very difficult to dismantle, and while we try to dismantle them, people are being harmed by them right now. So while the work to reduce harm is abolitionist in nature, it is not abolition.

This means that there is no "end point" of this work as long as these systems remain. And victories can be quickly undone when we forget that and take our eyes off our ultimate goal.

Ian Head has been a part of the efforts to end stop-and-frisk policing in New York. After a major court victory in 2013 declaring New York's policies that disproportionately subjected

Black and brown New Yorkers to traumatic and often violent stops and searches unconstitutional, many people considered the case closed—and assumed that stop-and-frisk was over. "The process of abolition, the process of whatever we want to call it—social justice and change, fighting the system—is an ongoing process," Head says.

Activists, advocates, and lawyers had worked for several years on this case. They had worked on outreach, movement building, case building, even before they got into the courtroom. And it all culminated in a nine-week trial, which ended up being a monumental victory for their team. But the court victory was just the beginning of the battle.

"People thought when that ruling came down, *Stop-and-frisk is over and the case is over.* But no," Head says. "Now we're gonna start a monitorship, and now we're gonna appoint a monitor."

Almost as soon as news attention turned away from stop-and-frisk, the NYPD began to work overtime to regain the power it had lost when stop-and-frisk was taken away. Head observes, "You saw how the reactionary parts of the system—especially, but not just, the neoliberal and reactionary parts of the system—work to claw back anything that was won."

The judge on the case had spoken strongly in favor of the plaintiffs. "She said—a quote we use from her remedial order often to this day—that impacted community members know better than anyone else what harms the police are doing to them and are better positioned to discuss and come up with the reforms, or whatever it might be, to address those harms," Head remembers. "They did not like that."

When the city appealed the case, the appellate court kicked the judge off the case.

Step one complete, the NYC carceral systems worked to further stack the deck in their favor.

"So," Head continues, "they got rid of her, the 'crazy liberal judge.' And then when we started the monitorship, the monitor that was appointed was a former prosecutor."

Dealing with a monitor who has deep, long-standing ties to police has made it very hard for the lawyers and community members working to end police abuses to make progress. Head has observed the city working in multiple ways to ensure that where progress is made, it is slow, and when it is made, they often find ways to make it work to their advantage.

"Between both the data and, obviously, the stories that we hear all the time from our partner organizations and clients—like, racial disparities? Not going away. Police abuse? Not going away. But you hear the city tell it: 'There's lots of reasons why we are gonna be in compliance soon,' et cetera.

"You see this clawing back." Head remembers, "First they hated the body-worn cameras. At first the cops were like, 'No, we don't want body-worn cameras!'" But Head saw the attitude toward cameras change as their use as surveillance devices increased. Body-worn cameras (especially ones that can be turned off and on at an officer's discretion) are a great way to record the actions of unknowing citizens without a warrant. "Now they love body-worn cameras, and now they want body-worn cameras everywhere, and now the whole department has body-worn cameras. And you see how things are co-opted, clawed back."

So while we build rest into this work, by taking on different roles at different times and coordinating our efforts, it's important to remember that the actual fight isn't over until these systems are dismantled and replaced with better systems.

What does it look like on the other side of this battle? Honestly, I don't know.

When I say this, it doesn't sit right with a lot of people, but I think it's important for us to be able to hold space for the unknown here. We've lived in deeply oppressive systems for the entire history of this country. It's all we know of our systems, and often of our relationships. When we create spaces and moments of safety and freedom, we get glimpses of what liberation *might* look like. But I suspect we'll be surprised along the way, and if we aren't able to get comfortable with that, we'll run back into the arms of the certainty of the oppression we already know.

The process of figuring it out is going to have a lot of trial and error. It's going to require that we be willing to try what has not been tried before and to trust that we can come up with something better than what exists now. But, unsure as the future might be, I feel like the right direction is pretty clear. Some examples of more abolitionist practices are already in place in our society—imperfect as they may be.

A few years ago, I was talking about abolition with Janaya Khan, co-founder of Black Lives Matter Toronto. In trying to describe what a post-cop world might look like, Khan, like Mannie Thomas, pointed to the experiences many people in white America already have. They describe a world where if you call for help because you have a family member in crisis, trained, caring professionals will show up at your door—not someone trained to kill, who will immediately see your loved one as a threat. If your child is in a rebellious phase and shoplifts from a store, they will have to show up on weekends to work off the debt by mopping floors, instead of facing down a cop's gun. Women being threatened or abused by partners can call for help without worrying about a confrontation with police that could leave somebody dead. You could get pulled over for speeding and be given a stern yet friendly reminder of traffic laws and the importance of driving safely, instead of gripping the steering wheel in fear that you may be arrested on a trumped-up charge, beaten, or worse.

This is the reality that many who think prison and police abolition isn't necessary already have—or *think* they have. Because no matter how safe they think they are, that power will have no problem turning against them the moment it views them as a threat.

And that brings me to the big question many have when we talk about police abuses: Do we *really* mean "Defund the police"?

Yes. Yes, we do.

One hundred fifteen billion taxpayer dollars are spent on policing in this country per year (Vera Institute of Justice 2020). Sixty-five of our nation's largest cities spend more than 40 percent of their budgets on policing (Buchholz 2023). This money is being used to terrorize populations of color, disabled people, queer and trans people, houseless people, and sex workers. This is not a system that rehabilitates people. This is not a system that addresses root causes of crime and violence. This is a system that simply punishes.

Meanwhile, our systems that can actually address the root causes of crime and violence are left to scramble for whatever dollars are left over. Our education system is embarrassingly underfunded, especially in majority Black and brown areas—areas that are also often over-policed. And our welfare systems receive less than half of the funding policing gets (Ingraham 2020). We spend twice as much money to lock people up as we do to feed people.

Defunding the police doesn't mean that we wake up tomorrow with no public safety entities. Defunding is the process of reallocating police funds to areas that can address public safety more effectively. Investing in healthcare, in education, in job programs, in welfare programs, in community conflict-resolution programs, in drug treatment programs, in housing. As we remove duties from police systems that they really shouldn't have and give the corresponding funds to those better suited to do this vital work, we are defunding the police.

If somebody robs you because they are broke and don't have

access to work, because they have an addiction that they're trying to pay for, because they're caught up in community cycles of violence, arresting that person and locking them away doesn't solve the issue that caused them to rob you in the first place. They're not given job training or access to job opportunities. They're not given addiction counseling or mental health counseling. They're not given conflict-resolution skills or access to healthier social dynamics. They're put in a space where they're regularly subjected to more violence and abuse, where their mental and physical health needs are ignored, where whatever family or community support systems they may have had before are stripped away. And when they're released, they're left traumatized, often disabled by the mental and physical violence they encountered while incarcerated, deeper in debt, and with a conviction record that makes finding a job or even safe housing nearly impossible.

Even if you're thinking, *Good. The person who robbed me doesn't deserve to be able to find a job or get housing. They deserved to be abused in prison*, remember: that person, now reentered into society, is even more desperate than they were before they went in because of that punishment you may think they deserve, and you have been made even more unsafe.

But if you're reading this book because you believe systemic racism and systemic oppression exist and are affecting how marginalized populations are able to navigate our society, then I hope you can recognize that the person who robbed you is not the only entity responsible for what has been done to you. Poverty, addiction, violence—all these issues have systemic contributors that must be addressed if we want to be able to reduce crime.

With abolitionism, we can address these factors, and as members of society, it is our responsibility to address them. Accountability is our responsibility, and if we're holding all those responsible accountable, then it's easy to see how unjust the idea is of locking up one person for a crime our entire society contributed to.

We can begin to see what an abolitionist world looks like now, by practicing it where we have the power to.

"Like, parent in your values. You know what I'm saying?" says Richie Reseda. "Teach or do your job in your values. The work of doing that—and building those accountability structures with people around you to see if you're doing that—is where I encourage people to start."

These words were a challenging spark that lit a fire in me. How can I act, every day, in a way that is in accordance with the values and ideals I've been fighting so hard for? How have I been utilizing abolitionist practices in my day-to-day life? These words had me thinking about how I've structured my relationships in life and whether or not they're truly abolitionist in nature. I started thinking about how my partner and I deal with conflict. I started thinking about how I parent. Do I use authority and hierarchy and threats to get my children to do what I want or need them to do? (Never physical threats, but what is the line between a consequence and a punishment, and what side of that line am I on?) Where can I turn that into relationship building, in which we work together to find solutions to issues based on how we want to move through the world and what relationship we want to have with one another? How do we want our family unit to function? In my work life, how am I working with the people I employ or partner with? Have we built abolitionist relationships and structures, or have we defaulted to traditional hierarchical ways of being? These are all beautiful opportunities to start building abolitionist realities right now in my life and my community.

It's really vital that I consider this in my writing and movement work. When I'm more purely externally focused in abolition work, the internal work that I do on autopilot will often default to harmful oppressive and even exploitative practices that we all have been taught. Many of our movements and organizations fighting for abolition and liberation are strictly hierarchical, patriarchal, and punitive in nature. The ways in which we deal with conflict with one another typically mirrors the same systems of punishment and revenge we're trying to battle in systems. If we want to win this battle, we must focus both internally and externally, and that means all of us must do our part.

## IAN HEAD

You know, I think there's a lot of ways I came into this work. One I always mention is hip-hop, which I think is true of a lot of—well, maybe not a lot of—white people in my generation." As odd as this may sound, Ian Head is definitely not the first white person I've spoken with who found the beginnings of a lifelong dedication to anti-racist and abolition work in hip-hop.

"In the '90s, coming up, getting open to hip-hop, especially Public Enemy, KRS, Queen Latifah, A Tribe Called Quest. That's what I was listening to—learning from, frankly. Those were like books for me. Those were not like, 'Oh, I look cool,' or, 'I feel cool listening to this music,' but this was actually leading me to read certain books, to look for certain things. To basically venture out of kind of my white Portland upbringing."

Some art is revolutionary by design. It sets out to tackle oppressive systems or harmful narratives. It is openly and intentionally defiant of the status quo. That art can be very effective in changing how we see the world. But there is also art that is revolutionary simply because it tells the truth when it seems like others cannot. And when that truth is coming from places that are often underrepresented—

especially places of struggle—it can be the most powerful form of art in the world. Hip-hop can be that and has been that for many people. An art form born from the storytelling and musical traditions kept alive in the breasts of enslaved Black people. It's an art form indigenous to Black America that has become a powerful tool of struggle for many oppressed and disenfranchised people around the world. And it has helped people outside of Black America see into and connect with the lived experiences of Black Americans.

"I was listening to hip-hop and hearing Black people talk about life experiences that are definitely different than mine—especially when it comes to law enforcement, what's happening with these prisons," Head tells me. "And I believed those stories. And I'm not saying I'm special for that, because everyone should believe those stories. But more that I feel like so many white people question and don't want to believe those stories unless there is three reams of data backing them up or whatever."

As a white kid growing up in Portland, Oregon, Ian Head listened to the stories his beloved hip-hop artists were rapping about and he believed them. A lot of his moral foundation—which opened him up for hearing and believing what he was hearing instead of dismissing it—came from his mother.

Head doesn't think his mom was politically radical, but her upbringing in Chicago's South Side had made her more skeptical of established systems and norms. She had taught her son to ask questions about the world. He credits her influence for his feminist and anti-racist beliefs.

Head became passionate about issues of racial injustice and began searching for ways to join the fight for liberation when he left home for college in New York City. After he graduated, he knew only that he wanted to be involved in racial justice and prison abolition work, and that he didn't want to be in the spotlight. "I felt it was important to play a support role," Head explains. "In the anti-racist work I wanted to do, in the kind of advocacy I wanted to do, in all these white supremacist systems."

While many white people are used to centering themselves and being centered in movement work, Head has worked hard to avoid that. "I definitely don't want to be the face," he tells me. And he doesn't think, for the most part, that white people *should* seek to be the face of anti-racist work. "But to the degree that I can be helpful, and sometimes I won't be, but to the degree that I can be an in-between for some of these organizers that I work with, advocates on the ground, and these lawyers who are up in their offices, or behind certain walls, or just behind certain kinds of barriers. Whether it's like the legalese or whatever, I can bridge those gaps. I take pride, I guess, a little bit, in that role."

He has a lot to be proud of, but even when I reached out to him to discuss his work, it took a bit of convincing to get him to agree. He didn't want to be centered, even here. It was only after explaining the full scope of this book and assuring him that the voices in it would be overwhelmingly BIPOC and there was a real need for his story did he agree.

One of the first post-graduation jobs Head got was with the National Police Accountability Project (NPAP). He worked part-time to support attorneys across the country who were trying to get justice and accountability in the courts for police abuse. When that job moved to Boston, Head decided to stay in New York. His connections with the NPAP brought him to the National Lawyers Guild.

In the group's Lower Manhattan space, Head was introduced to lawyers and legal advocates who were doing very radical legal work that he hadn't known existed before.

As he began this work in the legal field, he kept in his mind a powerful experience he'd had in college. Head and his associates had been leading discussions in a women's correctional facility. In one of their sessions, a woman began to talk about her experiences with her legal defense. Whenever she was arrested, her lawyers would insist there was little to be done for her case. She was going to serve her time. The woman explained how she would then go to the law library at the prison, research statutes that applied to her case, and figure out what she needed to do for her own defense. She would then often successfully gain her own release.

Even though this work wasn't able to address the systemic issues contributing to her arrests, this woman was able to find power and resources even when those much more empowered and privileged had written her off as a lost cause.

"She told us how she would continue to advocate and learn the law herself, and outthink her attorneys," Head recalls. "And that was really inspiring to me. I remember holding on to that for a long time . . . thinking, *There's a lot of different ways of learning and different ways of activating knowledge, right?* And so I kind of had that in my head."

That idea, that you don't need to have a law degree to be able to advocate for yourself or others, was still on Head's mind when he came across *The Jailhouse Lawyer's Manual*—a publication that incarcerated people without a law degree but who had legal knowledge (also known as jailhouse lawyers) wrote with attorneys in order to help incarcerated people advocate for themselves.

"It had been lying around in these paper copies, photocopied again and again, but no one had updated it since, like, 1980, and so a coworker of mine, another non-lawyer who was working, doing this kind of legal activism—this is back in 2002—was like, 'You should update this.'"

Head reached out to an attorney at the Center for Constitutional Rights (CCR) to help with the project. Together, they published *The Jailhouse Lawyer's Handbook*.

This project was a labor of love that involved many in the abolitionist community. "I wrote to a bunch of different jailhouse lawyers and just people inside," Head remembers. "Mumia, Sundiata, and a lot of folks that were kind of lesser-known names—just people who were members of the guild (they had members who were jailhouse lawyers)—for input."

Head wanted the handbook to be put to as much use as possible, since tools to help imprisoned people advocate for themselves were hard to come by.

"To be more specific about this handbook," he clarifies, "it helped with filing on your own civil rights lawsuits against the government for whatever conditions were happening within the place they were being held." The handbook wasn't going to help someone overturn their case, but it would help someone who was incarcerated utilize their legal rights while incarcerated. Legal rights that could help stop abuse, help gain access to needed programs or accommodations, and much more. And it explained it all in terms that people without legal degrees could understand. This sort of legal aid could help make prison survivable.

In order to get this handbook out to as many people who needed it as possible, Head and his teammates started organizing volunteer meetups, where attendees could go through letters from incarcerated people describing their legal issues and figure out how to best get them the tools they needed for their self-advocacy.

He was amazed by the number of volunteers who showed up over the years to help distribute the handbook. Some volunteers kept showing up for ten years straight.

The work was hard, but it was worth it to Head every time they heard back from someone who had benefited from the handbook. "One time someone came who had done about four, five years upstate, New York. Came to volunteer for a couple months. He said, in his time he had gotten three different copies. And whenever he got transferred, he would always leave a copy with someone at the facility he was leaving, so that they could use it."

Head continued to update and distribute *The Jailhouse Lawyer's Handbook* until the pandemic hit in 2020, and even with his decades of movement work on many important projects, he still feels honored to call his work on the handbook some of the most important work he's done.

The knowledge that Head gained from this project has made him a valuable asset in other abolition efforts, including the fight to end stop-and-frisk policing in New York City. He believes deeply in the work he does. "Twenty years later, I have a fairly good knowledge of prison litigation and how a lot of these things work. I never went to law school, and I got involved just because it was an important thing to do. Even just the basic administrative work was important."

In 2009, Head began working with the Center for Constitutional Rights (CCR) on their stop-and-frisk lawsuit, filed the year before. He joined the case as the CCR was in the middle of discovery for the class-action suit. In order to bolster the testimonies of the four named plaintiffs, the CCR needed more stories from others affected by the NYPD's racist and abusive policing.

Head tells me that the judges and officials on the case all wanted numbers. They wanted to try this case based on what the data said. And the data showed what the plaintiffs and the Black and brown communities in New York City already knew: that the NYPD was con-ducting hundreds of thousands of stop-and-frisk actions every year, and the majority of people being subjected to those searches were Black or Latine.

Even though the CCR felt they had strong data supporting their case, they wanted more, because every data point presented to the court was a human being who had been harmed and who deserved to be heard. "We felt strongly that you couldn't just go to court with data. That's not fulfilling our obligation as a kind of legal organization to our clients. We want to make sure the stories are up-front."

Head set out to help gather stories of Black and brown New Yorkers who had been affected by stop-and-frisk policies. Working in majority Black and brown communities, he had to go about this work with care, as many of the people he was hoping to get stories from had good reason to be distrustful of a white man showing up at their door in any legal capacity.

"I was once again playing that role of in between the lawyers and the activists, the organizers, the community, the leaders . . . talking with and then gathering stories from [them]. Whether it was in person or across the city, or whether it was calling people on the phone," Head recalls. "I think there has to be an acknowledgment that oftentimes I might not be the person that needs to go out there and talk to folks. . . . There's so many reasons, in the white supremacist world where we live, that when Black people, young Black folks in neighborhoods deep in Brooklyn or wherever it may be, they see someone like me and should not trust someone like me."

Head partnered up with Black and brown organizers when he went door-to-door to get testimonies. "We were approaching that super humbly. We had a little handout. We had a little spiel. Sometimes I would start; sometimes he would start. We were literally knocking on doors and asking these people if they knew about or had experienced stop-and-frisk."

Head also gathered testimonies by gaining invitations to community meetings about stop-and-frisk. He did this by building trustful relationships with community organizers. It was the strength of those relationships that helped him gain access to communities that may otherwise be reluctant to speak with him.

This work relied on Head trying to be as aware as possible of his power and privilege at all times. He would regularly check with the community organizers he had partnered with to make sure he wasn't overstepping. He would ask whether it was appropriate for him to be attending gatherings, and if so, how much time he should be speaking.

Head worked hard to decenter himself in this work and to remember that the ultimate goal was to gather these stories in order to battle abuses happening to Black and brown communities, not to make himself feel good.

"Frankly, sometimes it wasn't appropriate for me to be there. Sometimes it would be better for me to give some kind of spiel to the organizer and have them talk about it with others in their community."

It was also vital that Head be as transparent as possible about the risks of talking with him. He let people know that the process could involve months of work. It could require that people tell their story in front of a judge and prosecutors. Head wanted to give people who were considering talking with him as much information as he had.

Some people decided not to take the risk of speaking with him, but many others did speak. And the testimonies Head gathered helped build the case against stop-and-frisk. And in 2013 the practice was ruled unconstitutional.

This was a small but important victory. And even though, as we speak, the NYPD is trying to find more ways to violate the rights of Black and brown New Yorkers, and even though the legal battle is still far from over, nine years later, Head is proud of his work and still grateful for what he's been able to do.

"Despite the fact that we're dealing with harm reduction and not shutting down the system, despite the fact that there's frustrating things every single day, I do feel like I see little things change. I have hope, and I have made community with amazing people and see what they do, and there's kind of an ongoing inspiration, if that makes sense. I'm inspired by people around me. I'm inspired by what I see. I'm inspired by the youth. I think it's also an obligation. And I don't say that as a, like, 'Ugh. I have an obligation to do this,' but more that I think, as a white person, I have an obligation to stand up and fight against racial injustice and white supremacy."

As hard as this work is, he can't imagine doing anything else.

"It's exciting work, on a certain level. It's horrifically awful, on a certain level. But it's also, I think, when we get some wins here and there, when we are pushing back . . . it maybe comes back to the moral side, to some extent. This is the important work. How can we live our lives without doing this work?"

## What Is Beyond Punishment?

I've written before about how our family has been targeted because of the work I do. In 2019, our home was swatted—my own son put in serious danger when police officers were sent to our home by the swatters, expecting him to have a loaded weapon. But I don't talk a lot about what happened after this terrifying incident. We were continuously harassed in our home by these white supremacist terrorists—so much so that we had to move.

It was very difficult to get law enforcement to take the threats and harassment seriously. Their only advice was to not complain about it publicly in order to not draw more attention to them.

My older son was trying to heal from the trauma of being woken from his sleep to find six officers with guns at our door. I was trying to deal with the fear and heartbreak that the white supremacist response to my work had put my son in danger. My younger son had taken to sleeping under his bed, so the bad guys couldn't find him at night.

Eventually the group targeting me and other writers and journalists of color, as well as Jewish writers and journalists, was broken up by the FBI. Beyond targeting me, they had swatted other Black writers, threatened Jewish journalists with Nazi propaganda, and phoned in bomb threats to multiple institutions.

When news of the arrest and prosecution of members of this group reached me, I pulled up some of the cases. I looked at the face of one of the leaders of the group, one who had been responsible for a large number of swattings. He looked like a kid. He *was* a kid—or barely an adult.

I'm not going to lie. I felt like I could breathe a little easier after the arrests. But I was also very aware that the arrests hadn't really solved anything. Yes, I would have a little time to try to gather myself and heal from that terror campaign now that the main group targeting us would be disbanded. But I knew it was a very temporary reprieve. Because their punishment hadn't addressed the deep, systemic issues emboldening white supremacy against me and many others trying to create change. It hadn't looked at why these young white men had turned to such violence. It hadn't confronted the fear and hatred and feelings of desperation inside of them that had made them risk their entire futures in order to inflict such terror on someone they had never met. More angry and violent white men were out there, and they would continue to target those of us who were trying to fight the very oppression they depended on to feel powerful.

As one of few Black people who actually got to see some measure of "justice" for harm caused by white supremacy, I can tell you that I'm no safer for it. I can tell you that I didn't feel my safety or well-being was ever prioritized in my interactions with police or in how the case was prosecuted. Because that isn't what punishment is about.

But what if there is another way?

What if we could prioritize safety and healing when harm is done? What if we could have lasting accountability without causing additional harm?

What keeps you from hurting people? Is it fear of punishment? I know we sometimes like to joke in times of frustration or anger about what we might do if the law didn't apply. But really, is the fear of punishment what stops you from hurting your family members? Your neighbors? Your friends? A stranger who cuts you off in traffic or insults you in the street?

What keeps you from breaking laws? If there wasn't punishment attached, would you be out robbing a store right now? Would you be drinking and driving? Would you be smashing in the windows of the coworker who insulted you?

If we're going to talk about abolition, we need to talk about harm. What drives people to cause harm? What prevents them from causing harm? These questions are at the root of why we make laws: to deter harm. Well, at least they should be. Often there is very little connection between the causes of harm, the deterrents from causing harm, and the laws we build around it.

Almost nobody wants to go to prison. In fact, I've yet to meet anyone who wants to avoid prison *more* than the people who have already been there in the past. Prison is torture. It's violent; it's abusive; it's cruel. It's disabling and demoralizing. Nobody leaves prison unscathed. And yet we send more people to our prisons than any other country in the world. So if we've built some of the worst imaginable consequences for breaking laws—because that's how we deter people from breaking laws—then why are we still sending so many people to prison? I mean, by now the word about this whole prison thing has surely gotten out.

Part of what perpetuates this extremely violent and ineffective system of harm management is the idea that people who commit crimes are fundamentally different from those of us who do not. These are people with different motivations than us. These are people with different intelligence and different capabilities. These are people with different morals—if they have any at all. The idea that people who cause the type of harm that could land them in prison are *bad* is seen in countless books, movies, and television shows, and those who aren't *bad* are instead deeply flawed in a way that makes them incapable of being a part of "normal" society.

We don't send people to prison to get better. We don't send people to prison in order for them to get medical care or an education. We don't send people to prison for mental health treatment or job training. If we did, those services would actually be prioritized in prisons. Yes, lip service is given to a person's chances to "improve" themselves in prison, but what we're really doing is removing from us the people we think are beyond redemption and putting them with others we've decided are too defective to remain with us. And we hope their exile will serve as a warning to others out there who we are sure will only respond to the threat of the sort of violence that prison can provide.

These ideas about criminality have been deeply ingrained in our culture, in many ways that we don't investigate. And because we don't investigate them, we also don't investigate how often these ideas are informed by and strengthened by racism, ableism, and classism.

If we are to look honestly at what leads people to cause harm in our society, and if we are going to consciously try to address these issues without racism, ableism, or classism, then we must look honestly at what prompts those of us who view ourselves as "good" to cause harm, or to not cause harm.

Most crime is committed from a place of desperation, or from a place of deep harm that has already been done to the perpetrator. Crime is often a story of fear. It is a "choose your own adventure" with only one or two very unsavory paths on offer. When we look at who is committing crime, we often find survivors of abuse and neglect, people fighting addiction, people who have been made houseless, people who lack resources necessary for survival via "legitimate" means, people who are suffering from complex PTSD due to a lifetime of systemic violence, people whose connections to community have been severed.

I should be more specific here. Because the people who are being *incarcerated* for crimes often fit into these categories. A lot of people with power and privilege commit crimes and are complicit in horrific violence but do so because that is what is expected of their power and privilege, and those people are more likely to be elected to the US presidency than to see a day behind bars.

But for the majority of people, it is our connections to others, our sense of safety among our people, and access to resources needed for our well-being that keep us from perpetrating harm and that drive us to repair harm when we cause it.

And yet when we try to address harm on both systemic and interpersonal levels, the "remedies" we employ do nothing to confront the root causes of harm or strengthen the relationships and resources that would deter harm.

From early childhood on, we are often punished for behavior that causes harm—behavior that shows a breakdown in relationships, feelings of fear, and a (perceived or real) lack of alternative actions. But even with children, we don't teach how to repair relationships. We don't teach how to work through feelings of fear or try to address what is causing fear. We don't try to show children what other options are available to them. Instead, we remove children further from relationships with time-outs, or remove valued assets from the child, or even carry out acts of physical violence against them as punishment. Variations of punishment-based conflict-resolution tactics are found in just about all of our personal, professional, and societal relationships.

If lack of punishment is not why we cause harm, and if fear of punishment is not why we avoid causing harm, then why is it so often the only tool we turn to in order to address harm?

Many issues around harm require healing of a relationship. Whether that's a relationship between two people, between groups of people, or between people and institutions or governments. Punishment will not fix that relationship. You can't punish people into thinking that others are worthy of care or respect. You can't punish people into believing that a social contract that is harming them is actually for their own good. You can't punish people into suddenly having the resources that will keep them from feeling like they have to operate outside of social contracts.

Put simply: if your goal is a safer, more whole society, punishment can't be a part of your vision.

This doesn't mean that you're wrong or "bad" if you want people to be punished for harm they cause. This is a normal and common response to harm. It's what we've been taught and often all that we've been offered as recompense for harm done to us.

I understand that it doesn't seem fair that people can hurt other people—even kill other people—and not be punished.

But it's important to remember that punishment culture is inherently hierarchical, patriarchal, and oppressive. And it, like so many of our other systems, is too rife with racism, classism, and ableism to ever be applied in a way that won't contribute to great injustice.

"I do feel like there is that revenge element," says Theryn Kigvamasud'vashti. "And that piece, not having that, really pisses people off. And I do think that's based on a model of punishment that is very much part of our colonialized experiences."

Kigvamasud'vashti recognizes the deeper motivation for revenge that a lot of us have. "I recognize where the desire comes from. And it comes from a feeling of never having justice. Never feeling any kind of systemic justice. Anything that lasts. Anything that actually moves the community forward."

Part of why punishment has such strong appeal is because it's the only option offered to us for deterrence. But also because it's the only acknowledgment of harm and the value of the person harmed that we provide. Like Kigvamasud'vashti said, when even that is denied us, we are doubly harmed. And our desire for *just once*, for this fucked-up system to value us enough that it will punish those who harm us—the way it seems to want to punish us for just about anything—is strong.

Harm doesn't happen in a vacuum. We discussed many reasons that harm can occur. None of those are based solely on the actions of one person. This doesn't mean that the main perpetrators of harm are off the hook for harm caused. This means that if we're going to hold people accountable for harm, it's best to hold accountable all the parties responsible.

"When we look at folks, and we start seeing the totality of circumstances around a person, right?" Mannie Thomas says. "We can see that there are a set of circumstances that are not to blame. People can take personal accountability, but we as a society can also say, 'Okay, so what things were systems doing to this person in order for them to even think that they had to resort to that, or molded or shaped their behavior in that way?'"

This is, to Mannie Thomas, the essence of transformative justice. A way that many abolitionists have thought about healing alternatives to punishment and incarceration for many years.

"The thinking is, we're going to look at everything," he explains. "We're going to look at the person who suffered harm. We're gonna look at the person who caused the harm. We're going to look at the systems that were at play to contribute to that."

This isn't just theory that Thomas preaches. He and others who have gone through the Success Stories program are a testament to what transformative justice can do.

"Look at us," he says. "Living example of what it means to truly transform."

Transformative justice seeks accountability instead of punishment.

As Mariame Kaba states in *We Do This 'Til We Free Us*: "I want accountability. I want people to take responsibility. I want that internal resource that allows you to take responsibility for harms that you commit against yourself and other people. I want that to be a central part of how we interact with each other. Because while I don't believe in punishment, I believe in consequences for actions that are done to harm other people" (2021, 146).

Kaba goes on to further explain the difference between punishment and consequence:

*Punishment means inflicting cruelty and suffering on people. When you are expecting consequences, those can be unpleasant and uncomfortable. But they are not suffering and inflicting pain on people and you want them to suffer as a result. That is different. And what I mean by that is, for example, powerful people stepping down from their jobs are consequences, not punishments. Why? Because we should have boundaries. And because shit that you did was wrong, and you having power is a privilege.... But if we were punishing you, we would make it so that you could never make a living again in any context, at any point. That's inflicting cruelty, suffering, and making it so that people cannot actually live a life. (2021, 147)*

Transformative justice holds people accountable for the harm they cause, and it also holds communities accountable for how they contribute to harm, in order to prevent future harm.

Transformative justice takes resources that now go to punishment and repurposes them toward healing the persons harmed.

I want to live in a world where healing is possible. Where root causes of harm are addressed without causing further harm. I want to live in a world where the removal of someone from society is seen as a failure in the justice process, instead of a success.

I want to live in a world where the value of the people harmed is not measured by how much we're willing to punish the person who created harm but instead by how much we are willing to invest in healing and making sure that others aren't harmed in the same way again.

And we can live in that world. Every day, people—like many of the people you are reading about in this book—are pouring healing love into their communities. Into community members who may have been written off as damaged beyond repair. And with limited resources, and often with the entire power of the state working against them, they are saving lives and holding communities together. Imagine what could be done if even half of the resources we are currently pouring into systems that have trapped us into intergenerational cycles of harm were instead given to those who have been fighting to free us.

## MAHNKER DAHNWEIH

My name is Mahnker Dahnweih. My pronouns are she/her/hers. I'm a member of the executive team over at Freedom, Inc. And also the executive director of Freedom Action Now, which is our [501](c)(4) organization."

I was drawn to Freedom, Inc., for their work on getting cops out of Madison, Wisconsin, schools and was expecting our conversation to be around this sort of abolition work. Dahnweih begins by explaining that while, yes, a lot of work Freedom, Inc., does deals with the police and police abuses, and you will often see their name associated with large-scale protests against police violence in Madison, it's all just one part of a very large mandate for the organization.

"At Freedom, Inc.," she explains, "our work is to end violence and sexual abuse within and against our communities. By our communities, I mean Black and Southeast Asian, low- to no-income, queer, trans, and intersex folks in Madison and the broader state of Wisconsin. And by violence within, I mean focusing on intimate partner violence, and the interpersonal violences that we do to each other in our communities— very much based on the systems of oppression that we are enduring and living under. And then, by violence against, we mean state violence. And this is what we consider the 'big' violence."

Dahnweih feels like she was born into this sort of work. Her parents came to the United States seeking safety from the violence of the Second Liberian Civil War. Dahnweih was the first of their children born in the US.

Her family was resettled in Chicago's South Side, where from her birth—"I was born at Cook County Hospital, which is one of the worst public hospitals in the state"—Dahnweih was fighting for survival against oppressive systems and social and economic injustice.

The systemic oppression her community in Chicago was living under, combined with the stories of wartime violence her parents had fled, has shaped a lot of Dahnweih's struggle for justice.

In a place like the South Side, survival itself was a form of resistance that people practiced regularly. Dahnweih grew up with an understanding that "we do not fuck with the police. These people are not here to support us at all." The kids in her neighborhood did what they could to keep the police away. "If we see the police approaching, we're gonna go play at the end of the block in the middle of the street on our bikes or some shit, so they can't drive through. Or when we see somebody's car getting towed, we're gonna go call everybody on the block and go yell, like, 'Hey, your car's being towed!' You see somebody running from the police, 'Yeah, like, you can duck in my backyard real quick.'"

Dahnweih's neighborhood looked out for its own, and looked toward its safety outside of established systems that had harmed it.

"I'm not saying it was perfect or anything like that," Dahnweih says, "but there was still a lot going on that kind of predisposed me, I think, to always be seeking and wanting to seek, 'What can I do?'"

Dahnweih also learned how oppressive and abusive systems could amplify problems at home.

She shares a memory of watching her mother be arrested by police, who had shown up at their home after her father hit her mother, when he then claimed that her mother had tried to steal his car. She talks about how her older brothers and cousins were caught up in gun violence in their community while she faced harm inside her home as a queer person. Dahnweih struggled to understand the harm being done to her family while also fighting to survive the harm being done to her by her family. She remembers thinking, *I love my family so much, and I see how they're struggling and suffering under the state. And yet I'm also struggling and suffering under them.*

Dahnweih wanted to do something to change the circumstances her family and community were in. She first looked toward politics.

Around the age of sixteen, Dahnweih started volunteering with local congressional campaigns. She thought that if she could help get the right people elected to local government, they could create much-needed change in her neighborhood.

But Dahnweih was quickly disillusioned with politics, and especially political candidates. "Once you get up close and personal with candidates, you're like, 'This person just seems like a paper bag that somebody else put stuff in.' They're very shallow. They're not the ones who, like, you know, decide anything."

She found that it was actually the fundraisers and campaign officials who really called the shots and set the candidates' agendas. Money appeared to be king in politics, and whoever was able to bring in the money made the decisions.

Disappointed with political activism, Dahnweih began working with an environmental nonprofit that aimed to bring attention to environmental racism in Milwaukee. Dahnweih thought this would be a good place to land while figuring out next steps.

But in working with Milwaukee Riverkeeper, Dahnweih fell in love with grassroots organizing. In particular, the way Milwaukee Riverkeeper used data to inform its decision-making really appealed to her and her interest in geography.

When on a grassroots organizing fellowship, she met organizers from Freedom, Inc. They encouraged her to apply to work on their civic engagement initiatives. She applied, sure that they weren't going to hire her, but they did.

Dahnweih quickly got to work as their civic engagement coordinator. "I really took it upon myself to build a civic engagement program that centered our folks as experts." In her role, she worked with the community to help its members build leadership skills and then put those skills to work.

With the success of this program, Dahnweih moved up to manager, then to director of community power building. In June 2022, she became one of the executive team members.

Freedom, Inc., does a lot in its work to end violence in and against marginalized communities in the Madison area. This work is vital to preventing both internal and external violence in our communities. We're often motivated to "do something" about policing when a particularly horrific story of police violence is brought to our attention on the news or online. But Dahnweih stresses that we need to see beyond the headlines that sadden, scare, or outrage us and recognize the root causes of violence and harm in our communities. "By the time it gets to a news story, it's ruined so many people's lives," she says. "That person has probably been through so much other state violence leading up to this, and intertwined into their whole lives, that it's probably just the culminating moment."

That violence is often exacerbated by police actions many people outside of the community don't see.

"I would hope that when people see a single news story, they understand how insidious that act [of police violence] is. That one act that they're witnessing. How it impacts the rest of the community, and the constant state of terror and violence that we face from these people." Dahnweih says, "Because, even if you never had any interaction with the police besides they help you get your cat out of a tree or help you when someone broke into your car or whatever, it's not worth the harm that they're doing to ten thousand more people, when they may be helpful that one time."

Dahnweih also sees strong parallels between the gender-based violence in communities and the relationships between communities and the police. "They are out there abusing other people. And it is textbook abusive behavior. Because that's what happens too, when people are being abusive in intimate partner violence situations, too. People say, 'Well, I just can't believe it because he's such a nice guy to me. I don't know that he hits women, because he's never done anything to me.' And meanwhile, they are harming the people who they see as more vulnerable or that they can exert power over. So it's the same situation. They may not be able to exert their power over you, their force over you, because of your social status, because of your skin color, because of whatever else. But that doesn't mean that they're not doing it to ten thousand other people right now."

This abuse only continues when people are locked away.

"It's a sexual violation, too," she says. "Because there's no consent practice in what is happening. And there's so much physical—cavity search and whatever—handling of their physical body that happens. It is a spiritual assault, it is a physical one—it is horrible. It is meant to break people."

Dahnweih and Freedom, Inc., are taking this violent, abusive system on, investing in those who have been most harmed by our systems and challenging those systems causing the harm. "We're working with people who are incarcerated, being harassed by the police, families of folks who have been murdered by the police. And the systemic crimes that our state does to us. Like intentional poverty, food apartheid, pushing folks out of housing, and development plans that are racist, queerphobic, transphobic, and just against low- to no-income folks being able to thrive and live a good life." Dahnweih explains: "The ways that we end that violence, both the internal and the big violence, is through this cycle of providing direct services around intimate partner and state violence."

That support looks like a lot of things: helping people secure safe and affordable housing, working on safety plans for those experiencing interpersonal violence, providing court support for those targeted by our carceral systems, and more. Once people are past a crisis, they can then enter more long-term Freedom, Inc., programs, focused on support, healing, and education. Dahnweih says, "Folks are able to learn or really unlock leadership development skills and practices of restoring from harm, of mutual aid, within their support groups and across groups."

Once people go through this process, many become leaders of groups themselves.

From there, some leaders move into programs that show them how to become community organizers, in order to advocate for systemic change. This is, Dahnweih explains, the final part of Freedom, Inc.'s "theory of change." It's this part that Dahnweih currently leads.

This process isn't just vital to healing communities from harm. It's also a survival strategy for the organization. It has long been a tactic of oppressive powers to target movement leaders in order to create chaos in organizations and to slow or stop movement progress. Freedom, Inc., works hard to protect against that.

"We make sure that in designing our campaigns, there are many entry points and opportunities for our leaders to develop, to grow a base, to raise their status as a leader and be known in the community [as] a leader," Dahnweih says. "We are actually a *leaderful* movement, and we are bringing people in every day. . . . They cannot just target one of us and then the campaign dies. There are many of us, and there will always be someone to take our place and to move up in leadership."

As far as campaign priorities, those are set first by listening to people in their communities. Freedom, Inc., surveys community members and holds in-depth focus sessions to figure out what their top priorities are.

"We found that, yes, folks are more concerned about safety and things like that. But they don't see the police as a solution to safety concerns, or they don't see the police as the entity that's making them more safe." These aren't the only issues that community members feel city government can't handle: "People are concerned about food, but they don't think the city's the one that's gonna help solve that."

In talking with community members, Freedom, Inc., has been able to put together a People's Budget, to compete with the mayor's budget and the city's funding priorities. While their budget is much smaller than the city's, they can still make real change on a smaller scale, by investing in the priorities outlined by people in some of their most neglected communities.

This People's Budget works to not only help improve conditions in Black and Southeast Asian communities but also show the city that there is a better way. "This is what we want the entire city to look like, or the entire state to look like," Dahnweih says. Without the power or funds to make these changes for the entire city or state, they still do what they can.

In this work, Freedom, Inc., models an important abolitionist practice: building alternatives outside of policing. Freedom, Inc., fights violence by investing in community, instead of trying to control and punish community. And it's working.

"I'm going through candidate campaigns, I'm going through super PACs, I'm going through the basic, traditional, single-issue, white nonprofits. And I'm like, 'Those things don't actually work.' None of that shit worked," Dahnweih says. "[But] this is the thing that I've seen that's actually producing results. Beyond whatever our annual budget is, or beyond whatever big projects we say we're gonna do, what would last tomorrow and still be here tomorrow, if we had zero budget tomorrow? I think Freedom, Inc., would still be here. I think that our community, and the type of work that we do, we would still be doing it."

Dahnweih does this work because she believes in it, and so does everybody else at Freedom, Inc. They are building alternatives to policing in preventing violence, healing from violence, and building up community. They are showing what is possible when you empower people, and in doing so, they are meeting needs in their communities that the state could never meet.

"We've established ourselves as experts. And now, actually, it's time to hold you all accountable." Dahnweih says to those who have long failed in their responsibilities to her community: "You're gaslighting us and telling us everything is impossible that we want, and that's why you keep flip-flopping or not following through on promises. We're gonna show you that it's actually possible."

## BE A REVOLUTION

While most of us can agree that the ultimate goal of prison abolitionism is a world without prisons, this goal is huge, and one we may not see achieved in our lifetimes. But it doesn't mean that the work is hopeless or that there aren't many different ways we can make meaningful progress toward this goal.

The practice of abolitionism can look like a lot of things. Abolitionism means more than just the ultimate goal of closing down prisons and ending incarceration. Everything we can do to get people free—even if it's one person at a time, even if it's just helping people withstand the terrors of incarceration—is abolition.

Curious about where to start or how to join in the battle? Here are some common actions abolitionists are taking:

- **Target facilities.** Goals to shut down prisons, juvenile detention centers, immigration detention centers, and abusive mental health facilities are all valid and attainable. I myself have been a small part of work to prevent the building of new prison and juvenile detention facilities in Seattle—both of which were successful because of the dedicated work of activists and abolitionists.

- **Target spending.** You've likely heard the phrase "Defund the police." This call to take funding from policing services and put it toward community services that can actually prevent harm has increased in popularity in recent years. A lot of people may think actual measures have to be passed to take funds away. The truth is, every time a municipality puts together a budget, we're given opportunities to fight for defunding. Every penny going toward incarceration or strengthening the prison-industrial complex should be fought—even when government officials try to tie that funding to other spending that is more desirable or needed by communities. This is often done to make us (and more abolition-minded local legislative representatives) feel like we don't have choices. But by steadfastly refusing to vote for anything that would provide the dollars, we can show our representatives they have no choice but to separate out police and prison funding if they want their legislation to pass. Funding incarceration should be a poison pill for legislation.

➤ **Remove police.** The fight to remove police from specific places and situations is work we can and do engage in right now. Getting police officers out of schools and off university campuses is vital. Removing mental health and wellness checks from their responsibilities and requiring they rely instead on trained mental health professionals—who won't immediately turn to police in times of tension or conflict— is vital. Refusing to use police as protection or escort for protests and community functions is also vital.

➤ **Reduce sentences.** The fight to reduce sentences, both for individuals who are incarcerated and for crimes in general, is crucial work. Yes, people shouldn't be sent to prison at all, but anything we can do to reduce the amount of people in prisons and the amount of time people have to spend incarcerated is an important part of abolition work we can do right now.

➤ **Decriminalize offenses.** While it might be a hard sell to get people to agree to end incarceration today, we can and are getting agreement on decriminalizing certain offenses right now. Drug offenses are great targets for decriminalization. So is sex work. So are child support order violations.

➤ **Support defendants.** Providing support to defendants in their court cases—especially poor, disabled, BIPOC, queer, and trans defendants, who are targeted by our criminal justice systems and are less likely to have resources for defense—is very important. Raise awareness about prosecution efforts. Show up at court. Raise bail money. Raise legal defense funds.

➤ **End cash bail.** Cash bail only serves to ensure that poor people stay behind bars while rich people do not. It must be ended as soon as possible. Raise awareness about the injustice and abuse of cash bail and organize to have it ended wherever you encounter it. And support bail funds that aim to help victims of cash bail practices get out of jail.

➤ **Support prisoners.** People who are incarcerated are often forgotten by most of society as soon as those cell doors close around them. We must do what we can to stay connected to people who are incarcerated. We must support them during their incarceration so they can return home. Send letters. Send books. Support efforts to get incarcerated people transferred to facilities closer to their loved ones. Support funds to help loved ones travel to visit friends and family in prison. Support legal challenges of incarcerated people. Help incarcerated people advocate for their rights and protect themselves from abuse and neglect in prisons.

➤ **Divorce yourself from the prison-industrial complex.** We are tied to the prison-industrial complex in a lot of ways that we may not be aware of. Whatever we can do to limit our own support of this system will aid in abolition efforts. Boycott businesses and organizations that make money from prison labor. Demand that your university cut ties with service providers (like food service providers) linked to prison labor. Do not participate in media that aims to build better PR for police and policing. Don't share the heartwarming cop stories or the cute memes. Recognize propaganda for what it is: a tool to help further embed incarceration culture into our lives.

This is just a sample of some of the areas in which abolition work is being done. This is work you can join or support right now.

You may notice that items like "Reform police" weren't listed. That's because reform isn't abolition. And certain reforms may seem helpful on the surface while being detrimental to the fight for abolition in the long run. As Mariame Kaba says, "most prison reforms tend to entrench the prison system and expand its reach" (2021, 111).

Reform doesn't work, and it's something that has been tried over and over and over with few positive results. Racism and ableism are deeply entrenched in our prison and policing systems, and have been since their inception. Any meaningful attempts at reform are treated as the attacks on white supremacist capitalism that they are, and thus have never been allowed to be implemented in any substantial or lasting way. We've seen in this chapter how even mild reform is fought against—and often quickly rolled back—by the powers that be. We are often sold this light reform as revolution, and told that it's the most we can hope for, because those trying to sell it to us know it will buy them time to strengthen their hold on power and make real change harder to accomplish.

Some examples of reforms that may have seemed helpful on the surface but actually serve to further entrench policing in our lives are increased funding for police training (which just serves to increase the police budget and almost never leads to any measurable difference in police behavior) and body-worn cameras (which can be easily manipulated by officers to show them in a favorable light; are often conveniently "off" or facing away from the action when they wouldn't show officers in a favorable light; are increasingly becoming surveillance tools by police departments; and are another way to increase police budgets).

Often abolitionists have to do work that isn't abolitionist. In order to reduce harm that's happening right now, abolitionists sometimes have to work in systems that are carceral in nature or a part of the prison–industrial complex. This is the unfortunate reality of the world we live in.

Lawyer and abolitionist organizer Nikkita Oliver says, "For me, my abolitionist framework is not just about the vision of the world I want to live in; it is also about honestly assessing the work that we're doing. And if it's harm reduction or mitigation, let's call it that. This is not an abolitionist program; this is harm reduction and mitigation. And where it is abolitionist, where it's outside of the state, or it's building new tools and skills and networks and community, let's also acknowledge that and be about that."

Oliver continues: "I don't believe in inside-outside strategies. I believe in inside-outside harm reduction and mitigation. How can we keep the system from doing what the system does? And those of us who are inside, we play a role in protecting, stopping all the shitty shit. We're not gonna do the good shit. We might be able to release some resources to folks that are working outside the system, [who] are mobilizing networks and doing all the good shit. We get to stop the shitty shit. And I think that's what people from movements who get into office or start working in city or county government . . . don't realize. Because they don't hold that role in the place that it is. You're harm reduction. You're a stop-the-shitty-shit person. And that feels shitty, and you can only do that for so long."

This battle is a long one. It's at the core of systemic racism. There is a lot of power behind the idea that populations of color are inherently dangerous, unable to govern themselves, and must be tightly controlled in order to ensure safety for white communities. This is a powerful tool of capitalism, of our political system, of the gun lobby, of our incredibly resource-hungry prison–industrial complex. This is a system the powers that be will fight like hell to protect.

This means we will see a lot of defeats before we see wins. We will at times feel beaten down by the magnitude of what we're trying to accomplish.

This feeling of hopelessness is one that abolitionists like Talila Lewis battle all of the time: "I would explain to people some of the work that I was doing at the beginning, which was trying to support innocent, actually innocent, disabled/Deaf folks to get free from the cage, and they would be like, 'Oh, how many people have you gotten out?' Actually, none. Literally none. And I still been working on it ten years. But you don't understand that because your ideal of successful organizing around this is getting people out."

Lewis had to redefine success to be able to continue doing this work that seemed on the surface to have so few wins: "I created these metrics of success. Like: How many families have you kept together through the wires? How many children of incarcerated people still know that they're loved, notwithstanding these hundreds-years wars that are being waged against our communities to separate our families?"

Lewis encourages people to know what their achievable metrics of success are. "Because that is gonna be the question, and I need to have a good response—cuz otherwise it eats you alive."

These metrics aren't just trying to put a positive spin on work. They're also about understanding what progress really looks like and allowing ourselves space to celebrate that progress, even in what looks like defeat.

"Especially those of us who are in movement work, I think a good amount of our time should be sitting down thinking about that. If we really want to practice anti-ableist organizing, movement work, strategizing, et cetera," Lewis says. "Because some of these metrics just aren't successful. Even, like, getting a lot of our folks out on parole, clemency—it just doesn't happen. That's not our fault. We're doing all the organizing we possibly can. We've gotta be kind and generous to ourselves in our analysis of what it means. And when do we get to celebrate ourselves? Because if not . . . you could be very unhappy for a very long time, which I was. And I still am kind of coming out of that."

When organizers fighting the creation of a police- and fire-training academy in a Black community in Chicago's West Side were unable to stop Mayor Rahm Emanuel from moving forward with the project, Mariame Kaba wrote a beautiful love letter to the organizers. In it she counsels:

*Organizing is mostly about defeats. Often when we engage in campaigns, we lose. But any organizer worth their salt knows that it's much more complex than a simple win-lose calculus. (2021, 127)*

Kaba then went on to list many of the powerful things the #NoCopAcademy organizers accomplished and how much good they did in raising awareness about the academy and the dangers of further embedding carceral systems into our communities. She closed her letter with this beautiful note of appreciation:

*For myself, I say thank you to the #NoCopAcademy organizers. You have sustained my hope. I choose to emphasize the fact that you fought as a win because what we choose to emphasize determines our lives. Your protest, your refusal to be run over, your local actions, added to those of others the world over, will slowly tilt this world toward more justice. (2021, 129)*

Whether it's #NoCopAcademy in Chicago, #BlockTheBunker in Seattle, or #StopCopCity in Atlanta, people are fighting every day against the growth of our increasingly militaristic police system and its campaign of terror against our Black, brown, Indigenous, disabled, and poor communities. Some of these battles we win—at least for a little while. Some of them we haven't won, yet.

But every time we say no to the ideas that our communities need to be controlled by the state in order to be safe, and that our communities are made better by removing our people from them, we are pulling out the bricks of racism, ableism, classism, and patriarchy that make up the foundation of oppression in our society. And every time we decide to invest in our healing and our humanity, we are building up the foundation of our collective liberation.

## GENDER JUSTICE,

## BODILY AUTONOMY,

## AND RACE

I WAS TRAVELING ABROAD WITH my partner and younger son in 2022 when the news broke that *Roe v. Wade* had been overturned by the US Supreme Court. We had been enjoying a day at a museum in Paris, looking at musical instruments from around the world that spanned centuries. It was the first time all week that we had gotten some real engagement from our surly fourteen-year-old, who had been apparently too embarrassed at the reality that he had parents to enjoy a vacation in one of the world's most exciting cities.

There was little cell phone reception in the giant concrete building, so most of our visit was undisturbed. But the restrooms were closer to the entrance, and when I stepped away from my family to use the facilities, my phone started pinging away with notifications and anguished text messages from friends and community members.

I sat down on a bench by the doors, winded as if I'd been punched in the stomach.

I knew this had been coming. It was not a surprise at all. But still—damn, it hurt.

I sat in a daze, unable to figure out what to do next. Eventually my partner came and sat beside me. "I really don't want to go back," I said. He just nodded at me and began looking up reproductive rights in other countries. I started gathering abortion care resources to share online for folks at home.

A day or two later we got on a plane to head home. We had to transfer planes in Iceland before reaching our final destination in Seattle. We went through customs and were asked about our trip and what we had been doing abroad. We answered the usual questions and continued through. Then, at the final checkpoint, my partner was pulled aside. He had been flagged for additional security checks.

He was taken away from us to another room. My son and I weren't allowed to wait for him. We had to continue forward without him, they said. I didn't understand what was happening. I just knew that my spouse—a light-skinned Black person with a beard who, because of his skin tone and facial hair, is often mistaken for a Muslim man of Middle Eastern descent—was taken away from me in a foreign country as we were trying to get back to a place that had just stripped away an important measure of my own bodily autonomy and safety.

I paced around for what seemed like an eternity until I found my partner making his way back to us from the other end of the airport terminal. I tried to take deep breaths and quell my panic even while knowing that safety as Black queer people in this world is a very precarious and temporary thing.

Once my heart and my head calmed down a bit, I was able to sit more with the reality of this situation.

The reality is that I've never had bodily autonomy in the US— not as a Black queer woman. And there are many people who have had even less. Trans people. Disabled people. Poor Black, brown, and Indigenous people. Incarcerated people.

The shocking assault on our rights that came with the numerous anti-abortion bills and then the devastating Supreme Court ruling echoed previous attacks on marginalized and vulnerable people throughout our country's history. And only now—when cisgender, middle-class white women can feel the threat—is this considered an emergency.

But the same people right now deciding whether or not people will be forced to carry a pregnancy to term against their will are the same people deciding that Black, brown, and Indigenous people should be funneled into our prison systems, that the quality of life for disabled people doesn't matter, that trans people shouldn't have gender-affirming care or the ability to financially meet their basic needs or even use a bathroom safely.

The assault on our bodily autonomy didn't start with the Supreme Court ruling, and it won't end there either. And it is our racism, classism, ableism, and transphobia that have stopped us from coming together to fight this threat as hard as we should have.

I hope that in this chapter anyone who claims to be, or strives to be, anti-racist will see how vital it is that we recognize reproductive justice as a racial justice issue. And I hope that those who see themselves as feminist or pro-choice will understand that their work is doomed to failure if they're not willing to look at the racial intersections and influences in the battle to control the bodies of women and other people with a uterus. And finally, I hope that those who are concerned with the issue of abortion rights will understand that bodily autonomy does not begin or end with the right to have an abortion, and that their rights will remain at risk wherever they allow assaults on bodily autonomy to continue.

## TARANA BURKE

Tarana Burke is a lifelong activist. She is also an author and a mother. For many people, she is known as the founder of the Me Too movement and the chief vision officer for Me Too International. But Burke has been on the ground, fighting for Black people and all of the ways in which our bodily autonomy is threatened and attacked, for decades.

She tells me that she started her activism at a very young age, but when she was younger, her racial justice work didn't focus on the sexual violence or gender-based violence that Black and brown women and girls experience. Her journey to the work she does today is as much a personal journey as it is a professional one.

Burke grew up in a conscious, activist family in the Bronx, New York. Her parents and grandparents made Burke's political education a priority. This education, coupled with Burke's innate sense of outrage at injustice in the world, led her to activism early. Just like in recent years, the late '80s and '90s were a period of racial justice activism around issues of police brutality, especially in areas like Los Angeles and New York, where Burke lived at the time.

As a teenager, Burke joined the 21st Century Youth Leadership Movement, an organization started by veterans of the Civil Rights, Black Power, and land reclamation movements of the '60s and '70s.

The opportunity to learn from those who had lived through some of our most important civil rights struggles in recent history was a defining moment in Burke's life. "I don't get here for certain without having that training," she says to me.

Burke worked in nonprofits through high school and college, and felt certain that her future work would lie either in the nonprofit sector or in philanthropy. She had seen how 21st Century had suffered due to lack of funding, and she thought she would be able to create needed change from within funding spaces.

But it was elders in 21st Century Youth Leadership Movement who pulled her back in. "Some of the elders were like, 'We need you to come to the organization for a while. Cuz this is the whole point, for y'all to take over.'" Burke chuckles.

She heeded the call and returned to work with 21st Century, finding fulfillment, community, and healing she hadn't expected as a survivor of sexual violence. "I didn't identify this way then, but I recognized later: It had given me healing space that I needed from the sexual violence that I experienced. It had given me a place to pour my rage. It gave me a place to find validation and all these things."

Even though she found healing in that space, Burke saw there were barriers for other Black girls coming through the program to find similar healing, because the issue of sexual violence was never specifically addressed, even though it quickly became clear to Burke that it was a widespread problem.

Every time program members came together for leadership camp and the girls attending were able to gather for conversation, Burke noticed that someone in the group would disclose abuse or assaults they had experienced. They would try to support and comfort one another in the moment, but Burke remembers that the actual issue of gender-based violence in the community was never addressed on a larger scale.

Burke wanted to make more space for the girls in her program for healing, but she found it was difficult in mixed-gender spaces. "Patriarchy had us all in a choke hold," she says. "Even when we love the little girls in our programs, we tend to favor the boys. For good and bad. We give them a heap of attention when they do, quote, un-quote, 'good.' And when they are misbehaving, we try to give them a heap of attention to bring them in, you know. And girls, we just sort of expect them to do good. When they do good things, we're like, 'Right. That's what you should do.'"

The frustration with this dynamic led Burke, along with her best friend at the time, to start her own organization called Just Be, which focused on building leadership skills in Black and brown girls. She looks back on this productive and dynamic time of her life with wonder.

"I think about my twenties so much. I had so much fucking energy," Burke says with a hearty laugh. "It's ridiculous. At one point in my late twenties I was a full-time journalist, I was running two organizations, and raising my child. I don't know how. And still doing community organizing!"

Pretty quickly after she began working with these Black and brown girls, disclosures of sexual assault started coming in. These disclosures didn't look like the confessions of assault and abuse we see in movies or on television. They were more subtle, almost mundane, in ways that betrayed the terrifying normalization of violence against Black women and girls.

"We started meeting with these girls, and the more we met with them, the more disclosure we got. In random ways. It wasn't like, 'Oh, I have to tell you something. I want to confess.' It was kind of like a seventh grader is saying, like, 'Oh, Miss Tarana, meet my boyfriend.' And he's, like, a twenty-five-year-old. You know?"

As these disclosures piled up, Burke began to get a clearer picture of how large the issue of sexual abuse and assault was in her community.

"I had a fifteen-year-old once who was pregnant and I found out that the father of the child was a thirty-six-year-old married man. And I wanted to press charges obviously." But when Burke spoke with the girl's mom, she found the sexual assault wasn't treated like the violent offense it was. "The mom was like, 'Unh-unh, he gon pay.' You know? It was just, like, the normalcy. The way they had normalized sexual violence, and nobody addressed it with these kids."

It wasn't just parents who normalized sexual assault. Burke observed that these girls who were disclosing abuse and assault often blamed themselves for what had happened. They saw themselves as complicit in the abuse against them, even when that abuse was being carried out by adults. In talking with these girls, Burke was able to recognize the ways in which she had also blamed herself for the childhood abuse she had survived.

As Burke tells me this, I'm aware, even in my own experience as a survivor of child sexual abuse, how common this is and how deeply harmful it is. The first time I disclosed abuse I was told that it didn't happen in our community, that sexual abuse only happened in white communities. I was told that I was misinterpreting love and affection as something more sinister. I remember thinking then that I must not be able to understand what was happening to me, that I had done something wrong, or I was making a big deal out of something benign. If nobody else saw the abuse against me as important, who was I to make a fuss? This internalized blame and shame kept me from disclosing further abuse until I was in my mid-twenties.

Burke wanted to try to break this intergenerational cycle of harm, first by helping these girls understand what had been happening to them.

"I started a little workshop. Every week we did a different thing. And I just had a week—it turned into two weeks—of workshopping about sexual violence. I thought, *Oh, I need to teach them language first. Let's start with a really basic thing. These girls don't know how to identify what happened to them, cuz they don't know how to name it.* So literally we would be like, 'This is the definition of statutory rape.' 'This is what molestation means.' We gave them definitions."

To put those definitions into lived context, Burke brought in several high-profile Black women who had publicly disclosed a history of sexual violence to speak with the girls. Burke would share these women's stories with them beforehand, not yet revealing their identities. When the identities of the Black women were revealed, the girls in the workshop would be shocked to see that women they admired and respected had survived the same abuse they had. The women would then discuss how many Black girls had been harmed in our society, and how little had been done to prevent that harm.

Quickly the experience became overwhelming for Burke, due to the scale of the violence she was seeing. She estimates that 75 percent of the girls she was working with had experienced sexual violence. I cannot imagine how difficult it would be to hold the painful truths entrusted to you by so many children in your own community.

Burke knew that awareness, while empowering for the girls going through her program, would not be enough to create the safety and justice these girls deserved. In trying to come up with next steps, she turned to her roots.

"My training tells me that the response is some sort of organizing. It has to be something that we do collectively, that's not just me in a classroom trying to put Band-Aids on all of these wounds," Burke recalls thinking at the time. "Because I still hold these things to be true, that I wrote in my book, that it's nothing worse than being in a community and watching people actively not care. Most people have to still live and work and worship and learn in the places where they were harmed. That's bad enough. But to do that while watching people actively not care, actively be inactive about it, is another level of trauma that most survivors internalize. 'I'm not worthy of protection.' 'I'm not worthy of this care.'"

Burke first went to her elders for guidance, but she was repeatedly turned away. She realized she was on her own.

So Burke started looking at her own life and her own journey of healing after childhood abuse. What could have helped her understand what was happening to her when she was the same age as the girls she was working with now? What could have set her down a path of healing at twelve or thirteen, instead of twenty-eight or twenty-nine?

Burke began brainstorming: "I was feverishly writing in my notebooks every night and plotting out world plans of how we're gonna address this issue globally. In an apartment I could barely afford in Selma, Alabama, with no furniture," Burke remembers with a chuckle. "Trying to make sure I could make ends meet so I could feed my kid."

As a marginalized person trying to advocate for and with other marginalized people, Burke had to think beyond the limitations that had been placed upon her. She didn't know what she was capable of, because for much of her life the world had told her she wouldn't be able to do much. But if others weren't going to provide opportunities for her, Burke was going to create her own.

Burke started with what she knew, with what had worked for her: political empowerment.

"I did what I knew to do, which was activate the girls," she recalls. "We're not gonna get support from the community. We're not gonna get support from the elders. So . . . we're gonna just do it ourselves."

Burke laughs at the audacity of her plan and its success: "And that's what happened, and it was beautiful! It was great. It was hard, but I would do it the same way again."

In conversations with movement workers, I've seen how powerful—and difficult—this particular mode of creation is. Time and time again, our most effective and engaging work comes from this place of desperation. Where we've been so shut out of established organizing and change-making spaces that we have to create our own. And what is often created is more authentic, inclusive, responsive, and accessible than what existed before.

In going by her own personal experience and instincts, cut off from the advice and guidance of elders, Burke had stumbled upon one of the most important aspects of this work that is often neglected due to the patriarchy infecting even our movement work. "That was part of the lesson—now we talk about it all the time: Survivors should be centered. Survivors should be at the forefront. That language, that understanding. I didn't even have survivor language at that time, right? But I learned from actual experience that *Oh yeah, this is how it should be done.* Just like Black people should be the focus of our movements, women should be at the forefront."

In this moment, the Me Too movement was born. Burke built a

movement dedicated to identifying and interrupting sexual violence in healing and culturally competent ways. She has helped victims become survivors and then leaders.

Burke had been doing this work with Me Too for eleven years when the hashtag #MeToo went viral in the wake of high-profile cases of sexual violence, including Dr. Christine Blasey Ford's testimony during the Brett Kavanaugh confirmation hearings—a confirmation for the very court that would render its devastating ruling on reproductive freedoms. Suddenly, the name of the movement Burke and her team had been leading for over a decade was on everybody's lips, even if a lot of people saying it didn't know *her* name.

For a lot of Black women, the fact that many of the faces of #MeToo suddenly seemed to be famous white women rankled. It felt like a theft, once again, of the work of a Black woman.

But it is this common complaint that rankles Burke.

"Here's the thing that you don't realize," Burke tells me. "That it is disrespectful to me, first of all. And people say it to me in a way. They think they're trying to, like, support me. Like, 'A white woman stole Me Too from you.'"

But to Burke, it's impossible for Me Too to be stolen if we keep doing the work in our own communities.

"Toni Morrison told us a long time ago about deferring to white people's gaze," Burke reminds us. "If . . . something gets wildly popular [and] a Black woman comes to the forefront and says, 'Oh, you know I started that. And I started that for you,' then it is still a Black woman's and it is still for Black women."

To Burke, what white people think or make of Me Too shouldn't matter. She thinks many in our community don't realize how much whiteness is centered, even in our own thoughts. Even when discussing our own movement work, we tend to overfocus on what white people say or think about us. Burke is far too busy to care about what white women think about her or her work—work she was doing long before most people knew it existed and work she'll be doing long after people stop talking about it.

"Y'all over here crying for me. I'm not crying for myself. They're welcome to join. I have an assignment that I have been on for twenty-something years. This is another iteration of that assignment. I'm quite grateful for it. It's the biggest iteration of it. But if nothing ever happened in 2017, y'all would still see me with my black-and-pink T-shirts. Everybody who knew me from before, going around trying to put posters up about sexual violence. And you would not say white women stole it. You wouldn't say anything, cuz you wouldn't care!" Burke laughs.

Looking back at the rapid popularity of Me Too, Burke finds that the focus on whiteness also takes away from the contribution of those who shared their stories of sexual violence. "Me Too is not a part of the lexicon across the world now because of me. And it's not even because of Harvey Weinstein. It's because twelve million people had the courage to come forward and tell their story in two words. Which is why I used those two words in the first place. Because it's that powerful."

Burke laments that people had to do the painful work of sharing their stories at all. "Just looking at this country, the citizens of this country who propelled this issue into the mainstream by being able to tell their own stories—that's another set of labor that we put on survivors. We don't see that in any other issue. We don't ask the families, or the victims of gun violence—we don't ask people to do even more labor in the same capacity that we do survivors of sexual violence."

That labor, in order to not just be further harm and exploitation, comes with a debt: "What do we owe those people? In five years . . . there has not been a real formal, or formative, substantial response. To the millions of people who actually said, 'Me too.'"

## Why It's Often Race *and* Gender

In December 2022, Trevor Noah said goodbye to *The Daily Show* after eight years of hosting. In his tearful goodbye, Noah advised his audience to listen to Black women. Black women would lead us in the right direction, because they "can't afford to fuck around and find out."

This message, and this understanding of why we are so often at the front of fights for justice in the US and around the world, made many Black women feel seen on a platform and scale in which we aren't often seen.

In recent years, there have been repeated calls by many in progressive circles to "listen to Black women." Listen to us, follow us, even elect us. We will save you.

And yet the ways in which so many in the US look to us for salvation is often extractive and exploitative. It's exhausting and infuriating.

While we are looked toward to save everyone else from themselves and the destructive choices their own communities are making, we are—time and time again—the only ones who will save us.

I write this only a few short days after Brittney Griner was freed following ten months in a Russian prison.

Griner, a Black queer professional WNBA player playing in Russia during the US offseason, was arrested on highly suspect charges of marijuana possession. She had been playing in Russia because women's sports—especially sports dominated by Black women—aren't valued by the general public in the US. The pay being two to three times higher in countries like Russia has pulled a lot of WNBA greats like Griner—who to many is considered the greatest active player in the game—overseas to supplement their incomes (Feinberg 2022).

Griner was not detained because of marijuana—not really. She was detained at a time when Russia needed a political bargaining chip. And Russia decided that one of the greatest players in the WNBA would be that bargaining chip.

Suddenly, white and non-Black people of all political persuasions who had been waving the Ukrainian flag and sharing anti-Russia messages all over social media were vocal supporters of the Russian justice system.

Suddenly, Black men whom Black women had marched for, fought for—to protect them from our racist criminal justice system—were pro-Russian Cop, saying that Griner "shouldn't do the crime if she couldn't do the time."

As a Black woman engaged in both racial justice and gender justice work, I'm often told by people in my own community that my focus on gender is a distraction at best, and a weapon of white supremacy at worst. I'm told that gender justice and feminism are the invention of white women, and that this work cannot exist with anti-racist work and has no place in discussions of racism. Not only are we not supported in the work we are forced to do on our own in order to save our own lives; we are also punished for taking away from what many view is our real purpose in movement work: supporting the men in our community.

It's no surprise that in the end it was the unwavering dedication of Black women—led first and foremost by the amazing efforts of Griner's wife, Cherelle Griner—that kept the world from forgetting about Griner's imprisonment, and kept pressure on the Biden administration to secure her release.

While Black women are often uniquely expected to be political and social nursemaids to not only our own community but non-Black communities as well, many other women of color have experienced similar expectations of labor from their communities while knowing they cannot expect anything near the same in return.

But it's not just that. We are expected to fight for everyone else and stitch our communities back together after white supremacy has torn them asunder while also often facing some of the worst of systemic racism in very specific ways. Issues like poverty, work discrimination, and exploitation are compounded by our gender. Our political and social power is further marginalized by patriarchy in very devastating ways.

Sexual violence has a particular history in communities of color—especially in the Black community. Sexual violence has been a regularly utilized tool of white supremacy for hundreds of years. This violence has been used against people of all genders, up to and including the present day. Our prisons, which are disproportionately filled with members of our Black, Indigenous, and brown communities, regularly subject their wards to sexual violence—from assaults carried out by other inmates and staff members but also in the everyday violations (like cavity searches) seen as "routine" prison procedure. Just a few generations ago, enslaved Black men and women were both regularly exposed to sexual violence and exploitation, and forced to participate in the sexual abuse and exploitation of one another. Indigenous women were regularly abused and exploited as well.

But it is women, trans people, and nonbinary people of color who are most often subjected to sexual violence both inside and outside our communities in ways that are directly tied to the violence of racism, colonialism, and patriarchy—and the sexual violence women of color are often subjected to may well be tied to the ways in which men have been subjected to sexual violence by white supremacy.

"I've been really trying to unpack the power dynamic in sexual violence and its relationship to white supremacy," Tarana Burke tells me. "There's one side that is about an abuse of power. And I think that another side is about longing for power."

The dynamics of sexual violence in the Black community are difficult for Burke to come to terms with.

"I struggle with Black women having the second-highest rate of sexual violence experience in this country. And it happens largely at the hands of . . . Black men. That's a reality, and it's a reality across the races. Just like every other crime, it's a reality across the races. . . . Our rate is only second to Indigenous folks, and Indigenous women are largely assaulted by people from outside their community—80 percent of the sexual assault that happens in Indigenous communities happens from people who are not from those communities.

"Knowing that there's no special depravity in our community, and there's no special depravity in Black men, [I'm] trying to unpack where that violence comes from, bringing it back to power. We've seen the mimicry of white supremacist thinking and ideals in our community across the board in so many ways. And I think this is another way that it manifests, in that there are people who abuse power. And then there are people who want power so they can abuse it, will take power in any way, shape, or form they can. Look at the history of Black people, and Black men, in this country. You can point to a group that has been devoid of power or had power stripped from them."

I, like so many other Black women, have experienced this myself. Not only was my first experience with sexual violence at the hands of a Black man, but also I regularly encounter Black men who are trying to heal their own harm from the violence of white supremacy on the backs of Black women. I've seen Black men come home from a day out in the world that has made them feel diminished and powerless, and try to make up for that by holding and abusing power over Black women. I've talked with Black men who have made it clear that their vision for racial justice has them sitting right next to white men in positions of power over the rest of us.

When I talk to other women of color, of non-Black races and ethnicities, they often communicate similar experiences. And that is shown by statistics of how women of color fare in health, wealth, political power, and personal safety across the US and in so many other countries harmed by white supremacy and/or colonialism.

As Tarana Burke said, many Indigenous women face sexual violence from men outside of their communities. In this, not only are the perpetrators often white or non-Indigenous people of color but also the circumstances for that abuse are often created by white supremacy.

When I talk with Indigenous environmental activist and movement leader Matt Remle about his work to protect Indigenous lands from the destruction of pipelines and other environmentally harmful projects, he mentions how some of these projects aren't just endangering land; they're also harming Indigenous people.

"I'll use where I'm from as an example," Remle says. "In the Dakotas, in the Bakken oil field, you have these massive man camps." Remle explains that these camps house, in close quarters, hundreds or thousands of men from all over the world to work in the oil fields and fracking sites. "There is a direct connection with these man camps and the issue of missing and murdered Indigenous women, because a lot of Indigenous women and girls are being trafficked into these man camps." Remle points out that inquiries into the issue of missing and murdered Indigenous women in Canada have named some of these sites as central to the disappearances of Indigenous women.

While many women and queer, trans, and nonbinary people are more at risk for sexual violence across racial lines, it's people of color from these groups who are often criminalized for that abuse in ways and degrees many white people are not.

In her enraging and indicting book *Pushout: The Criminalization of Black Girls in Schools*, Monique W. Morris looks at the ways in which Black girls are often punished for the sexualization of their bodies in school. Pushed out of school for that sexualization, Black girls are then frequently driven into the arms of sex traffickers or into survival sex work.

From there, these Black girls and women are criminalized by our white supremacist, patriarchal criminal justice system, and even subjected to further abuses by police and in our prison systems. Morris cites statistics that show an astonishing 40 percent of sex trafficking victims in the United States are Black, and in areas like Los Angeles County, that figure reaches 92 percent (Morris 2018).

Many social issues that are thought to affect all populations of color equally often affect women and other people of marginalized genders more, and in very specific ways. We are harmed in particular and gendered ways by the prison-industrial complex, by our racist government, by our racist healthcare system, by our racist employment industries, by our racist education system, by our racist media.

Many issues thought to have an impact on all women, or all queer and trans folk equally—like employment and wage discrimination, reproductive rights, sexual violence, and exploitation—have more of an impact on BIPOC within those populations, and in very specific ways.

When it comes to social issues, we are typically the first and hardest hit, and the least helped.

So yeah, we can't afford to fuck around and find out. We have to treat all of these issues as if our lives are on the line, because they often are, and we know that from our lived experience. We have almost always had the most to lose, and have had to put forth the most effort to try to recover ourselves and our communities when people refuse to heed our warnings.

But nobody else in our communities—nobody at risk of white supremacist patriarchy at all—can afford to fuck around and find out either, even if they don't know it yet.

Because white supremacist patriarchy has been honing its blade against us. White supremacist patriarchy builds its systems against us first, not only because it knows that nobody else will care but also because it knows that to defeat it, we are the strongest weapons you have.

## NORMA TIMBANG

The Asian and Pacific Islander Women and Family Safety Center was founded from a place of deep rage, fear, and heartbreak around the murder of Susana Remerata. Remerata (called by her married name of Blackwell in news reports) was a Filipina immigrant who was trying to divorce her husband. She was trafficked into the United States through international marriage brokerage, a practice once known as mail-ordering brides.

Remerata was a beautiful young woman looking for a better life through a marriage with an American man. She corresponded with her future husband, Timothy C. Blackwell, for a year before agreeing to come to the United States to marry him. But her dream quickly turned into a nightmare.

Remerata reported that Blackwell tried to choke her. After two weeks of violence, she left him. After leaving, she met another man and became pregnant. Blackwell felt that his "investment" in Remerata—in time and money spent on the marriage broker and bringing Remerata to the United States—had been wasted.

At the time of Remerata's marriage, approximately four thousand American men found their wives through international brokerage services every year (Egan 1996). Women being trafficked into these marriages (especially women from Asian countries) are often advertised as more naturally docile and subservient than American women. The violence and poverty of the colonization of the Philippines has forced many women into these often abusive and exploitative experiences, and their economic and political vulnerability once they're in the United States can make it very difficult and even dangerous for them to try to leave these marriages.

On March 2, 1995, as Remerata (eight months pregnant at the time) was waiting with two friends for Blackwell to arrive at the divorce hearing, she and her friends Phoebe Dizon and Veronica Laureta Johnson were all gunned down by Blackwell in front of the courthouse.

The murder of Remerata and her friends sent shock waves through the local Asian community. Norma Timbang, Emma Catague, and others came together to hold vigils for Remerata, Dizon, and Johnson, and to discuss the violence that women in Asian, Pacific Islander, and immigrant communities of color were subjected to—a violence that many of these women knew personally.

"The moment that we started working on the vigil . . . I just really wanted to support," Timbang tells me, "and it was hard because I had two small children at the time, and I was a single mom. And I had escaped—as a survivor I took my two little children all the way from Florida to Seattle."

Norma Timbang is a community organizer, a DEI (diversity, equity, and inclusion) trainer and consultant, and a co-founder of the API Women and Family Safety Center, which would later merge with Chaya and become API Chaya. Timbang would help API Chaya to grow into one of the most respected and important BIPOC- and immigrant-centered gender justice organizations in the greater Seattle area.

But in 1995, Timbang was a mother trying to find safety for herself and her children. As hard as it was to show up in these spaces while having also fled gender-based violence herself, Timbang quickly found community and some measure of healing with the other women who had come together after Remerata's murder.

"Having these people around me was just so motivating, so inspiring. And such a great place for me to feel like, *Yes, I can do these things*."

Hundreds of people came to the vigil for Remerata and her friends, Timbang says. Their goal was to increase visibility about the violence that immigrant women like Remerata are more vulnerable to, due to language barriers, immigration status, lack of community or family support, and lack of knowledge about how to navigate local systems.

From these meetings and conversations, the API Women and Family Safety Center was born.

There was a lot of pushback from their communities as Timbang and the other founders of the center tried to get people to talk about such a taboo topic. But they were determined to not only support people in their communities facing gender-based violence but also do what they could to prevent future violence as well as empower others to interrupt violence.

"Community was the place where a lot of us focused," Timbang recalls. "One of the things the API Safety Center created was called Natural Helpers, a program [that] exists today. It was the baby of Emma Catague." Catague wanted to figure out how to get people in the community to recognize the signs of abuse and exploitation in order to be able to interrupt it. So she started having community-level conversations—first in the local Samoan and Filipino communities—to discover what the signs of abuse looked like in these communities and to develop interruption strategies. Then the Safety Center started training community members in these strategies and techniques. Natural Helpers has since expanded to serve people from many BIPOC and immigrant communities in the Seattle area.

Throughout the Seattle community, graduates of the Safety Center and API Chaya's Natural Helpers program are doing what they can to interrupt gender-based violence. "We teach them, 'Here's what you're looking for,' 'Here's how you can support,' 'Here are the resources you can give to the person who's asking for your help.'" Timbang explains that it's not just what Natural Helpers can do to help but also how they provide that help that matters. "We teach them to not judge, and to not tell them what to do. But to just listen and have them sort of figure [it] out. 'Here's some options. What would you like to do?' Have them decide. Because that place of self-determination, as it's facilitated through community conversations, was actually the place where API Chaya is now continuing to bring in that tradition that API Safety Center had started earlier on."

Most people will disclose gender-based violence to someone in their community or family before they will to authorities, so it's vital that there are community members to turn to who are known to be good resources when people are ready to disclose.

"If you're known as a Natural Helper, someone might just come to you and say, 'Hey, this is happening,'" Timbang explains. "While also listening in community and being able to get the vibe, get the pulse of what's happening, with certain families, with certain people."

In communities of color, in order to do this work well, a person has to be not only culturally competent but also a part of the community they're working with. This practice is something that other, more traditional violence prevention organizations and entities funding such work have struggled with.

Timbang says the API Safety Center was the first organization in Washington State to receive government funding for its work in fighting violence against immigrant women being trafficked into marriage. With that funding, the center trained more people in various violence prevention organizations and positions on how to recognize this sort of trafficking and how to support and protect the women who were being trafficked. This helped greatly increase the amount of resources in the state for immigrant women in marriages similar to the one that resulted in Susana Remerata's murder.

After years as API Chaya's executive director, Timbang eventually moved away from its day-to-day operations but still contributes to the organization through training and consulting. And after decades of this work, also as a therapist helping people heal from trauma and violence, Timbang has been trying to find ways to protect her own emotional well-being and heal from the abuse she fled over three decades ago and its lingering effects in her life. Effects that are often triggered by the trauma and violence she has witnessed repeatedly in her work.

"I have two adult daughters. And one of them understands substantially that this is not something that she wants to do. She doesn't want to be involved with somebody who's gonna control, who's gonna abuse her. And yet, generationally, it still happens," Timbang tells me. "I would just love to see things not happen generation after generation after generation. And that's hard, right? And in so many ways, I have to heal from that guilt."

I know what that guilt feels like. More than twenty years after leaving an abusive marriage and learning how to create a space of safety in my home for me and my family, I wasn't able to fully shield my own child from the impact of those early years, or from the ways in which his later relationship with his father had harmed him, even while he loves his father dearly. So many times I found myself asking why I didn't do more. *Why didn't I move farther away? Why didn't I step in sooner?*

I share these feelings with Timbang, thoughts that still haunt me to this day. I tell her that the only comfort I can give myself is the knowledge my sons got to live in a home that, for most of their lives, was headed by a woman who didn't let anyone pass the threshold who disrespected her. Not anymore.

"I think one of the hardest things about being a parent is the fact that you also have to be a human being who is growing and going through things at the same time that you're responsible for another person," I tell her.

"Yeah," Timbang replies. "I had a therapy practice for eight years.

And a lot of folks who came to me were survivors. Some of them survivors of heterosexism, homophobia. Some of them survivors of mental health struggles or emotional struggles. And, you know, I had to stop and say, 'Okay, my turn. I love all of you, and I'm still here for you, but my practice isn't gonna be there.' Cuz it's a lot. We sit with our children, we sit with the people we work with, we sit with our colleagues and our friends and our chosen family. And we hear so much already. . . . And then we have our own stories at home. And that makes it doubly hard."

Today, Timbang is a lecturer at the University of Washington, teaches and consults for API Chaya, consults organizations on DEI, and more. Her most passionate work right now is political action, trying to address the racial implications of mandatory reporting for teachers, therapists, social workers, and in many other fields.

This difficult, sometimes traumatizing work is what Timbang still finds a way to do because of all that it can bring her and others. "It brings a lot of rewards," Timbang says with a laugh, after she finishes telling me about how difficult the work is. "It brings a lot of rewards in supporting not just each other, but realizing that it's a very mutual and interdependent practice."

One of the first things abusers will do in a relationship is try to isolate their partner or family member from others, in order to gain greater control over them. Racism and xenophobia increase that isolation. The violence of patriarchy tells us that being abused is something to be quiet about, to be ashamed of. All of this silence, all of this isolation, can kill in so many different ways, quickly or slowly. Norma Timbang has been fighting for her life and for the lives of others for decades, and here she is, a living, breathing example that she's winning that fight—that maybe we all can.

## Abortion, Bodily Autonomy, and the
## Racism That Endangers It All

I'm going to share more of Theryn Kigvamasud'vashti's story and the story of the amazing organization Communities Against Rape and Abuse (CARA), which she co-ran for years. But first, I'm going to tell you how CARA ended.

CARA ended because they wanted to help BIPOC facing gender-based violence without putting them at risk of further violence from carceral systems.

For years, CARA had done amazing work in educating about and interrupting gender-based violence in Black and brown communities. They worked with women and girls and people of marginalized genders, who are often the most vulnerable to sexual violence. They worked with the people many others wouldn't. But they couldn't get enough funding.

"We rejected certain monies because it required us to partner with police, and we weren't gonna do that," Kigvamasud'vashti tells me. "It required us to partner with police in terms of mandatory reporting. That mainstream movement was also very tied up in Child Protective Services."

Organizations that serve BIPOC populations receive much less funding in general than organizations that serve white populations, so whatever funds did come CARA's way were not turned away easily. But CARA also understood that many people in the communities they were working with had been harmed by the racism deeply embedded in police and social services organizations like CPS, and that working with these entities could put their already at-risk communities in even more danger. They were determined to find a way to serve their community in other ways and maintain their autonomy, even if it meant turning away from much-needed funds.

For a while, CARA was able to get by. But eventually, it wasn't.

"When the money became more and more hostile, we eventually walked away from it," Kigvamasud'vashti recalls. "But the organization didn't have the resources needed to fill in the gaps from that government money. So eventually, it ran out of money."

And that was the end of CARA.

Carceral solutions to gender-based violence can make many women of color and other BIPOC of marginalized genders less safe.

When a call to police or social or child services is made, BIPOC survivors of gender-based violence are brought face-to-face with institutions that have been harming their communities for generations. Often that call can put an entire family, including the person seeking safety, at risk.

Women of color—especially Black and Indigenous women—are more likely to experience intimate partner violence, and far more likely to die from that violence. And yet they are less likely than white women to call the police or reach out to traditional services for victims of gender-based violence (Women of Color Network 2006).

For many BIPOC, especially queer and trans BIPOC, safety in times of crisis must be found outside of established systems. This means that those organizations that try to serve BIPOC without involving potentially harmful entities are often underfunded, while organizations that rely on more carceral solutions or partner with carceral entities are rewarded for practices that alienate vulnerable BIPOC at best and endanger them at worst.

When larger, white-led organizations have tried to listen to BIPOC demands for more abolitionist approaches to ending gender-based violence, they can find themselves targeted by the very groups they were once affiliated with.

In 2020, after the horrific murders of Breonna Taylor and George Floyd by police officers, dozens of anti-violence and anti-sexual-assault organizations signed on to an open letter written by abolitionist feminists calling for a more abolitionist, BIPOC-centered approach to addressing violence. They faced a swift backlash. As described in *Abolition. Feminism. Now.*:

> *Calling the statement "offensive" and "dangerous," the Idaho Prosecuting Attorneys' Association, the Idaho Sheriffs' Association, and the Idaho Chiefs of Police Association withdrew their support for the Idaho Coalition Against Domestic and Sexual Violence. Funders called into question the focus of their work, legislators pushed back against the analysis of how laws have interfered with safety, police chiefs objected to being identified as part of the problem, and local service partners distanced themselves because they feared a loss of status if they identified with the brave coalition members who dared to speak out about the carceral orientation of those feminist anti-violence activists standing in the path of emancipatory strategies that would require taking abolition seriously. (Davis et al. 2022)*

Racism doesn't just complicate efforts to end gender-based violence. It's also a contributing factor to that violence in BIPOC communities, which is important to understand if we want to prevent that violence or effectively aid BIPOC victims. But many traditional feminist movements are resistant to the inclusion of racial analysis in their work.

Norma Timbang understands why these conversations can be uncomfortable for many white feminists. When we're trying to build solidarity around social issues, talking about fundamental differences in how we experience these issues can feel like a threat to the work or like a distraction. "There is real hope and desire that all women are the same. And that's true in many circumstances," she says. "However, without understanding the intersectionality of it, we are just doing a quarter of what we need to be doing to support people in their survivorhood."

It's not just the fight against gender-based violence that is threatened by this failure of intersectionality. When it comes to one of the battles central to feminist work—reproductive freedom—racism and lack of racial awareness have led to incomplete understandings of reproductive justice by many in our mainstream feminist movements, and undermine reproductive justice efforts.

While much of the focus of mainstream feminist reproductive rights work has been on abortion, the truth is that abortion rights are only one part of reproductive freedom (and yes, an important one). And often the fight for abortion rights represents "choice" for people with more relative privilege than that of the many BIPOC who may need abortion access the most.

Abortion rights represent reproductive freedom and choice only when multiple options are made available. Those options need to not only exist for you; they must be accessible. When your ability to have children has been taken from you by force or coercion, that is not choice. When you don't have access to reliable birth control, that is not choice. When your options to have or not have a child are limited due to lack of safety, or lack of economic means to support yourself and said child, that is not choice. When you cannot trust that you can raise your children free from state, interpersonal, or economic violence, that is not choice.

The restriction of reproductive freedoms has long been used to control women and to protect patriarchal power. Less discussed is how the restriction of reproductive freedom has been used to control populations of color and protect white supremacy. Whether or not populations of color can have children, or whether or not they get to raise their children, has been a powerful tool of oppression and colonization for centuries.

The rape of enslaved Black people and the theft of Black children were not the only ways in which white enslavers and white communities were able to build entire economies off of the forced labor of Black people. These were also the means by which they kept many Black people, especially Black women, under control.

The myth of the dangers of the unchecked innate sexuality of Black women and Black men helped justify violence and subjugation of Black people even after slavery was legally abolished. Those same myths are used today to justify everything from gun rights (white fathers must be able to protect their white wives and daughters from dangerous, hypersexual Black men) to lack of both economic support and support for reproductive freedoms for Black women (welfare will only encourage Black women to have more babies out of wedlock; so will abortions).

The white supremacist idea that populations of color cannot be trusted to understand their reproductive health needs or make their own sexual and reproductive choices also shows up in more subtle and yet devastating ways, like the large numbers of Black women who report not being listened to when they bring concerns or side effects about their birth control to their doctors (Bellamy 2022).

It's not just Black people who have been denied reproductive freedom in the service of white supremacy. For hundreds of years, countless Native women have found that the decision to have or raise their children has been taken from them.

Native women (as well as many other poor and incarcerated BIPOC women) were often sterilized against their will, beginning in the early 1900s and continuing on until the 1970s (Silliman et al. 2016). After the practice was outlawed, many health service providers continued to pressure and coerce Native women into undergoing permanent sterilization, or unsafe long-term contraception procedures.

In the 1980s, the use of long-acting hormonal injected birth control Depo-Provera was prohibited over concerns of increased health effects. Though it was banned at the time, Indian Health Service (IHS) physicians admitted to injecting disabled Native women with the banned birth control without their consent (Silliman et al. 2016, 119).

Native people have also been disproportionately affected by national efforts to restrict reproductive rights. When the Hyde Amendment blocked federal funding for abortions, some of the hardest hit communities were Native communities, who rely on the federally funded IHS for the majority of their healthcare.

Even when funds are provided to the IHS for abortion through state Medicaid funds, many IHS providers were found to be non-compliant with IHS abortion policy. Of the IHS facilities surveyed, 62 percent did not provide abortion services even in cases of rape or when the pregnant person's life was endangered by pregnancy. This same 2002 study found that only 5 percent of IHS clinics performed abortions, and most did not make abortion medications available (Silliman et al. 2016, 120–21).

Native people who have children often find their families targeted by social services. The violent intrusion into Native families and the theft of Native children by local governments, social services programs, and white faith-based organizations have been horrific practices for hundreds of years, practices that continue to this day.

In recent years, the lasting trauma from violent residential schools in the US and Canada has dominated many headlines, even as we still have not uncovered the full scope of the murderous devastation of the hundreds of thousands of children stolen from their homes and families and tortured by white organizations and churches with the active support of the US and Canadian governments.

But less discussed in white-led press is the shocking number of Native children stolen from their families in current times by state-run social services programs.

In 2014, the American Civil Liberties Union (ACLU) filed suit against the state of South Dakota on behalf of Oglala Sioux and Rosebud Sioux families whose children were removed from their homes by South Dakota judges. At the time of the suit, Native children in South Dakota were eleven times more likely to be taken from their families by the courts than non-Native children. The ACLU found in reviewing 120 transcripts of custody hearings involving Native children that these hearings lasted on average only four minutes, and that the children were removed from their homes almost 100 percent of the time (Pevar 2014).

While statistics from other states may not be quite as alarming as they are in South Dakota, they still show nationwide patterns of anti-Native bias in our child welfare systems that continue to have devastating impacts on Native families and communities. Even though Native people make up only about 3 percent of the US population, they make up almost 6 percent of the children in foster care (Wildeman et al. 2020).

While claims of concern for child welfare have long been used to justify the theft of Native children, similar claims have been used to justify the sterilization of Black and brown people. One of the larger activism projects that Theryn Kigvamasud'vashti worked on with CARA was to try to shut down an organization aiming to prevent women addicted to crack cocaine and other substances from having babies.

The organization was called Children Requiring a Caring Kommunity. (*Just* in case you thought for a second that the acronym was a happy accident, they decided to spell Kommunity with a *K* so that it was painfully obvious that it was not. The name has, in recent years, been changed to Project Prevention.) It put up fliers in Black, brown, and poor communities offering people addicted to drugs or alcohol two hundred dollars to be sterilized or put on long-term birth control.

This is not a family planning organization aimed at providing education and options to people struggling with addiction. The goal of this organization is to get desperate people to give up their reproductive rights for cash—evidenced by the fact that the organization paid more to people who chose permanent sterilization (tubal ligations and vasectomies) over long-term birth control. And it was only after public backlash that they made the payment amount the same for permanent and long-term options.

The founder of this organization, a white woman named Barbara Harris who had adopted four Black children born to a mother struggling with drug addiction, claimed to be doing this purely for the welfare of the children.

But offering cash to incredibly vulnerable Black people to make permanent medical decisions that will affect the rest of their lives, instead of offering, say, treatment options, counseling, safe housing, or other important basic needs that can actually help them down a path of recovery, is not helpful for Black and brown communities, and therefore not helpful for Black and brown children.

And in case you might think that Harris is just misguided in her approach and actually deeply cares about these communities, here's a quote from her in *Marie Claire* in 1998: "We don't allow dogs to breed. We spay them. We neuter them. We try to keep them from having unwanted puppies, and yet these women are literally having litters of children" (Vega 2003).

While CARA was able to shut down the Seattle chapter of CRACK, they were unable to shut down the entire organization. It is, at the time of writing this book, still in operation, and still encouraging people in the throes of addiction to give up their reproductive rights for money, which has recently been raised to three hundred dollars (Project Prevention, n.d.).

The fight against CRACK made it clear to Theryn Kigvama-sud'vashti how deeply intertwined issues of reproductive justice, gender-based violence, and systemic racism are. "What was really compelling about us turning our attention towards this work, as part of our bigger project for Black liberation, was recognizing that our work was intersecting with reproductive justice," she recalls. "And the history of reproductive control over Black women's and brown women's bodies has a long legacy in this society. And that legacy is very much tied to our experiences of sexual assault."

It's clear even from the previous examples that reproductive justice is a vast issue, encompassing so many different ways in which the bodies of women, BIPOC, disabled people, and queer and trans folk have been harmed and controlled by white supremacist patriarchy. And yet time and time again it's all reduced to abortion and the "choice" that it represents to those with more privilege.

Even the decision to frame the fight for abortion as a matter of protecting "privacy" and "choice" has limited the ability to intersectionally approach the issue, and has led to unintended legal and social consequences.

In the early 1980s, abortion rights organizations conducted a national poll of voters in search of a way to split conservative votes on the issue of abortion rights. They found a racial divide in support of abortion, with Black communities narrowly approving of abortion and white communities overwhelmingly disapproving of it. In figuring out where to grow support for abortion through messaging strategy, organizations decided—not surprisingly—to try to cater to more conservative whites. The approach they took was meant to appeal to those in favor of "small government" and who were averse to the idea of "government interference" in their personal lives.

In *Undivided Rights: Women of Color Organize for Reproductive Justice*, the authors argue that

> *adopting privacy as the rubric for long-term pro-choice organizing backfired politically. It undercut demands for public access to abortion that had characterized the feminist struggle for legalization in the 1960s and '70s. It also played into the hands of conservatives who were denouncing "big government," thus reinforcing the federal government's position, under the 1977 Hyde Amendment, that it had no obligation to pay for women's private decisions to have abortions. (Silliman et al. 2016, 37)*

As the debate over COVID-19 vaccines raged across the country in 2021, I was reminded of this passage from *Undivided Rights* and the lesson that we had perhaps failed to learn. As I was urging people to please do their part to protect their families and communities, to help protect disabled and immune-compromised people, I was met with the following argument, over and over:

"My body, my choice."

I shook my head at the different ways in which deciding to appeal to whiteness with promises of individual choice (that takes a certain level of privilege to even be called a choice), instead of a fundamental right and a medical necessity for the well-being of society, had found another way to harm our most vulnerable communities.

## THERYN KIGVAMASUD'VASHTI

Me: "So, I would love to, if possible, profile you in the book as one of the people I talk to. If you're not comfortable with that, then on background. But, you know, I would love it if—"

Theryn: "Girl, I'm a Leo."

Thus began my interview of Theryn Kigvamasud'vashti.

Kigvamasud'vashti is a teacher, a community movement worker, the proud mother of a "young African man-child, who is nineteen, and who has chosen to fight fires in the woods and jump out of helicopters," and for years she co-ran the organization Communities Against Rape and Abuse (CARA).

In the 1990s, Kigvamasud'vashti was working in sexual-assault and violence prevention for a different organization, one that often cooperated with police. Her boss was what she calls a "really problematic white woman."

She explains: "I was really desperate for a non-temp job when I applied for that one."

Kigvamasud'vashti's distaste for working with police was obvious to those close to her. So when some friends were looking to start a new sexual-assault prevention organization that was more abolitionist in nature, they reached out to her and asked if she'd like to apply.

The CARA Kigvamasud'vashti joined was not the CARA she would one day leave, and not the CARA many Black people in the Seattle community came to know.

"I was at the gig for ten years," she tells me. "The last four years, I was the co-director of the organization. And by the time I left, the organization had decided that they were clearly an organization that supported Black people. Like, it went from an organization focused on disabilities and young people to focusing on Black people with disabilities and Black young people and Black folk. And it was run by Black women, queer and otherwise."

In trying to apply their original goal of ending gender-based violence to their work in the Black community, CARA quickly found that the issue was much more complicated than just the violence between two people or in an interpersonal relationship.

They started looking at the causes and contributing factors to sexual assault in the Black community and other at-risk communities. In their research and observation, they were able to see that these were communities disproportionately affected by institutional violence like systemic racism, medical abuse and neglect, and carceral violence. This violence made people in these communities more susceptible to sexual assault.

As the causes of gender-based violence in Black communities were complicated by systemic violence, so were the solutions.

"We knew right away that our work of ending rape in the Black community was going to intersect with calls for an end to police violence. With calls for an end to prisons," Kigvamasud'vashti recalls. There weren't a lot of examples of sexual-assault prevention organizations that were also trying to address carceral violence, so CARA had to build a lot of their work from the ground up. "So we read. We really dug into the fourth chapter of Freire's *Pedagogy of the Oppressed*. We talked about this vision of praxis, this idea that not only can we build the movement and make plans for where the movement should go but that we can be on the front lines ending violence at the same time."

This meant that Kigvamasud'vashti and the rest of CARA had to think about the long-term systemic changes they should fight for as well as how to address the immediate ways in which that systemic oppression was causing harm in Black communities. Vital to liberation work is the idea that, yes, we have to fight for the big changes every day, but we also have to create the future we want now in whatever ways we can, in our own communities.

So CARA worked on multiple levels to try to address sexual violence more holistically. They focused on women and youth who were directly affected by gender-based violence. They partnered with other abolitionist organizations across the country—like INCITE! Women of Color Against Violence; Critical Resistance; and the Committee on Women, Population, and the Environment—for larger-scale projects. They also aimed to educate and empower the local Black population through community events.

"We did this thing called the Nat Turner Teach-In," Kigvamasud'vashti tells me. "I loooooved doing the Nat Turner Teach-In. It was every August, near the anniversary of Nat Turner's murder as a result of rebelling. And we organized to put that on for ten years—minus, I think, one year."

Kigvamasud'vashti's goal with the Nat Turner Teach-In was, in her words, to "ground Black liberation in a historical context."

She also hoped to address inaccurate and harmful narratives written by white historians about Black history. Narratives that painted Black people as perpetual victims who never fought for their freedom, especially in times of slavery.

They discussed how common rebellion actually was among enslaved Black people, and many of the forms that rebellion took. "We talked about ways that people were subversively trying to survive and actually thrive in those climates," Kigvamasud'vashti recalls. "We did classes on women who were enslaved who were in the house, who actively tried to kill the families. We centered the experiences of enslaved children."

Kigvamasud'vashti told attendees that the different slave revolts helped pressure Lincoln to act to end slavery. "Cuz Black folks was burning shit down," she says.

At first, the Teach-Ins focused only on the Black experience, even though the sessions were open to all people of color. But attendees told CARA that they wanted a more diverse conversation on liberation, one that reflected more of their BIPOC community. "There was some folks that were like, 'You guys are talking about liberation movements. You got all these people of color here. We need to talk about the Mexican–American War. We need to talk about the Mexican Revolution.' And it was like, 'Oh. Well, if you got that, bring that.'"

The Teach-Ins grew from there. Eventually they were discussing liberation movements of countries all over the world who had battled European colonization.

As the scope grew, so did the attendance. "I dropped in one afternoon, and it was packed." Kigvamasud'vashti was pleasantly surprised to see so many people in a room that had had only about twenty Teach-In participants in its first year.

In CARA's work to interrupt gender-based violence in their community, they led and advised on accountability processes, to try to end abusive behavior and help facilitate healing for the person(s) harmed. CARA also led workshops on sexual assault prevention for sex workers and provided support for Black girls trapped in the prison system.

Though the work was often rewarding and always purposeful, it was also stressful and at times emotionally traumatizing. It took a lot out of Kigvamasud'vashti. Eventually, the toll began to add up as she struggled to take care of her clients, her team, her family, and herself all at the same time.

"I thought, *I can't be present fully in my life and do work to organize to end rape*," she remembers. But it wasn't really her work with the community that was wearing her down: "It was the hustle for the money and the conversations with mainstream organizations that I was supposed to be partnering with that was exhausting."

Kigvamasud'vashti had personal goals she wanted to accomplish, and she knew she wouldn't be able to accomplish them while still leading CARA. So after a decade, she left CARA to go to graduate school.

While Kigvamasud'vashti was in school, CARA closed down due to lack of funding. While there are abolitionist-minded efforts in the Seattle area still working to end gender-based violence, there hasn't really been an organization to come along to fill the hole left by CARA's departure, especially not in our Black community.

Even though she knows that transition is a part of movement work, and that all efforts have their seasons, Kigvamasud'vashti still sometimes wonders, *What if.*

When Charleena Lyles, a pregnant Black mother of four who was in a mental health crisis, was gunned down in front of her children by Seattle police officers in 2017 after she called them for help, our entire Black community was devastated. In Lyles, Kigvamasud'vashti saw the women she used to work with at CARA.

"When Charleena Lyles was murdered, I couldn't help but think, *I wonder what that would have looked like if CARA was still around.* What would it have looked like to be able to support her with services? Cuz we supported survivors at Sand Point [the location of the transitional housing where Lyles and her children lived]. I used to go out to Sand Point and visit with some of our clients."

While Kigvamasud'vashti can find herself thinking of what could have been, she also gets to see what *is* because of the work she did.

"There was a couple times where sistas would pull me aside," she recalls. "One time at QFC, I was buying chicken for the kids right after tae kwon do practice. And she saw me. She said, 'Theryn.' And I said, 'Yes?' She's like, 'Do you remember me?' And I said, 'You look familiar, but I'm terrible at names and I'm growing old, so can you help me out?' She's like, 'Well, you did a workshop that I was a part of.' And I said, 'I did? Did it help?' And she goes, 'I loved it.'" Kigvamasud'vashti pauses with a smile. "She goes, 'I loved it. I felt seen.' And then later, as I was leaving, she pulled me aside. She says, 'I was a sex worker in one of those workshops.' And she was like, 'I felt so heard and so seen. You know, I want to thank you for that.'"

## Intersections of Racism, Queerphobia, and Transphobia in Gender Justice Work

J. Mase III is a Black trans masc poet, educator, writer, and movement worker currently living in Seattle. I have been fortunate to be in community with him for years now and have always been impressed with how one person can have such talent, humor, knowledge, and insight all at once. I'm always happy to sit down and chat with him.

When I share with Mase my thoughts on the Supreme Court's *Roe v. Wade* decision, he quickly points to connections, not only the attempts to restrict the rights of trans people but the specific ways in which transphobia has been used to police the body of cis women as well. "I'm always curious how people don't see the connection, especially when we're talking about trans people in sports, especially trans women in sports. Like, 'Oh, all these rights around abortion, abortion access, all these things are being attacked.' Well, do you not remember when they were just trying to define what womanhood is? And did y'all not realize that a lot of cis women don't fit into that? Especially Black and brown women. I think so much about, you know, obviously Caster Semenya and Serena Williams, who are cis women, and yet they face lots of trans antagonism because of the ways that white cis bodies and white cis systems are trying to rigidly define what womanhood is and who gets to be a woman."

Conservatives have been able to exploit anti-trans bias on the "Left" to divide movements and pass anti-trans legislation as a gateway to more widely reaching oppressive legislation. They have even been able to use the anti-trans bias of larger lesbian and gay organizations and movements to gain support for ideas and even laws that harm all queer people as well as so many others by weaponizing the respectability politics many mainstream groups have utilized in hopes of seeming "acceptable" enough to be worthy of rights.

"I think trans people have been depicted as people who are just *irrationally* asking for things," Mase explains. "Like to have our names and pronouns respected. To have access to facilities. To have bodily autonomy rights. And that is seen as egregious in the eyes of people who fought for their rights off of the backs of seeming 'normal.' So I think of how many cis queer women and lesbians I've seen fighting against trans rights, because trans people's very existence—especially trans women's existence—was somehow an affront for them to be around."

Norma Timbang also sees these divisions in social change movements as a real resistance to true inclusivity, preventing us from tackling issues effectively and intersectionally. "A lot of times when we center racism, people get really fearful of that. They want to distract. And I hate to say, but sometimes it's 'Don't bring in LGBTQ because you'll distract from the racial struggles.' 'Don't bring in immigration because you'll distract from the racial struggles.'"

This division means that often those with intersecting identities, people who are often the most marginalized in society, are also the most marginalized within our movements. Even though it's these very people—disabled, queer, and trans BIPOC activists—who have long been some of the fiercest fighters in our movements.

Much of the modern LGBTQIA+ movement we see today was built off the labor of Black and brown activists, yet you wouldn't know that to look at the leadership of the larger organizations. This disparity is not an accident; it's by design.

"We take all these stats, all this history, and erase the actual people from it," Mase tells me. "I think about Daughters of Bilitis, I think about the Mattachine Society, I think about HRC [Human Rights Campaign], I think about GLSEN [Gay, Lesbian, and Straight Education Network], that started and exist because they were able to profit off of the labor and activism of Black people, of Indigenous people, of brown people, that were trans and queer, that were gender expansive. Without ever wanting to actually honor our leadership, wanting to honor us."

It's not just that the most marginalized from queer communities have been erased from the history and leadership of mainstream queer organizations. It's also that these organizations use the plight of these same people they've ignored to fundraise for themselves.

"To me, it's not possible for there to be a white queer organization that *doesn't* exist because they took from the labor of—or have been telling the stories of—Black trans people, while also erasing them," Mase argues. "It's not possible. Like, when I hear white queer organizations talk about houselessness among queer youth—what youth are you talking about? *Who* you talking about? You can't talk to me about joblessness and not be talking about Black trans people. *Who you talking about?* You can't talk about murder and homicide and not talk about Black trans women and femmes or trans people. Who are you actually talking about?"

Many Black and brown trans movement workers try to work with more mainstream organizations that give lip service to greater inclusivity. Not necessarily because they love the organizations, but because the organizations take up such a large percentage of movement funding that they feel they have to in order to gain the resources to help their community.

While many of the larger white-led LGBTQIA+ organizations have long excluded Black and brown queer and trans folk, the same groups are also often excluded from more mainstream anti-racist movements. This is something I've seen quite a lot in Black liberation movements—even though queer women and femmes have been at the absolute center of vital Black liberation work since forever.

"There can't be gender justice for Black people without understanding how it's related to disability justice and trans justice," Mase wants to make clear. "It is so vital for us to be honest about our bodies. It is so vital for us to be honest about our identities, about who we are, who we have historically been, and what liberation means. To have all Black people being free. That it's not possible to exist in a world where Black trans people, Black disabled people, are being treated poorly and other Black people will be fine. That's not real, okay?" Mase adds with a laugh, "Not real."

This points to something that has always been so confusing to me. In all of the ways in which the bodies of Black, brown, and Indigenous folk have been abused and exploited and controlled over centuries . . . the ways in which women's bodies have been abused and exploited and controlled over centuries . . . how can you look at Black trans folk or Indigenous trans or two-spirit folk, who represent survival over hundreds of years of violent oppression, who still face some of the worst oppression our systems have to offer, and still live in their entire truths, truths that stand in more direct opposition to white supremacist patriarchy than just about any other . . . how can you look at these people and not see your liberation tied to them? There is no world in which they get free and the rest of us do not.

But this opposition to white supremacist patriarchy I speak of is not one that many trans BIPOC were given a choice in, Mase stresses.

"We don't get the option of blending in," Mase says. "And while many of us do or can and want to pass in cishet society, you know, for all the different reasons of safety, or all the different types of things that come up, a lot of us can't. A lot of us came into this world not having that option."

And so while trans and gender-expansive people in our communities are vital for our society and our movements to survive, we are often told the opposite.

Mase sees this erasure as a powerful weapon of oppression: "I think that the more that Black people, brown people, Indigenous people, can be lied to about the role of trans people, the more that we can be kept from our own freedom, from our own liberation."

## EMMETT SCHELLING

I met Emmett Schelling at the TIME100 Summit, an education and networking event for TIME100 honorees. He introduced himself to me shortly before the summit began and said that he had appreciated *So You Want to Talk About Race*. We parted ways as the summit began, only to find ourselves locked in conversation just a few hours later.

I was excited to reconnect with Schelling for this book, and he was as well, as we were now obviously besties.

As joyous, openhearted, and friendly as Schelling is, the work he does is very serious and often quite difficult. He's the executive director of Transgender Education Network of Texas (TENT).

"We are one of the largest statewide BIPOC trans-led policy, education, and engagement organizations in the entire country," he explains to me. "And we really do our work from a place of understanding that the best advocacy that you can ever provide is education, is meeting people where they're at and bringing them forward."

Doing this work just about anywhere in the US would be challenging, but doing this work in 2022 in Texas—the state currently leading the nation in anti-trans rhetoric and legislation—seems unfathomably difficult.

It was in this climate—when he was trying to balance the need to fight dangerous anti-trans legislation while also working to tackle all of the other ways in which trans people in Texas are harmed by anti-trans bigotry and systemic oppression—that Schelling was honored by *TIME* magazine for his work.

While on the surface it may seem like TENT is a trans political advocacy organization, it's far more complicated than that for Schelling, because the ways in which trans people experience systemic oppression can be complicated.

"Transness is a component of what makes us a whole and full individual in this world," he tells me. "That makes us inherently who we are as people, as human beings."

And yet that one component, often seeming the most targeted by systems in a state like Texas, is intertwined with race and class. Schelling knows this personally as an Asian trans man but also from the Black trans folk who have mentored him, advised him, and make up a large part of his community in Texas.

When Schelling moved to Texas, he was himself in crisis. "Two major events happened in my life that were devastating, for one, but also were solely based on my transness being the factor of unleashing the disaster."

It was in this place of crisis that Schelling started volunteering. Often, when it feels like we have little control over the issues affecting our personal lives, we can find empowerment and even healing in working toward justice that is larger than our individual selves. Schelling threw himself into work, addressing issues that were affecting multiple marginalized communities in Texas.

"Things were really boiling along in Texas," he recalls. "Houston was going through a very ugly repeal of the Equal Rights Ordinance."

In 2015, conservatives decided to weaponize anti-trans bigotry and ignorance in order to repeal the Houston Equal Rights Ordinance, which the city council had passed earlier that year. The ordinance was not unusual for a major city like Houston; it was aimed at preventing bias against fifteen protected classes of people. But by framing the ordinance as a law trying to put "men in women's bathrooms," repeating dangerous lies about transgender women and sexual predation, Houston conservatives were able to turn voters against the ordinance. By playing off the bigotry against one group of marginalized people, they were able to take away protections from a large portion of the population (Fernandez and Smith 2015).

"That included pregnant people. That included veterans. That included the homeless," Schelling says bitterly. "Just another example of how you can get people to literally throw their support against their own interests by preying on this stereotype and this fear."

It was in the midst of all this harmful stereotyping that Schelling found a surprising personal advantage in his work. A transgender Asian man who grew up in a rural community, wearing a button-down shirt and a bow tie, is not what people who are ignorant and afraid of trans individuals expect to encounter. It has thrown people off their defensiveness, sometimes long enough for Schelling to get in a word or two.

"I certainly don't fit in their stereotypes!" he says.

When he first started volunteering with TENT, they had few resources, and yet they still fought hard day after day against an onslaught of anti-trans legislation. In 2021 alone, the state of Texas introduced nearly eighty anti-trans bills. Through the hard work of TENT and other LGBTQIA+ activists and advocates, only one of those bills was passed into law that year.

Schelling is still amazed at all they were able to accomplish, and he feels immense pride, especially considering everything that has been stacked against them. "And don't get me wrong," he says with a laugh. "I would never want to do it again."

Schelling continues with a deep, demonstrative sigh, "But it's like, looking back—we fucking did that! This ragtag group of transgender people in Texas. All volunteering. Nobody's getting paid. Nobody's getting their travel comped. Nobody's getting their food comped. That kind of shit. This is the thing: You can under-resource us—please don't—but you can do all these things, and all these realities can be put in place." And still, Schelling says: "Loss is not an option."

While a lot of national attention has been on the anti-trans laws in Texas aimed at preventing young people from getting medical support for their transitions, Schelling worries this exclusive focus overlooks what's most endangering trans young people in Texas, especially Black and brown trans youth. "I go back to this frustration for me. . . . We're still not actually focusing this conversation where we really need to, which is: What happened to all of the transgender kids who are in CPS care?"

Schelling points out that a lot of the focus of activism for transgender children has been set by upper-middle-class white families with trans children. These parents are often the most visible spokespeople for trans youth, and that focus has often left a lot of the serious issues affecting poor trans youth of color out of the discussion.

This is not because upper-middle-class white parents care more about their transgender kids. It's because they have greater resources and greater access—and are less likely to be simultaneously targeted by multiple systems in the same way many families of Black and brown trans kids are.

And yet many Black and brown trans kids are the most vulnerable in the trans community, as they have to battle both transphobia and systemic racism. Black and brown families are regularly targeted by our child protection systems, and once Black and brown children are removed from their home, the picture can be quite bleak—especially if those kids are queer or trans.

Of the youth population in the US, queer youth make up approximately 11 percent and trans youth about 1 percent, yet they make up 30 percent and 5 percent respectively of the youth in child welfare systems. Queer and trans youth often end up staying in child welfare systems longer than other youth, and are more likely to experience abuse within them. Many queer and trans youth flee these abusive systems, ending up homeless and vulnerable to even further abuse and exploitation (Youth.gov, n.d.).

Texas has the highest rate of murders and violence against transgender people—specifically, Black and brown trans women (McGaughy 2019). To Schelling, this is directly connected to systems that abuse Black and brown children and leave them more vulnerable to violence. "It's the same folks that are disproportionally impacted by maternal mortality." He wants to reset the conversation around those in the trans community who are most at risk for systemic harm.

Schelling cites unemployment rates and more as further examples of how Black and brown people in Texas are disenfranchised and made vulnerable. All of which often hit queer and trans youth the hardest.

"Again, we go back to who gets thrown onto the streets. What does the youth homeless population look like?" Schelling asks. "We have, like, forty-something percent out in the streets. So what is happening?"

To Schelling, anti-trans legislation being brought up by Texas lawmakers is dangerous and deadly, but not nearly as deadly as the ways in which trans people have already been targeted by and disenfranchised from much of society.

Schelling recalls how writer and Black transgender community leader Monica Roberts used to refer to trans people as the canaries in the coal mine. "But I think, even further, the canaries in the coal mine are the poor trans folks. They're the trans folks who don't have access to quality healthcare."

Schelling argues that for many, the right to medically transition is not the number one concern that cis people may think it is. "You're talking about: they don't have access for diabetic medication." When transgender people can't meet their basic needs for survival, issues around hormonal medications or gender-affirming surgery take a back seat.

Schelling stresses that trans people are still trans people without medical transition, and they are still being violently discriminated against because of anti-trans fear and hate. "When you have been thrown out on your fucking ass, simply for who you are, it doesn't matter the facial hair. It doesn't matter that my body will go through hell, my mind will go through hell. You will put me through hell, as an individual, absolutely yes. But you will not change who I inherently am, because that medicine doesn't fucking change whether or not I am who I am. And I know who I am."

Schelling stresses that it's the isolation, it's the poverty, it's the lack of access to healthcare, the lack of access to safe housing, that's killing Texas's most vulnerable trans people. And that is reflected in who Schelling *doesn't* see in the trans community.

"Where are Black trans women in their seventies?" Schelling asks. "Where are they? This is that connection to access to quality healthcare. We're not talking about gender-affirming care. It's not the transition-related care. It's the day-to-day care. It comes back to this fundamental three. Everything's just access to employment, housing, and healthcare. How do we achieve this for everybody? And what does that look like?"

It's these fundamentals that drive Schelling.

He is guided in his quest by Black trans movement workers like Rocky Lane and Lais Milburn, who have helped advise and educate him, and are officers on TENT's board. Lane and Milburn have helped turn TENT into the pro-Black organization it is today and aims to be in the future.

"Trans or not, we are gonna be unapologetically pro-Black," Schelling says. "And that means—and this is where people really get pissed at me—that means understanding a cultural humility of how homophobia and transphobia very uniquely impacted the Black community."

Schelling believes strongly that non-Black people in the LGBTQIA+ community need to understand this. Especially considering how many communities of color were violently forced away from more expansive definitions of gender and sexuality that their communities had long had and toward the more rigidly patriarchal ideas of gender and sexuality of white supremacy.

"We talk about generational trauma, but we just say the tagline," Schelling says. "And we don't talk about how men, women, and children were forced in families to watch their husband, their father, their brother, be emasculated in cruel, calculated, and intentional ways. [About] how the criminal justice system has preyed upon especially little Black boys. And Black women, Black people, Black children."

Schelling wants non-Black queer and trans people to investigate the parts they play in harm to Black trans people. He wants people to look at how transphobia in the Black community in particular is weaponized by white and non-Black trans people to perpetuate anti-Blackness, and how these practices divide the trans community and weaken the fight for trans lives.

I've seen versions of this myself as a queer Black woman. I've been told many times by white queers that I shouldn't be fighting for Black lives when my Black community is more likely to be unaccepting of my queer identity than the white community—as if my queerness, and not my Blackness, is ever the first thing that non-Black people see about me. Yes, I absolutely feel and fear the queerphobia in my community. But I'm always aware of the full weight of systemic racism that any white person, queer or not, can bring against me and my family at any time should I displease or even inconvenience them. That is a danger I feel every day of my life.

In this work and these difficult conversations, Schelling hopes to build lasting change with TENT. He hopes the legacy of TENT will be the ways in which the organization has evolved to advocate for and with the most vulnerable trans people in Texas, and that it will be able to stay true to its intersectional, pro-Black mission.

As proud as he is of all that he and TENT have been able to accomplish so far, and with all they still hope to be able to do, Schelling still laments the great toll this work takes on the entire community. "The world would be so much better if we didn't have to apply all this labor and money and bullshit to simply teaching us as a community, as a society, as a culture, how to bring ourselves back to kindness," he tells me. "And I just think to myself, every day, *What kind of world would we live in if we could take all of these brilliant minds and apply them to something other than having to advocate for survival for themselves and their community?*"

---

## BE A REVOLUTION

---

Black queerness, Black transness, and Black womanhood have existed at the center of who we are since time immemorial. And it is all a part of Blackness that can never be removed from all that Black people are.

When we look at the harm of violent white supremacist patriarchy, we must recognize that so much of it was accomplished by convincing many of us that we shouldn't exist, that we are not sacred.

We either get through this together, whole, or not at all.

If there's one thing that I hope I make abundantly clear in this book, it's that everyone has different roles in this revolution.

Those roles will be determined by skill, by will, by ability. They will be determined by our privilege. And they will definitely be determined by our race and ethnicity.

This is no more true than at the intersection of gender justice, sexuality, and race.

➤ **Understand your lane(s).** Battling queerphobia, transphobia, and misogyny in communities of color and in our racial justice movements is vital to our survival. Battling racism and transmisogyny in our mainstream feminist movements is vital to our survival.

But it's always important to focus attention on the structural mechanisms at play in our communities and what privilege we may have with respect to these mechanisms, if we are to address these issues in a way that does not cause harm.

➤ **Understand the root causes of racism, patriarchy, queerphobia, and transphobia in our communities.** Many of our current understandings of race, gender, and sexuality have been shaped by white supremacist, capitalist patriarchy. These understandings were forced upon us in so many ways, and benefit the white supremacist power structures while also harming us.

And yet white allies who claim to stand beside us will often blame us for how these understandings look in our communities of color.

Misogyny, queerphobia, and transphobia in Black and brown communities are regularly used against us. They are used as excuses to not support us, excuses to not fund us, excuses to make decisions for us.

But these are our communities, and as a Black queer woman, I am not made more safe by the condemnation of or condescension to my community—even toward those who may also be harming me. Misogyny, queerphobia, and transphobia in communities of color are manifestations of the violence of white supremacy we need to heal from. That healing requires space, safety, and resources.

➤ **Center those most affected.** For white people, this means prioritizing political and social objectives that are informed by the lived experiences of queer and trans BIPOC and seeking to remove structural barriers to our healing. For queer people of color, it means we have to center queer and trans voices in our communities and know that our liberation will be collective or it will not exist at all.

➤ **Support queer and trans movement workers.** Where queer and trans BIPOC are informing our objectives, their work must be compensated. Support should have a tangible impact on the lives of those doing the work—a like or a share or a "You're so brave" won't cut it. Time spent helping whiteness move away from violence and oppression is time not spent on ourselves and in our communities. While we're spending time educating cisgender and straight people in our BIPOC community (which is often expected to come second to educating whiteness), we're not spending time on our own rest and healing. That work means something.

➤ **Hold white-led gender justice and LGBTQIA+ organizations accountable.** "One in three [Black trans people] makes less than ten thousand dollars a year," J. Mase III tells me. "I've been asked by so many people, like, 'Oh my God, we need more people, more Black trans people to talk, to share stuff. Can you speak on this panel? Can you do this thing?' And again, 'Can you do it for free?' And it's, like, 'Do y'all work for free? What do y'all—you think my landlord accepts rainbows and sunshine?' She expects a check, okay?!"

For so long, white-led organizations have been able to take up the lion's share of funding while BIPOC-led organizations struggle. This pretty much guarantees that communities of color will be left behind in gender justice and queer justice efforts.

Emmett Schelling offers up an example: "Instead of giving money to Lambda Legal, give it to Transgender Legal Defense and Education Fund. That's led by a trans woman of color." He finds a lot of hypocrisy in what people *say* they support versus where their money goes. "You can say, 'I want to see trans people be able to succeed and be supported, but I keep giving my money to an organization that is literally predominantly white and cis.'"

White-led organizations must be open to hearing about how they have contributed to harm and still may be, and they must see the success of BIPOC-led movement workers and organizations as crucial to their success as well.

➤ **Move away from carceral approaches to gender-based violence.** As part of understanding harm that traditional gender justice and violence prevention organizations have caused, it's important to understand that all BIPOC are put at risk by carceral systems. And often it's those facing violence in their own homes, relationships, and communities who are put at the most risk.

This means that if you're a white person working on issues of gender justice or sexual violence, you must investigate all partnerships with police, prosecutors, Child Protective Services, social workers, and other entities that have long histories of causing harm in our communities. These relationships must be limited as much as possible if you hope to be in partnership with communities of color, and the boundaries of those relationships with carceral systems should be set by those most at risk.

➤ **Support abolitionist solutions to gender-based violence.** As we work to find abolitionist alternatives for ending violence and harm, that work needs support, protection, and resources. This is going to be messy, and whenever we talk about abolitionist alternatives for preventing violence, many who are invested in carceral narratives will demand guarantees that any alternatives will work perfectly from the beginning, every time, in order to be of value. But we're trying to forge new paths, and we're trying to do so with limited resources and in a culture that has long discouraged any skill-set building in truly nonviolent accountability practices. It will not be perfect, not even close, and not for a long time. But our carceral systems cause harm almost every single time they're used to try to address violence. Investing even a quarter of the resources we currently use for carceral solutions to violence in abolitionist solutions instead can make a world of difference and result in lasting positive impacts on our communities.

➤ **Reject shame and stigma and approach gender-based violence with caring community.** As we move away from carceral solutions to gender-based violence, it's also vital that we move away from isolation and shame. So often in cases of gender-based violence, the victims of violence are ignored, disbelieved, even punished for being victims. We cannot end gender-based violence this way.

Tarana Burke recognizes a marked difference between how Black communities address police violence or gun violence, and how they address—or don't address—gender-based violence: "If the police were out of order, we going down to the police station to protest. If the mayor said something crazy, we going to city hall. We respond to everything. We are very proactive in that way. So then what happens when you have what I see as a crisis [gender-based violence] and there's no response?

"But what I tell people is, think about gun violence. The response to gun violence that we've seen, in the last ten years in particular, has been heightened with all these mass shootings. So much of the legislation, or lack of legislation—it is now at the forefront. People understand gun violence as a political issue. Just think about the individual who was shot in our community: we now connect that to lack of legislation, to capitalism, these other systems that exist and uphold this violence that trickles all the way down to your homeboy who was shot on the corner. And so that analysis took time for some people to grow to. But I think they could see that—largely a lot of people see that now.

"And so when there's gun violence in our community, because we have that broad analysis, we feel a sense of collective responsibility, right? If a child is shot in our neighborhood, people rally. People are like, 'We will not tolerate our children being shot in the neighborhood.' Parents are like, 'I want my child to be able to get to school and back safely.' Community organizations are like, 'We have to get these guns off the street and keep our community safe.' For a singular incident. And they should. That's exactly what we should [do]. Because [if] any one person in our community is not safe, it has repercussions for the whole community not being safe."

But that same sort of analysis and sense of responsibility doesn't happen when someone in the community is harmed by sexual violence.

"When somebody falls victim to sexual violence within the community," Burke says, "we have nowhere near the same response. Instead, there's an interrogation of the individual's complicity in that."

➤ **Focus on accountability instead of revenge.** Tarana Burke stresses that we need to see gender-based violence as a community-level problem with systemic roots that needs both community and systemic solutions. We need to know that gender-based violence affects the entire community, and that the entire community must address it, while still centering and supporting those most directly harmed.

"There is a role for everybody to play in dismantling sexual violence and dismantling rape culture, which leads to sexual violence," Burke insists. And this starts with us building community relationships that center accountability, and building processes for that accountability to happen.

"When you harm somebody, you have to be accountable. Whatever it is. If I hurt your feelings, in order for us to be in community again, I have to figure out how—what you need from me—so that I could be accountable, so that you feel made whole again. If I care about you, if I care about being in community with you, even if we're never good girlfriends, you know, the relationship doesn't turn to whatever it was, but I resolve that harm. That's what we owe people on a basic level as human beings. Very, very basic level. That absolutely applies to sexual violence in a lot of its forms."

➤ **Know that gender justice *is* racial justice.** In BIPOC communities, not only do we have to move away from carceral solutions to violence; we also have to separate our feelings about white supremacist, carceral solutions from the important work of community healing and accountability.

What I mean is, yes, carceral solutions to violence have been imposed upon us by white supremacy, but that doesn't mean every approach to ending violence or every fight for gender justice is also white supremacist.

Because of how much harm has been done by these carceral solutions, some people are wary of any justice or accountability processes. I've heard quite a few times that attempts to hold, say, BIPOC men accountable for gender-based violence is "racist" or "white supremacist"—even when thoroughly abolitionist in nature and originating solely from within our communities.

I've also heard people claim that our own BIPOC feminist and womanist movements are white supremacist in nature, as well as our movements for queer and trans rights—even though not only do we have a long history of our own indigenous versions of this social justice work but also we have long been pioneers of the work itself.

Some of these concerns and dismissals are from a place of genuine fear and trauma from the harm of white supremacy, and some very clearly are disingenuous and aimed at keeping us from addressing these issues in order to maintain current power hierarchies within our communities. It's vital that we're able to distinguish between the two, and vital that we repeatedly check in with ourselves and one another to ensure harmful, punitive practices aren't working their way into our processes.

Issues of women's rights and LGBTQIA+ rights aren't just national questions to be debated at elections or topics for white people to argue about. These issues affect our communities because the people most affected by these issues are in our communities—and we get to decide what the discussion around these issues looks like and what the solutions are.

➤ **Build community-specific approaches.** "Start local first," Emmett Schelling advises. "It can never be a blanket strategy of how to address things on the ground. Because every region, every locality, has its own specific nuance. . . . Where has the harm shown up? What are the obstacles? And that's different for somebody that lives in Rio Grande Valley [versus] somebody who lives in Austin."

Community by community, we can move forward to address issues of gender justice and LGBTQIA+ rights, while also coming together to fight systems that seek to hinder our progress and our healing.

We must recognize how these issues are essential to all of our liberation, and we must find our sphere of influence to address them. While we establish our sphere of influence, based on who we know, what skills we have, our privilege, and more, it's important that we do this work as publicly as possible. It's important, too, that we normalize this work and make it a part of our collective values.

"Where do you light the fire?" Tarana Burke asks. "Your sphere of influence is a perfect place to start and end. . . . And if that is where you are a revolution for the rest of your life, that's okay. What this moment in time tries to tell us is that your work is not real, your efforts aren't big enough—if it's not the Me Too movement, if it's not Black Lives Matter, if it's not that, then you haven't done your job, you haven't done enough. But I think that people need to understand just how important it is for people to see you *want* to be a revolution, for you to understand the people who you are influencing right around you. And that's enough."

## HIERARCHIES OF BODY AND MIND: DISABILITY AND RACE

I T WAS THIS CHAPTER that broke the entire book for me. In my head, I had all of these neat chapters organized by where people were fighting systemic racism. Were they fighting at the intersection of labor and race? Easy—that goes into the labor chapter. Were they fighting at the intersection of race and incarceration? Goes into the abolition chapter. Were they fighting at the intersection of gender and race? Goes in gender justice and feminism.

And so I approached my interviews with disabled BIPOC activists in this mindset. Yes, there would be some bleed-through to other chapters because of the intersectional nature of the world. But disabled BIPOC activists would go into the disability chapter.

Pretty soon into my interviews with disabled BIPOC activists, I realized how silly my assumptions had been.

The truth is, a huge amount of the important work in racial justice and liberation has long been carried by the work of disabled BIPOC activists. And the work they do—and have done—intersects not only with race but also with every other oppression and system we can think of.

If there's a chapter in this book that has truly changed me—changed how I see activism, how I see the world, and how I see my place in it—it is this one. Until now, I did not fully appreciate how vital a disability justice framework is for any social justice work and *especially* for racial justice work. And I don't think I had seen how internalized ableism limited the ways in which I see myself and my work.

My hope, then, for this chapter is that you will see yourself in it and that you might be similarly changed.

## DR. SAMI SCHALK

Dr. Sami Schalk and so many other people I interviewed for this book reminded me of the many multitudes we really do contain, and how many multitudes those who have been marginalized must contain for their survival.

So let's see if I can summarize the work Dr. Schalk does. She's a researcher, scholar, and educator. She has researched and published books on disability in Black women's speculative fiction and most recently in *Black Disability Politics*—a book on, well, Black disability politics. She has also been researching sexuality and pleasure activism from a Black, queer, disabled perspective. She teaches courses on disability, gender, and sexuality as an associate professor of Gender and Women's Studies at the University of Wisconsin–Madison. She's a board member of Freedom, Inc., the Black and Southeast Asian activist and advocacy organization. When she's not doing all that, you may see her out on the streets, providing food, water, and other vital resources to protestors in the Madison area in order to make protests more accessible.

She also twerked with Janelle Monáe once.

It's easy for those of us who have not twerked with Janelle Monáe to feel intimidated by such a résumé. But one of the things I love about the breadth of Schalk's work is that, while a lot of it does utilize her specialized skills and scholarship, a fair amount of it is accessible to many of us looking to create change. In fact, a lot of her work is about making movement work more accessible to more people.

For Schalk, all of the activities that fill her robust life started quite simply: in a disability studies class.

At nineteen years old, Sami Schalk had just come out to her friends as bisexual, and you couldn't tell her *nothing*. She was a fired-up, political young adult. "I thought that I knew everything there was to know about oppression at that point," Schalk remembers with a smile. "As you do at nineteen."

When she signed up for the disability studies class, she thought she would come out of it a better ally. She didn't realize that she would not only find herself in the stories of disability and disability politics but also gain a far greater understanding of how all systemic oppression works.

"Ableism became the lens that helped me understand the relationship between all kinds of oppression. It became, really, that nexus for me, where I was like, *Oh, inside of all these other things I experience, I see how ableism supports them and makes them function.*"

Schalk was able to see connections between disability studies and the Black feminist theory she had been strongly influenced by in her life. She naturally then expected to see a lot of collaboration and intentional connection in the fields of study and activism themselves—but she didn't see those connections.

In her feminist theory classes, issues of health and disability would repeatedly come up, but they weren't discussed in the same way they were in her disability studies class. And in that disability studies class, she could count the attendees of color on one hand.

"I was like, *What?* It was so different. I became so invested in bringing these things together, because it just made sense to me in a way that I wished other people could see."

In that frustration, Dr. Sami Schalk's life of teaching, learning, and activism began.

"Nineteen." Schalk laughs as she remembers these events that set her on such an important path. "It just broke open my little brain."

Now Dr. Schalk is the creator of similar life-changing moments for younger generations in her popular Disability, Gender, and Sexuality class. Remembering how a disability studies class had helped her become more comfortable in her own disabled identity, Schalk works hard to create a safe environment for students to open up about their own disabilities in ways they may not feel safe to do in other classes. In Schalk's classes they also discuss the systemic causes behind a lot of the shame and guilt disabled people are often made to internalize.

"One of the things that these kinds of classes bring to the students is that it makes them realize that things they thought were specific to them—personal failures—are actually connected to these much larger systems. . . . It empowers them in a way, that they can point to the thing and be like: 'This thing is making me feel bad!' 'That's actually the problem over there.'"

It's not just disabled students who benefit from these lessons.

"Even the non-disabled students say that it changes things for them. To just realize that their version of sex, the way they think about sex, is so narrow and ableist. . . . They realize that even if they are not disabled, they can expand the way they think about and engage with sex in a way that benefits them. And that's all I want." Schalk adds with a laugh, "I tell them, 'If the only thing you take away from this class is that penis-in-vagina sex is not the only kind of sex that you can have, great!'"

While Schalk is working on helping disabled students understand the systemic oppressions affecting their lives and their communities, she is also working to make it easier for disabled people and many others to join the fight for systemic change through protest.

When people think of protests, they often picture long marches through cities or people circling in picket lines or perhaps participating in sit-ins. But all of these forms of protest often require different abilities that many non-disabled people take for granted, even as those requirements keep many of the most affected by systemic oppression from being able to participate.

Standing and marching for long periods of time, for example, requires a level of mobility and physical stamina that many don't have. Others are physically excluded from activities that require sitting or lying on the ground. Large, loud crowds can make it hard for neurodivergent people to participate. Hours spent in heat or direct sun can be dangerous for people whose bodies don't regulate temperature well. Being without access to food or water for hours can be very dangerous for those who are prone to overheating or who need to keep their blood sugar regulated.

Schalk wants disabled people to be able to participate in protests for social change. In 2020, as millions of people around the world took to the streets in an uprising for Black lives, many Black disabled people—those often at most risk of police violence—found themselves excluded both in presence and in organizational demands.

To be clear, when we neglect to consider the needs of disabled people in our movement work, a harmful message is sent. As Schalk explains: "We're communicating that folks who cannot meet these particular able-bodied, able-minded standards and be in these spaces are not the people that we want to connect with, they are not the people that we want to join."

But it goes deeper than just failing to send a message of inclusion. When we exclude disabled people of color from protests for racial justice, we also exclude the issues they highlight and prevent our fully understanding how systemic racism is affecting communities of color. If you're marching for Black lives, and yet you have no real understanding of how issues like police brutality are disproportionately affecting Black disabled people—and therefore you have no way of including their needs in your demands for accountability, reform, or abolition— are you really marching for Black lives . . . or just *some* Black lives?

"There is no way to end white supremacy without addressing ableism," Schalk stresses. "The way that race is understood and med-icalized and pathologized is so tied to ableism and the way that we determine norms of body-minds. It's just so essential. I really want non-disabled people of color to understand how deeply tied our lib-erations are. . . . There's no way for folks of color to get free without addressing ableism."

While not every protest action is going to be accessible to all, al-most all protests can be made *more* accessible. And Sami Schalk has shown how easily that accessibility can be achieved.

"What I have now become known for in Madison is that I am there with food and water," she says. "I just try to make sure that people have basic supports to be there. To be there as long as possible. And I try to talk to people about why having these various forms of care work, including medical support, at protests is so important."

Where protests can't be made more accessible, Schalk stresses that it's important to communicate this clearly so people know what to expect and where they can participate and where they cannot. This clear communication can encourage out-of-the-box thinking that expands the scope and effectiveness of protests and makes them accessible in ways that couldn't be visualized before.

"Be clear with people about what's happening," Schalk advises. "If you want to do a five-mile march, and you're gonna shut down the city and you have this plan, just let people know: 'Hey, we're gonna be walking for five miles. And if that's not the action for you, there are other actions.' Even if there's a five-mile march—which I can't do—there might be people who are driving in front of the march. Vehicles for protection. And disabled people can be in the vehicles. There are lots of ways to engage."

In fact, the work Schalk often does at protests—passing out food and water to protestors—is one of those ways she has found to stay engaged in protests she otherwise may not be able to physically par-ticipate in.

It's not just disabled people who benefit from these considerations. Food, water, restrooms, shade, places to sit—these are all things many non-disabled people need at protests as well. Schalk adds: "It is for disabled folks. It's for people who are pregnant, who have children, young children. All of these folks need food and water."

Accessibility considerations may seem like a lot, but usually we can very quickly adapt to them. When I first started taking speaking gigs on issues of race and gender, accessibility was rarely talked about. In all honesty, it wasn't something I thought about very often, until Sonya Renee Taylor stood onstage at a speaking engagement we were both in and talked about the fact that we were discussing inclusivity and social justice on a stage that didn't have a wheelchair ramp.

I realized how often my platform was given to me in part because I could—literally—walk onto it. In not considering accessibility at my engagements, I was helping to block important voices from the discussions I was trying to foster.

So I talked with some of my friends in the disability justice world about what accommodations I should look for when taking a gig, and I added a standard accessibility clause to my contracts. For years now wheelchair access, seating to accommodate larger bodies, sign-language interpreters and captioning, gender-neutral bathrooms, and more have been a part of pretty much every speaking agreement I sign. It was wild for me to experience pushback on these simple requests. Organizations that had professed a dedication to inclusion and social justice when trying to hire me for an event were almost offended I would require captioning or adequate seating for people. Sign-language interpreters would come up to me at events, asking what was up with my gigs, because they were almost never booked in those sorts of venues and yet they had interpreted for me twice, or even three times, within the span of one year.

My requests for accommodations at speaking events were met with surprise or even hostility for years. It was depressing how often institutions and organizations would try to tell me that for an event that they had spent tens of thousands—if not hundreds of thousands—of dollars on, often flying in speakers from all over the country, they "didn't have the budget" for a sign-language interpreter.

But suddenly the COVID-19 pandemic happened. Captioning became a necessity for everyone as we all tried to understand one another via our shaky internet connections over Zoom. In-person events suddenly had very flexible seating as we tried to keep a safe distance from one another. So many accommodations that disabled people had been asking for in their schools, organizations, and workplaces for years were everywhere seemingly overnight. In recognizing that we could completely change the way we communicate while also meeting the needs of non-disabled people, conversations opened up about how to accommodate disabled people—conversations that were both badly needed and incredibly infuriating.

People don't bat an eye at the accommodations rider in my contracts anymore. I hope, as I write this and our society tries to return to "normal" after years of the pandemic, we'll continue with these accommodations and more, especially considering that we're barely beginning to understand the ramifications of Long COVID on long-term health and on society—and with more than one hundred million people infected in the US in the first three years of the pandemic, if even a small percentage of those people develop Long COVID, we could be living in one of the most disabling events in this country's history.

We can change. We can change a lot in a short period of time. But unfortunately, we only seem to be willing to do so for some in society and not others.

Integrating disability justice work into our anti-racist work, and vice versa, is really the only way to do this work well. And while these considerations may seem daunting or complicated, they actually just open up more beautiful opportunities for meaningful change.

"The system is meant to erase all the small wins," Schalk says, referencing advice that Talila Lewis had once given her. "And so I think really focusing on what's the small win, the intervention that I can make—and then grow that, and I can grow that—that is the way to go."

## Why Disability Matters

It might seem strange to some people to see an entire chapter of this book dedicated to disability justice, especially if you're not a disabled person of color. But even though many people try, the truth is that we really can't separate racism and ableism in the struggle for liberation—not if we want to win that struggle. Systemic racism and ableism serve the same core purpose in society: to justify the oppression, exclusion, and exploitation of people based on a manufactured hierarchy of value—one involving people's bodies and minds. Historically, Black, Indigenous, and other bodies of color were deemed expendable, were seen as either tools or obstacles. Our bodies were reduced to our productivity or to a threat, nothing more. Where we couldn't produce a profit for white supremacy, we were disposed of. To justify the violence enacted upon our bodies, our minds were deemed less valuable, less capable of feeling, comprehension, and self-control. It was argued that we were, literally, built for exploitation and our value disappeared when we couldn't continue to, or refused to, work in exploitative conditions. Our brains were considered incapable of the higher thought that would allow us to be full members of society. We were unable to rise above base, animal instincts and therefore must be controlled or exterminated. These were all ableist justifications for violence that are still used against disabled people and many non-disabled people of color.

Further, ableist images and racist images became intertwined—with disabled white people often despised for having traits that matched racist ideas of populations of color (especially stereotypes of Black and Indigenous people). People of color were also despised for having traits that resembled ableist ideas of disabled people. And all of it, the ableism and the racism, reduced our bodies and minds to productivity and profit, or a threat to productivity and profit.

Which came first—the ableism or the racism—is a chicken-or-egg-type question that many people have differing opinions on. At the end of the day, the two oppressions often work together to serve the same greater purpose. Abolitionist and disability justice advocate Talila Lewis calls this relationship between racism and ableism an "Escherian stair"—invoking the drawings of the visually daring artist M. C. Escher—with ableism at the heart of the construction of marginalized identities, and vice versa. One oppression begins as another one ends so seamlessly that you can't pull them apart; they are instead stuck in a loop of harm.

"It is co-constructive," Lewis says. "So it's not like it's in this vacuum: one and then the other. It's like, no—all the time, at the same time, constructed together. You can't disconnect them, and if you try, you're actually harming everyone."

When we aren't aware of the links between racism and ableism, we can fall into ableist traps in the name of anti-racism—traps that harm us all.

We often trade in ableism, hoping that will buy us safety, but it never does.

Lewis says, "What I argue is that a lot of folks who are doing work that they don't see as directly tied to disability work—dismantling racism, dismantling trans misogyny . . . are boxing ableism's shadow. And so what ends up happening is that they're often reinforcing ableism, even as they fight racism or classism."

Our instincts to prove white supremacy wrong about our perceived value, or lack thereof, end up often reinforcing ableist ideas of conditional human value.

Lewis points out that the way ableism is used against communities of color is what makes us feel compelled to regularly prove our value. We have to show we're upstanding, taxpaying, hard-working people instead of feeling like we can insist on our safety and dignity simply because we're human beings.

When we keep trying to prove that there are reasons why we deserve safety, food, shelter, even our very lives, we reinforce the ableist idea that our worth as human beings is tied to external definitions of our contributions to society—our "productivity." When we insist there are things we can do that justify why we should live, we reinforce the idea that there are also things we can do—or neglect to do—that justify why we should die.

This is very harmful to anti-racist and anti-capitalist work, because it provides our oppressors a way out—a justification for their violence against us. All they have to do is paint us as unworthy of basic human rights—due to measurements of value *that they set*—and they are free to do with us as they wish.

"Ableism does all this work and doesn't even receive honorable mention," Lewis says with a chuckle. "And that's why it's been so successful. It's so nimble and timeless. It's a shape-shifter. It can operate as any single form of oppression, or it can operate as itself to do the harm it needs to do."

Disability also matters to anti-racist work because, to put it plainly, disabled people of color exist. There are quite a lot of us. And when disability and racism collide, it's disabled people of color—especially disabled Black and Indigenous people—who suffer the most.

Data has shown that BIPOC have increased rates of asthma, mental illness, and disability, and that disabled BIPOC are more likely to experience disparities in accessing healthcare, housing, and other basic needs. Forty-one percent of people incarcerated in US prisons have a self-reported disability, and considering that BIPOC are less likely to have access to medical and mental health professionals that would be able to provide diagnoses, that number is likely higher. Black people are five times more likely to be incarcerated than whites, and Latine people are 1.3 times more likely (Crowe and Drew 2021; Nellis 2021).

Because of how vulnerable to both systemic racism and ableism disabled BIPOC often are, it should not be a surprise to hear that disabled people of color have long been at the forefront of our racial justice movements. Yet for many it will be, because those people have often been written out of our history due to ableism.

"Black disabled people have always been a part of this work," disability justice activist and macro social worker Vilissa Thompson tells me. "Whether they are visibly disabled or have non-apparent disabilities. A lot of the people that we look up to in history—like Harriet Tubman, Fannie Lou Hamer, and so forth—they were disabled."

Thompson adds, "One of my favorite stories I love to share is about a disabled Black Panther named Brad Lomax, who was instrumental in the 504 Sit-In that happened in California in the '70s, and how he got the Black Panther Party to assist in the protest. The Black Panther Party fed the protestors, and without their involvement, many consider that the protest may not have been sustainable."

Brad Lomax was the founder of the Washington chapter of the Black Panthers. He helped to organize the first African Liberation Day demonstration march on the National Mall. When Lomax moved to Oakland, he found that the Bay Area transit systems were not accessible to him and other disabled people, so he began protesting for disability justice as well as racial justice. The 504 Sit-In was aimed at getting the government to enforce Section 504 in the Rehabilitation Act of 1973, which prohibited recipients of federal aid from discriminating against disabled people. Lomax reached out to the Panthers and convinced them to provide food and other resources to the protestors, which helped them sustain their protest and made it the longest peaceful occupation of a federal building in US history. The protest was successful, and on April 28, 1977, regulations to enforce Section 504 were signed by the Health, Education, and Welfare secretary (Connelly 2020).

It's not just non-disabled people who don't know how valuable the contributions of disabled people of color are to liberation work. They've been so erased from popular culture and our education system that many disabled people also don't know their value. Even when disabled movement workers are included in our histories, often their disability is erased from the story.

"I think that does a great disservice when their disabilities are ignored, or placed as a footnote, and we don't get a fullness of understanding of our ancestors," Thompson tells me. "It should not have taken me being an activist to learn about Brad Lomax and other Black disabled folks who were at the very beginning of the disability rights movement."

Not only have disabled activists of color long been at the forefront of social justice work for many generations; they also have some of the more creative and innovative solutions to many of the problems we face, because they're used to having to operate outside of established systems and norms that have never served them.

Writer, poet, and disability and transformative justice worker Leah Lakshmi Piepzna-Samarasinha uses climate change as an example of an area where disabled people often have knowledge and experience that could be vital to us all: "There's been a lot of writing out there by disabled people about how we are both the canaries in the coal mine about climate change and we are also people who have figured out, 'Okay, here's how you create climate respite spaces.' Because we are those canaries who are perhaps more at risk to extreme heat and extreme cold, massive changes, flooding, et cetera. Nobody's coming to save us. So if we don't wanna die in a nursing home in bed, we've gotta figure out how to get the survival systems out there."

If your vision of liberation for people of color doesn't include disabled people of color, it's an incomplete vision. Piepzna-Samarasinha argues that at the end of the day, when our work is truly inclusive, it's just plain better for all of us. "Don't we *want* everyone to be there?" they ask. "And wouldn't it be great if there were chairs that are comfortable, and you don't have to climb up a mountain to get there and stuff? And no one's shamed for having a fucking feeling or whatever?... Sometimes care is a pain in the ass. But this isn't just this grinding thing we have to do as a duty. We're actually making this really joyful, loving space of communion."

## ALICE WONG

My name is Alice Wong. I'm forty-eight years old. I'm the daughter of Chinese immigrants. I was born and raised in Indianapolis, Indiana, in the '70s, and I think that the time and place is important. To try to ground myself and to give you context into the world I was born into."

Alice Wong is very intentional and yet very genuine in how she talks about herself and her work. She believes in the power of story—in the power of her story and the stories of so many other disabled people of color. So it's important to her that you see her story clearly. Her identity and experiences as the disabled daughter of Chinese immigrants, raised in the Rust Belt, are important to how she sees the world and what she wants in the world.

Wong was born with a form of muscular dystrophy. That condition has defined a lot of her life and her work, and it informs a lot of her future as well.

"[The condition] is progressive, so, you know . . . it's forever," she explains. "It's definitely a one-way trajectory. It progressively gets worse. That has always been a reality of my life."

As someone who has always been very physically disabled, Wong learned early on about power—who has it and how to get it. So many people seemed to have power over Wong and her well-being, so she needed to find her own power in order to be able to get what she needed to navigate the world.

"I think the advantage—I call it an advantage—is knowing at a very young age my relationship with the world, and my relationship in terms of power dynamics. Whether it's within the university or within the medical–industrial complex or with other adults. I was acutely aware of my difference and of the way people saw me. And also of the way that, because I need help with things, my relationships to other people are different. With my siblings, with my parents . . . Even though all children need help, this is a different level of help. So I grew up really understanding politics before that word or concept was even a thing in my mind."

As the progression of her muscular dystrophy has caused her to become more and more dependent on medical professionals and health aides, as well as an increasing amount of medical machinery and implements (a progression she has referred to as her "cyborg existence"), Wong has had to become an even stronger advocate for herself in order to be able to manage her healthcare.

"I think I developed a very sophisticated set of skills, including executive functioning, because I constantly had to manage, think ahead, assess people's emotions, assess people's receptiveness. The mental load was a lot. That's how I grew up. I need to survive and figure out how to communicate with people, and in many ways get people to do what I want."

This has been the reality of Wong's life for as long as she can remember. So when I ask her about what led her down a path to the amazing work she does now, it's clear that she bristles a little at the question.

"When people started asking, 'How did you get into activism?' I feel like I didn't really have a choice. I was born disabled in a non-disabled world."

The choice to become an activist having been made for her, Wong wants other disabled BIPOC to be able to make different choices. "I don't want disabled people to feel like they have to be activists. And I feel like the world that we want and deserve will allow us to just be, rather than [us] always working towards being accepted or fighting for space or just being valued."

I met Alice Wong the way many writers and disabled people meet these days: online. Years ago, when I was working as an editor at a now-defunct online magazine, I started seeking out more disabled BIPOC voices in an effort to make our magazine more intersectional and inclusive. We were, like so many other publications, woefully lacking in disabled representation, even as we claimed to be an intersectional feminist space.

A bit of online research brought me to Wong's Disability Visibility Project (DVP). There I found so many voices that had been overlooked by mainstream media and even smaller indie media like our little website.

The DVP is more than just a blog site. Even though Wong's blog posts about her life and work are amazing, it's also a community space with regular contributions from other disabled writers. The project is described by Wong as "An online community dedicated to creating, sharing, and amplifying disability media and culture" (Disability Visibility Project, n.d.). There are blog posts, essays, reports, and more "about ableism, intersectionality, culture, media, and politics from the perspective of disabled people."

As a Black woman and Black writer, I've always felt that all issues are Black issues and all issues are women's issues. And I've long felt frustrated by how often people try to silo my voice into one particular area, as if Black women don't interact with the rest of the world, as if their hobbies and interests and concerns don't exist outside of strictly "race- and gender-specific" areas.

Wong has taken on similar racist and ableist assumptions with the Disability Visibility Project. Some recent blog titles include "Taking the Edge Off: Navigating an Ableist Pandemic Through Mixology,"

"Making a Case for Self-Description: It's Not About Eye Candy," "How Radical Acceptance of My Disabled Body Made a Mess (and Clarity) of My Gender Acceptance," "Accessibility and the Lack Thereof in the Film Industry," and so much more. And because of DVP's commitment to intersectionality, a majority of the voices you'll read there are of disabled people of color.

The DVP was born from Wong's lifelong love of books and writing. "I felt many times excluded as a little child, as a student, on the playground . . . all these places," she explains. "Books were freedom. Books were a gateway. Books were the multiverse. I escaped through books. I felt like I could do anything through books. Books really fed my imagination and my creativity."

That love of writing took Wong through a degree in English and sociology. From there, she went on to graduate school, earning her master's in medical sociology, and then worked on research projects focused on disabled living and community. This and her activism work dedicated to the disabled community has brought recognition in the form of numerous awards, including the Disability Service Award by the University of California, San Francisco, and AAPD's Paul G. Hearne Leadership Award. She also served on the National Council on Disability, advising President Obama on policies affecting disabled people.

But with her impressive résumé, Wong still credits the influence of her Chinese immigrant community for how she works in the disability justice community. "I think a lot about immigrant communities," Wong reflects. "Because it's about sharing communities, sharing cultures. These are cultures of sharing, right? Before mutual aid was called mutual aid, this is what people did."

The small community Wong grew up in revolved around the church. Church wasn't just about worship; it was also about connection. It was a central place for community members to come together, support one another, and share resources. Wong recalls, "Whenever there were new people arriving, my mom and other aunties—you know, aunties are very powerful—all the aunties would be like, 'Here's what you do to get to the DMV to get your driver's license.' 'This is what you do.'

'Let's have a potluck.' 'Let's have a wedding in the church basement be-cause these two graduate students don't have money.' 'Let's just throw things together.' And I feel like that's a way of sharing resources or wealth or capital, in ways that's really just sustained our communities. I think that's what we do as people—we want everyone to do well, not just do well within this capitalist framework but just . . . be well. I think that's the thing. We take care of each other."

This upbringing underscores Wong's insistence that people have different roles in revolutionary work and everyone has skills they can bring to the table. She remembers how every Sunday, after services, members of the community who were doctors would set up a make-shift clinic in the church to help community members who didn't have healthcare. This is just one example of how people brought their different skills to the table to help their community where they could, and how those who had more resources recognized the need to support the community that had supported them. Wong points out that this model of caring seemed to come naturally to the com-munity, and that many immigrant communities have their own inter-nal support structures.

"Our church was a real mix of people," she says. "People who were newly arrived, people who were working-class, people who were graduate students or who lived there longer . . . Those of us who were definitely more established, I saw them give a lot. There would be these Sunday clinics, and it wasn't a collective, it wasn't a founda-tion. They just kinda did stuff on their own. I feel like there's a lot of immigrant communities who have these philanthropic structures as well that are sort of formalized, like giving circles."

As communities invest in their people, people are then able to give back in turn. This is how immigrant communities have survived and even thrived in environments that are often hostile. And I believe white supremacy views this as a threat—a threat to white supremacy and to capitalism. We are told time and time again as people of color that if we want to get far in this country, we have to be independent and make it on our own. We are told to put our own personal success above the health of our communities. We are told that the instinct to commune and to work as a collective will only lead to failure. But that can't be true, because, against all odds, we are still here.

It's writing that makes up a majority of Wong's work these days, whether for the Disability Visibility Project or her books. The DVP has led to two books: *Disability Visibility: First-Person Stories from the Twenty-First Century* (along with a young-adult edition) and the upcoming *Disability Intimacy*. She also released a memoir, *Year of the Tiger*, in 2022.

And while to some this might seem like a departure from her earlier work in research and policy, it's all part of Wong's lifelong work in helping to create a world where disabled people are able to live with full dignity and as autonomous yet fully connected members of society. She believes there is a special place for story in that work.

"Activism absolutely requires imagination and creativity. And that's what I think I'd really like to emphasize, is that I do believe that creative culture plays a big part. We need to tell our ancestors' stories, we need to tell our own stories, because it's not just for us right now. It's about honoring our elders and also looking ahead to future generations. That's the lineage, that's the kinship that's furthered by blood, by chosen family. By chosen communities. I think that's really another form of activism."

The stories Wong writes and publishes not only offer ways of looking at the world through important, intersectional lenses; they also underscore the fact that our stories are worth telling and preserving. We've been told for so long that our stories are insignificant, that others matter so much more than us.

"Often, marginalized people don't realize that they are creating history every day, and that our stories and that our tweets are worth archiving. This really challenges the notions of who gets to create knowledge. What is knowledge? Who produces knowledge? We have to be prepared to constantly repeat, over and over, that we feel that our knowledge is fine, that our knowledge is sacred."

## Ableism in Anti-racist Work

"I have the experience of somebody who walks with a limp, uses a cane, walks 'slower' than a lot of people," Leah Lakshmi Piepzna-Samarasinha tells me. "I'd go to the protest march, and I'd be at the front. And then we'd start marching, and for over an hour, everyone would march faster than me, so I would be at the end. And there would be some marchers who would be like, 'Keep up, keep up! The cops are gonna catch us!' And I'm literally watching the revolution walk away from me."

The thing about institutionalized oppression is that it can seep into *everything*. And the more integral it is to our history and major systems, the more ubiquitous it becomes. The US was founded on hierarchies of bodies and minds, and the exploitation of and violence against those bodies and minds. And so—just as it shouldn't surprise you to find racism in every system in the US, as well as in most businesses, in most neighborhoods and towns, in many families, and even internalized within ourselves—it shouldn't be a surprise to find out that ableism is also almost everywhere we look.

Our progressive movements are in no way exempt from this. Just as we often find racism in mainstream feminist and disability justice spaces, we will also find ableism in our racial justice spaces. Further, the ways in which marginalized groups are often pitted against one another means we are incentivized for participating in this division and oppression within our movements. For disabled people of color who face racism in many spaces and ableism in many others, this can mean that there are very few places where they can feel safe, let alone prioritized.

When protests erupted around the killing of Mike Brown, and

attention and resources started coming to groups and organizations associated with the Black Lives Matter organization and movement, Talila Lewis and many other disabled Black organizers quickly became frustrated with the lack of disability inclusion in these movements. Black disabled people were *the most* likely to be targeted in the Black community by police violence, and yet they weren't being given a voice or resources in this rising movement for Black lives. They were overlooked by white disabled activists as well as by mainstream Black abolitionist movements. Lewis, Lewis's partner Ki'tay Davidson, and Allie Cannington decided to challenge this erasure.

Lewis, Davidson, and Cannington first challenged the silence of white disabled people with the hashtag #DisabilitySolidarity on social media. They aimed to educate people on how racism, police violence, and carceral violence were issues the entire disabled community needed to take action on.

"We ended up posting a Twitter storm that took off," Lewis remembers. "We were talking about #DisabilitySolidarity being this call for people to understand disability in a more critical way, ensuring that anti-racism was part and parcel of anti-ableism, and vice versa. All of this was happening while we're also trying to bring in and sit with our own communities—Black, brown, Indigenous communities, and migrant communities. About our own ableism."

While many made excuses for their lack of disability inclusion in these organizing and protest efforts (when it occurred to them to discuss disability at all), this small group, with little more resources than their own experience and creativity, figured out how to bring disabled Black organizers together to discuss their needs and wants, to make sure disabled Black people were included in the struggle for Black lives.

"Somebody was like, 'Yo, here's a Google doc. Let's put this stuff in order. Let's coalesce. Let's get on some calls.' Mind you, there were Deaf, Deaf-blind, disabled, multiply disabled Black folks engaged in this. And we figured it out on our own—no resources—how we were going to communicate with one another. Even though we were using these different languages and modes—some signers, some text writers, some speakers. It was beautiful," Lewis remembers.

Out of these discussions, the Harriet Tubman Collective was born.

The Harriet Tubman Collective aims to get larger Black liberation spaces to understand and add some focus to how disabled Black people experience both ableism and racism at the hands of the state, society, and our movements. But the collective was also a chance for connection in work that can be quite isolating at times.

"I see it as a way for us to connect as Black disabled people," collective member Vilissa Thompson tells me. "There's not a safe space for us to be in. We're kind of ignored, and dealing with the racism in one camp or the ableism in the other. . . . For me, being part of the Harriet Tubman Collective is about finding community for Black disabled folks who are doing incredible work in their respective areas. And figuring out: How do we push the [broader] community forward when it comes to race, anti-Blackness, misogynoir issues?"

In 2016, BLM released a platform statement they called *A Vision for Black Lives*, and disability was notably left out, much to the frustration and dismay of Lewis and many other Black disabled activists.

The collective came together to discuss how police brutality was affecting their lives and their communities, and what they saw as missing, not only from the BLM platform but also from Black liberation struggles in general. They released their own statement. In it, they shared statistics and specifics on how Black Deaf and disabled people are disproportionately targeted for state violence. They pointed out recent high-profile police killings of disabled Black people. They listed many of the ways in which disabled Black people were erased from the BLM platform by their failure to include adequate mention of the risk of police violence to the Black disabled community, or to even include disabled movement workers who were already trying to address this violence in the platform process. They reminded BLM that the inclusion of Black disabled people in the fight to end state violence was nonnegotiable, stating:

> If a staunch political stance is going to be taken about the Black experience, it is a grave injustice and offense to dismiss the plight of Black Disabled and Black Deaf communities. This platform and work is wholly incomplete if disability is not present. To be sure, no successful movement has existed without our leadership, and no movement will be successful without us. (Harriet Tubman Collective 2017)

Their efforts helped shift some of the focus in the fight for Black lives toward the most vulnerable and under-resourced in the struggle: disabled Black people. Their statement was picked up by media and sparked many conversations on how disabled Black people are uniquely affected by police violence. For years the collective regularly shared information on how Deaf and disabled Black people were being targeted by state violence, as well as resources for Black Deaf and disabled people. Members of the collective wrote articles and gave talks around the

United States on issues of violence against the Black disabled community.

THE WORK THE Harriet Tubman Collective has done has been vital to our understanding, not only of how police violence is both a disability justice issue and a racial justice issue but also of how ableism within our racial justice movements is a serious threat to our fights for liberation. When we don't investigate ableism in our work, even our proposed solutions intended to decrease violence against communities of color can actually *increase* violence against disabled people.

Leah Lakshmi Piepzna-Samarasinha points to the 2020 uprising for Black lives as an example: "During the rebellions... [there were] massive, at least temporarily successful calls to defund the police. And then there's the 'What can we do instead?' 'Okay, let's put [police funds] into health- and community-based alternatives.' And that can mean a lot of things.

"And then you saw some people in the movement being like, 'Oh, we actually need more psych institutions,' and 'We need to, in some cases, push back on laws that protect mentally ill, psychiatrically disabled people's rights to refuse treatment. Because if they'd just be locked up, they'd be safe.'"

If we were to set aside the basic fact that Black and brown people are absolutely *not* safe in a large amount, if not a majority, of mental health institutions in this country, we must also recognize that if liberation is our goal, arguing for forced treatment and confinement is counter to that goal.

Piepzna-Samarasinha explains: "If you replace prisons with a psych institution that you can't get out of—okay, yeah, you're less likely to get shot in the psych ward. But if you're locked up for your whole life and you can't, you know, express your gender, refuse treatment, say 'I don't want that med,' or speak back against forced restraints or forced treatment—these are two different forms of carceral treatment."

Often when our movements try to be more inclusive of disabled people, we end up being condescending and patronizing instead.

"One of the many insidious ways ableism shows up is this idea that disabled people are not agents," Piepzna-Samarasinha says. "We are people who are pitiful, who need to be helped. . . . 'Oh, I'm smart. And I'm able-bodied. So that means I can do more, and better! I should do that for you!'"

Piepzna-Samarasinha also sees that when able-bodied people enter disabled spaces, condescension often comes with them in ways that can make disabled organizing more difficult. "I've seen able-bodied people and neurotypical people come into disabled spaces and be like, 'Oh, everything's so slow, everything's inefficient. I'll help you speed up with this!'" But Piepzna-Samarasinha points out that the slowness of disabled activism is one of its biggest strengths. That slowness comes from care, from knowing that vital people and perspectives are lost when everything is rushed, and that our movements can't afford to treat their members as expendable. "It actually lends a depth and breadth and a strength to the organizing that is not there when everyone's being left behind."

It's important that we recognize and address ableism in our movements and communities, while also recognizing ableism as an integral part of white supremacist, capitalist patriarchy. It's also important to recognize that the ableism in our movements and communities was often forced upon us. This is my way of saying: white readers are not let off the hook here. It's incumbent upon you to address how you may be bringing ableism into BIPOC spaces and how white supremacy itself contributes to ableist practices dressed up as "respectability," while also giving our communities space to address our own healing without interference.

## VILISSA THOMPSON

Vilissa Thompson introduces herself first as a proud Southerner from South Carolina. That geography is important to her, as a Black disabled woman, because growing up disabled and Black in the South underscored the racial lens with which she does her work as a social worker, speaker, writer, and DEI professional.

None of the work that Thompson does today was anywhere on her radar when she was in grad school. In her social work program, she wanted to become a therapist. But that all changed when she found out about macro social work.

Macro social work looks beyond an individual and the challenges they seem to present, and instead looks to society at large and moves toward creating change in environments that can then better help people who are at risk. Macro social work's focus on community organizing, community building, and policy activism really appealed to Thompson.

She got more traditional social work experience interning with organizations focusing on people living with HIV/AIDS and renal kidney disease. In that, she was able to see the individual cost of systemic failures macro social work hopes to address. "I saw in those experiences what happens to individuals who are very marginalized through their disabilities or chronic illnesses. The level of care that they receive or not, and how it impacts their lives."

Thompson was also able to see the impact that lack of care and resources had on those who were tasked with their support, like nurses, social workers, caseworkers, and family members. "What does it mean for them to not just engage with clients but to also deal with the systemic things?"

This understanding of the micro-social impacts of ableist systems combined with a macro-social understanding of how those systems work helped Thompson find focus for her work. "It's really nice to have that micro understanding of what's happening 'on the ground' with individuals," Thompson reflects. "How do the systems in place impact that, and what is your reaction to those systems?"

After she graduated, Thompson tried her hand at some more traditional social work jobs, but they weren't really a good fit for how she wanted to practice. In addition, many roles were not inclusive or accommodating of her disability and her needs as a wheelchair user. So she decided to create her own space.

In 2013, Thompson launched Ramp Your Voice!, which highlights voices of disabled people of color as well as offers consulting and speaking services for people and organizations looking to better serve the needs of disabled people—especially the needs of disabled Black girls and women. "My real focus in my activism work is centering Black disabled women, since we are grossly ignored in both the disabled community and the Black community—and in feminist spaces as well," she explains.

Thompson doesn't just talk with people in areas related to social work; she also spends a lot of time in Black liberation and anti-racist spaces. In all of them she is often trying to get people to understand the importance of including disability issues and disabled people— especially Black disabled people—in any and all movement work.

It's also important to understand, Thompson stresses, that Black disabled people have always been integral to the fight for liberation, even if their contributions or their disability are erased from the broader narrative.

Not only have Black disabled people long been instrumental to our resistance movements; they are also often those most at risk from the systemic oppression we are fighting against. Disabled and Deaf people make up over half the people killed by police in the US.

When you add the fact that Black and Native people are four times more likely to be killed by police than white people are, you can easily see how very vulnerable Black and Native disabled people are to police violence.

And it's not just police brutality. Disabled people of color are especially vulnerable in just about any system. "This system is disabling towards us," she says. "So I think it's very unfortunate that many people who do that type of work, that focus on the criminal system, as well as those who care about these issues in general, fail to make the disability connection."

Disability is a large part of communities of color, and issues of ableism regularly exacerbate issues of systemic racism, and vice versa. Because we are often excluded from or even abused by many traditional disability spaces and conversations, we have created our own disability language and often more subtle recognition of disability in our community. The truth is, disability is so common and in many ways normalized in our communities as we deal with the multigenerational impacts of systemic harm that we don't see it clearly. And it can be harder for us to recognize the systemic oppression that specifically affects disabled people in our communities, and therefore push for political and systemic change that truly will serve everyone.

This is where Thompson works—in bringing what we know deep down to light, and getting us to start saying it with our chest.

"Once you see that lens," she says, "it's hard to unsee it. It's hard to unknow it. And I think that is everybody's responsibility to Black liberation work, Black progressive work, to really look for that lens."

When we fail to look at social issues through this intersectional lens, it can be disastrous. Thompson sees this all of the time in the social work field. "A perfect example of this is social workers in a medical setting, like hospitals, who are utilized as agents of harm—as I like to call it—when it comes to disabled people who are parents. Instead of taking the proper assessment . . . to see what kind of support a disabled parent might need, based on their disability and the support that they might have, they are written off as incompetent. Simply because they're disabled. And then that involves CPS getting involved and taking away children. Harming families and creating trauma."

It's not just social workers. Thompson continues: "It's the doctors and nurses, too, who have a responsibility when they are dealing with disabled people who are parents or deciding to become parents. Just how that ableism that exists in that setting creates trauma. I really think about how we do not do enough to hold members of the profession accountable to the ways in which we look at marginalized communities, and how we write them off so quickly based on our own perspectives. That does not align with the code of ethics that we're supposed to uphold no matter what setting we're in."

While a lot of the blame for the lack of knowledge about issues of race and disability can fall on the shoulders of our white supremacist, ableist education systems, the ultimate responsibility for bridging those educational gaps lies with individual practitioners. This is something Thompson takes seriously. "It's our responsibility to get updated," she insists. "So that we do not unknowingly create harm."

Until social workers and those in social services fields can address the ways they have contributed to harm and educate themselves in order to do better, there will always be a divide between social workers and the communities they aim to serve. And that divide will continue to leave disabled people of color underserved.

"A lot of people in this space do not like social workers. And I completely understand that," Thompson says. Many people in marginalized communities have been harmed their whole lives by social workers and the systems social work is often a part of. But Thompson observes that many social workers don't understand this history and the mistrust this harm has reasonably led to; they therefore don't understand how it affects how well they're able to work in these communities. This puts marginalized communities at even greater risk for further harm.

Part of how Thompson has tried to tackle this issue in her field is by helping social workers become more aware of their gaps in knowledge. Early on, she began presenting at social work conferences. She remembers that they were surprised and intrigued by her frank and honest discussions: "They had no one who was actually disabled talk about it in this way. They had social workers—non-disabled and white—talking about disability from a very medicalized standpoint, but not really bringing the social aspect into it."

Social work is an overwhelmingly white field in the US—largely due to its roots as an avenue of philanthropy for middle- and upper-class white women. It's important for social workers to be aware of this often-problematic history and how the field can still encourage paternalistic behavior. "Particularly if they are white and not in tune with racial things and other marginalized identities," Thompson stresses. "A lot of people have the Good Samaritan savior complex. These communities don't need you to save them. They can save themselves if they [have] the resources and support."

## What Is Disability in Communities of Color?

I didn't identify publicly as disabled before I began writing this book. I'd long been open about my ADHD and anxiety disorder and my battles with chronic illness. And yet when I'd been asked to speak on issues of disability from a personal perspective, I often felt uncomfortable.

When I spoke with Britney R. Wilson, a civil rights attorney and associate professor of law at New York Law School and a disabled Black woman, she talked about how hard it is to make legal progress in fighting ableism when so many people in our communities who are disabled don't identify as such. "People right in front of you will be part of those communities. Will be disabled. You might not know it. It's not obvious. I think we have gotten more comfortable in recent years with certain aspects of disability that we still don't really label as disabled. Like, we're having all these conversations around self-care and anxiety and mental health. Those conversations are around disability. I'm happy those conversations are happening. But I don't think it gets translated to a broader understanding and acceptance of disability. I still don't think those people are really labeling necessarily what they're going through as disability. I still think there's a stigma attached to that."

Ouch. Call me out already.

But while I think part of my own personal reluctance to identify as disabled might indeed lie in stigma, I think it also has a lot to do with (a) the fact that I didn't know for a long time that conditions like ADHD, anxiety disorder, and chronic illness "counted" as disabilities at all, because often non-disabled people will write off a lot of these types of disability as personal failure or weakness and not an actual condition; and (b) once I became aware, I was worried that, as someone who tries to be aware of my privilege and the space I take up, talking about my less visible and less discriminated against disabilities in a disability justice context might take space away from people whose disabilities put them much more in the crosshairs of systemic ableism.

When I share my personal experience of this with Wilson, her response catches me off guard.

"To a certain extent, I'm like, 'Okay, I respect that.' But... that's so interesting to me for you to say that, as a Black woman. Because we know that there are segments of the community that do not worry about taking up space at all."

I have to laugh at the truth of her statement. As a Black woman, I know what it feels like when people sit stubbornly in their privilege and insist on centering themselves at the expense of others. And I don't want to do that, even though I know that despite my best efforts I still sometimes do. Privilege can work like that. But other times—and perhaps in this instance—because I know so deeply what it feels like and the harm it can cause, I may overcorrect to a point that does a different kind of harm.

I can't deny Wilson's point, even if it's causing me to have a lot of self-reevaluation. The truth is that when people who are disabled and don't identify as such are able to gain rights and accommodations that they need, the rest of the disabled community can be cut off from those gains because they aren't recognized as a part of broader disability issues.

Wilson next surprises me by bringing up my own words to make her point further: "I think about something else I think I heard you say in an interview once. You said... privilege is relative. And it's the same thing with disability, right? There's a spectrum of disability. I think one thing we try *not* to do in the community—most of us, anyway—is police who gets to say that they're part of the community. Especially because we want people to understand ableism."

But it's not just neurodiverse people in our community who often don't identify as disabled, and it's not just because of internalized stigma or a question of privilege: it's also about safety.

"There's a reason why we navigate the world in the ways that we do," Talila Lewis explains. "There's a reason why our parents don't want us identified as disabled. There's a reason why our parents encourage us to mask for various things. There's a reason why they try to intervene in advance of society finding out about what could be termed a disability. There's a reason to reject those things. And the sooner we all come to grips with that and have those conversations, the better off we will be as a collective."

Leah Lakshmi Piepzna-Samarasinha has experienced this in their own life, encouraged to mask their disabilities as a child by their parents, and then as an adult by their own community. They remember being advised by other disabled people—especially before the Affordable Care Act made it harder to deny coverage to disabled people—to avoid official diagnoses for their disability in order to be able to continue to have access to medical care. They have seen, in their disability justice work, that many disabled people in BIPOC communities avoid any disability diagnoses for similar reasons of accessibility and affordability of care.

"Mia Mingus has that quote from years ago now," Piepzna-Samarasinha says, "where she's like, 'Over and over I meet disabled women of color who do not identify as disabled, even though they have the lived reality of being disabled.' It can be really dangerous to identify as something when your life depends on you denying it. When your survival depends on your denying it. So then, in terms of organizing, number one, you're gonna be working with a lot of people who are like, 'Don't call me that. I have a condition. I don't wanna talk about that.'"

While all disabled people are harmed by ableism to various degrees, there's a specific vulnerability for BIPOC who are disabled that often differs from what white disabled people experience and that often requires more caution when identifying as disabled. This can cause conflict in disability justice spaces that don't respect these nuances.

"White disabled people are screaming, 'Say the word "disability"!'" Talila Lewis explains, "and I'm like, 'Nah, you don't decontextualize our lived experiences, our histories, the things that y'all have done'–that is including white disabled people–to make it such that it is not safe in many cases, in many instances, in many settings, for Black people, Indigenous folks, and Black Indigenous folks to be like, 'Yo, I'm disabled, too.' Even me. I'm disabled, and you're not gonna find me admitting that in every single space. We gotta be safe about who we're sharing what with, when we share it, and how we go about it."

But even if in our communities we may be reluctant to use the word "disabled" to identify ourselves, it doesn't mean that our community has less disability or that we're unfamiliar with it.

Systemic racism is disabling. It causes poverty, stress, trauma, medical abuse and neglect, violence, illness, and so much more that disables people every day. Systemic racism complicates and deepens the effects of disability on the body and mind as well. Even if we don't *say* disability, we *know* disability.

"We actually talk about disability all the time as Black people," Lewis says. "But we'll say things like, 'I'm feelin' off,' 'I can't come today–you know I had a flare-up,' 'You know it rained today.' We have ways to talk about disability. . . . Disability is so normalized for us. We often don't have to name it."

Lewis points out that when looking at disability and disabling events in communities of color–especially Black and Indigenous communities–society will often try to place the blame on our communities or act as if these issues are purely rooted in our bodies and communities, instead of looking at the contributions of external harm: "They'll be like, 'Oh, biological factors. All these Black people in this community have hypertension.' No shit, Sherlock! The next generation, we're still anxious about the exact same things [as the previous generation], sometimes worse. Yeah, we've got the same disabilities. But this shit isn't biological. This shit is ecological."

## BRITNEY R. WILSON

While many people find themselves surprised to be in movement work, it was the opposite for Britney R. Wilson. She went to law school to become a civil rights attorney, expecting her job to include disability justice work. "I sort of just assumed that civil rights and social justice work would necessarily include disability," Wilson remembers, "and I was surprised to find out that it didn't."

In her early post-graduation work with organizations like the ACLU and the Center for Constitutional Rights, she explains, "I was always the person saying, 'And people with disabilities . . .' 'And people with disabilities.'"

If Wilson had been expecting to find a better home in disability rights law, she was disappointed there as well. Whenever she was in disability rights spaces, the work they were doing didn't relate to the lived experiences of disabled Black people. This wasn't just about who they were representing; it was also about their lack of understanding of how race influences disability rights issues.

This was the work—work at the intersection of race and disability—that Wilson had felt called to law to do, and she was having trouble finding spaces open to that work.

As a Black disabled woman growing up with cerebral palsy, Wilson spent a lot of time and effort in her youth learning to advocate for herself and watching others try to advocate for her. She wanted better for other disabled Black people and disabled people of color.

"Law wasn't a career choice for me," she says. "It was something that I felt like I had to do."

So here she was, after years of hard work to get her law degree, unable to find a space for the practice that she knew from personal experience was so needed. "I felt like there really was no country for me in these social justice spaces, and that is part of what motivated me to move into academia."

If spaces didn't exist for Wilson to practice the type of civil rights law she felt was needed, she would create that space—for herself and for others. She decided to set up a legal clinic that recognized the importance of disability justice in all civil rights cases.

"I saw clinics as, one, a space where I would have a little bit more autonomy to create the sort of work that I wanted to do. And also, it occurred to me that maybe one of the reasons that the profession was as siloed as it is, is because people aren't really taught about disability in law school, when they should be. I know I wasn't."

In fact, Wilson wasn't able to take a single disability law class in her law school days, because one wasn't offered.

Wilson has worked on cases covering a broad range of civil rights topics over the years. She's worked on discriminatory policing cases in Missouri and New York—including *Floyd, et al. v. City of New York, et al.*, aka the "stop and frisk" case. She's worked on cases dealing with immigration detention practices, the school-to-prison pipeline, and more. And she understands from this work and from personal experience that these are all disability issues.

"We talk all the time about intersectionality—and as Audre Lorde said: 'We do not lead single-issue lives.' . . . I think that is the basic summation of it all," she explains. "The issues that you think about being in one category affect people across the spectrum that have different identities. Even if we're talking about immigration, that's not just a racial justice thing. That's a disability justice thing as well. It doesn't matter what the issue is. Different groups are gonna be impacted by it in different ways."

It's this structural oppression that Wilson is concerned with in her work, and that she wants people to focus on as well, especially when it comes to disability, which many non-disabled people neglect to put a structural analysis to.

Wilson believes that many conversations around disability are still focused on representation and inclusion in various spaces. And while she stresses that representation and inclusion are important, they are just the very beginning of disability justice work, and are not enough to create change that disabled people can actually feel in their day-to-day lives. "It doesn't change any structures," she says. "What I think people need to understand is the structure of ableism, because I think that ableism actually includes structural racism."

Like many of the other disability activists I've spoken with, Wilson refers to Talila Lewis's work in describing how she sees the relationship between racism and ableism.

"The definition of ableism that I teach to my students," Wilson says, "is basically a ranking of bodies and minds according to societal definitions and constructions of what is normal, what is intelligent, what is productive, what is beautiful. And that, to me, by definition includes racism, because, you know, race is but one construct or one way in which to rank people's bodies and minds. And so, if we were thinking about these issues along structural lines, we would have to include disability, because ableism is part of those structures."

While she and other disabled activists and advocates of color can clearly see the unbreakable links between racism and ableism, many people—and many of the systems that control so much of our lives—insist on always seeing them as separate issues. This makes it very hard for Wilson to push forward legal cases dealing with both race and disability.

She tells me that she feels like her legal work on race and disability discrimination hasn't been as effective as she had originally hoped it would be. A lot of this difficulty, she explains, stems from the way our legal system has been set up: "Many people don't know how hard it is to actually bring race discrimination claims. It's very difficult. And then when you try to bring that in the context of disability, it's even more difficult. The legal system isn't really set up ideally to bring intersectional claims."

Wilson's explanation, while new to me, makes perfect sense. Our legal system likes things to cleanly fit into one bucket or another. Trying to argue that a precedent dealing with discrimination actually fits into two buckets or even three seems almost impossible.

Further, it's hard to push forward on cases involving both race and disability because legal cases often require a certain level of privilege and access. Disabled people are less likely than non-disabled people to have privilege and access, and people of color are less likely than white people to have privilege and access. It stands to reason, then, that disabled people of color are much less likely to have the privilege and access necessary to launch successful legal suits.

"Being part of a lawsuit is work," Wilson elaborates. "It takes time. It takes resources. And so, oftentimes you see certain people being represented over and over again in certain ways in these fights."

She hopes her law clinic can help to change that, by supporting a new generation of lawyers who can understand the importance of an intersectional approach to civil rights law. "[So] the next lawyer doesn't have to keep saying: 'And people with disabilities . . .' 'And people with disabilities . . .' They can be the ones who say: 'What about how this impacts this population?' Or: 'Are we thinking about it from this angle?'"

Wilson also hopes the lawyers who come through her clinic will start to listen more to the communities they work with. She has confidence in her students, that they will be able to represent much-needed change in the legal field.

Wilson aims to challenge the idea often taught in law school that the relationship between lawyers and clients is a hierarchy of knowledge, with lawyers having all of the answers that they are able to bestow upon and use on behalf of the less knowledgeable communities they work with. "We always talk about being 'a voice for the voiceless.' People have voices. They have different abilities to actually amplify and use those voices because of the structures of our society. I think hopefully what my students have learned from working in community and with community is: don't underestimate people, including people with disabilities."

Even though Wilson is herself disabled, she tries to practice what she preaches in her legal work. "That's something I've been intentional about in some of the public health work that I'm doing. The disabled community were the ones that started organizing around it, and I just came in and said, 'Hey, how can I help? You need somebody to write a letter? You need somebody to do X, Y, or Z?' Let's collectively strategize about how we want to approach these problems.... It's not just like: 'I'm helping the disabled community. Let me feel good about myself. Yay!'"

Wilson tries to offer what communities need: access and resources that have been denied to them due to systemic oppression. Help that they have actually asked for.

"This is a community that's already empowered," she explains. "We're just here to use a particular skill set that we're cultivating to amplify them, or to give them whatever it is they might need."

## BE A REVOLUTION

There is a uniqueness to disability in comparison to other identity groups in that we are more likely to move across spectrums of disability in our lifetimes. We don't usually move out of our racial group (and no, passing doesn't count, because that's a completely different phenomenon steeped in pain and trauma). We don't usually move far in class—even generation after generation it is unlikely. But people can and do move in and out of disability and from mild disability to more severe. And yet many non-disabled people act like it can never be them, as if "disabled" is this separate group outside of them, their communities, and their lives.

Chances are, disability touches all of us, whether we're disabled or not. And there's a good chance that if we're not disabled now, we'll become so as we age. While that's a reality we should understand—especially when it comes to looking at the scale of issues affecting disabled people and what it will mean for our communities in the coming years—Britney R. Wilson stresses that it shouldn't matter whether or not you one day find yourself disabled or caring for a disabled loved one.

"There's a quote—not my quote, somebody's quote: 'Disability is the only minority group that most people will join at some point in their lives.' Something like that," Wilson says. "I used to like that quote. I don't like it so much anymore, because that sort of says, 'I can only care about this if I think it's going to impact me.' And maybe it won't. Maybe you'll be the person who lives to eighty and you're gonna be in perfect health generally. Okay, great. Wonderful. I still want you to understand this issue."

➤ **Join and support online disability justice groups.** A huge part of understanding disability and disability justice in our anti-racist movements starts with understanding ourselves. While the instinct may be to just "get out there" and do the work, a lot of "the work," Sami Schalk advises, will be internal initially: "The first part, I think, of becoming a disabled person who wants to do political work is to start to address your own internalized ableism. Because you don't even know how much you have."

Even if you're not disabled, or don't identify as disabled, it's important to do this work, because when we don't investigate our ableism and aren't open to learning about our ableism, it will not only make it impossible to do effective anti-racist work but it will also lead us to cause harm to disabled people in BIPOC communities.

For many disabled BIPOC who want to get started in this work, almost everyone I talked to recommended the internet as a great place to start. While access to the internet is a barrier to some, it's a great tool for those who may not be able to come together easily in person. It's also a great way to fight isolation and connect with other disabled BIPOC outside of your local area—especially if you live in an area with few BIPOC.

Vilissa Thompson remembers when it was harder to find connection and community as a disabled person of color and has appreciation for her experiences in groups like the Harriet Tubman Collective: "I'm very lucky to have found community at this age, in my thirties. But I wish that [I'd] had something like that in my twenties, particularly in college. I know that when I was in college I saw other disabled folks, but not many of them were Black. I feel like these type of spaces allow that connection to be full and not feel so fragmented."

➤ **Join groups that match your interests, that have a disability justice focus.** After years of being left behind by so many anti-racist movements and activist groups, Leah Lakshmi Piepzna-Samarasinha was relieved and surprised to find inclusion and care in groups like Sins Invalid and the Allied Media Conference (AMC). "I just remember being with the whole crew of us at AMC, and we were just this wild pack of slowness; we just filled the entire street. Everyone either had to walk as slowly as us or they had to, you know, walk behind us. And I was just like, *Wow. I'm not being abandoned*." They remember, "I was like, *I can be my whole self. . . . I'm not letting the movement down by being disabled*."

➤ **Add disability justice to the work you're already doing.** Another way to get started is to integrate anti-ableism into your existing anti-racist work or the anti-racist work you want to do. This work is important and benefits all BIPOC, disabled or not.

For movement work that is already in progress but hasn't had enough disability focus, that's something you can bring to it. Sami Schalk advises that any activist work can be made better with the addition of disability justice: "If you are interested in tenants' rights, if you're interested in unionizing—all of that should be included in disability justice. Say 'One thing I want to do is bring more disability justice into this particular space.'"

Piepzna-Samarasinha shares a powerful moment of inclusion and solidarity with me, when their friend disability justice leader Stacey Park Milbern sent them video of a march against Trump's efforts to end DACA and the DREAM Act: "It's these, like, fourteen-year-old undocumented youth, these Dreamers leading the march. And they were like, 'Okay, the ASL is right here. We have one hundred chairs for people to sit at the front—for elders, for people with chronic pain, anyone with kids to stay there. We have this huge space for people in wheelchairs. We have sage because we really want to use medicine, but we know some people have asthma, so we're not gonna light it. Guys, if the revolution is not accessible, it's not the revolution!' And they were fourteen years old. Stacey was like, 'We won! We kind of—we didn't win yet, but we kind of won. These kids get it!'"

➤ **Take accessibility seriously.** Access is crucial to the success of our movements, and working with disabled people in BIPOC communities to create as much access as possible will allow them to actively participate in movement work and provide vital viewpoints. ASL, captions, wheelchair access, comfortable seating, food, water, and more can make a huge difference. And where you can't be fully accessible, communicate that so disabled people can decide if and how they want to participate.

➤ **Be honest about what accessibility you can and cannot provide.** "I hands down state that total accessibility is impossible, or there's no such thing," says Alice Wong. "But I think that it's the most important thing to be up-front about. Many people's access needs are in conflict with others. So if you're organizing something, or just writing or creating or producing something, there are limits.

There are constraints. I think that's the thing that's the most important to me, is to be as transparent as possible."

❧ **Be open to feedback.** Wong stresses that it's also important to be open to hearing how your work can be more accessible, and correcting where you've caused harm: "To think about accessibility, to think about storytelling, to think about all the things that I try to do, I just try to keep it real. I just like to say, 'This is what I can produce. This is what I've designed.' I welcome critique. I welcome feedback. Of course I expect that. And if anything I've done harmed people, I want to be accountable and just do what I can to repair the harm."

❧ **Plan ahead.** It's beneficial to start thinking about accessibility as early as possible in any movement work or projects. That's Wong's approach: "Build in access from the onset. Before I start something, I try to think about all the different things, but also what is possible."

❧ **Don't be afraid to start small.** These additions may seem small, but small is often where people should start. Dr. Sami Schalk says, "People want to start off so big sometimes, and it's beautiful. And then you burn out so fast and get overwhelmed."

Alice Wong offers similar advice: "So much of the work that happens on the ground is really small things. Sometimes it's just small, intermittent things. It doesn't have to be a website. It doesn't have to be fully formed. Some things have a particular life span. And that's okay, too."

Becoming aware of disability justice practices and staying updated with how racial justice issues are affecting disabled people in communities of color, as well as being vigilant in trying to stay aware of our own ableism, will continue to offer up opportunities to be a part of real, revolutionary change.

❧ **Support on-the-ground disabled BIPOC-led disability justice work.** Because so much of the work of disability justice in BIPOC communities is being done on smaller, more local levels, it's really important to look smaller and more local if you want to financially support this work.

White-led or white-centered disability justice groups often get the lion's share of the limited funding that goes to disability groups. It's important to be aware of where your money is going, and where it isn't.

"There's nothing wrong with donating," says Vilissa Thompson, "but be very mindful of where you donate, where you support. How involved in the communities are they? Are they only utilizing Black and brown faces just to market their donation efforts? Or to look like they are very intentionally inclusive and intersectional when they're not? I think people need to ask more questions and pay better attention."

Even disability organizations and programs that try to provide for and work with disabled people of color often fall far short.

"People don't understand the ineffectiveness of these programs," Thompson says. "I understand intimately the gaps in society, and dealing with what we have, as an educated disabled person. There are a lot of things that our systems are not keeping up with. Inflation—they're not keeping up with the cost of living. And they're not keeping up with the transition of disability and power and access that disabled people are now able to do."

Thompson points out that these organizations are also often disconnected from the more complicated needs of disabled people of color and fail to look at those through an intersectional lens: "Sometimes somebody's disability might not be the biggest obstacle that they endure socially. It may be their race. It may be their gender identity or their sexual identity."

Because so little funding actually makes its way to disability justice activists of color, many of our most dedicated movement workers struggle to pay for their basic needs. It's not at all unusual to see disabled activists crowdfunding or taking on unhealthy levels of additional work to pay rent or cover their own medical expenses, while also working hard to raise funds to help others in their community.

➤ **Support mutual aid efforts by disabled BIPOC.** Mutual aid is the imperfect bridge attempting to span massive resource gaps that are leaving many disabled people of color struggling to survive. People come together to pay rent, to pick up groceries, to hand down medical equipment, to find more affordable medications.

And even though mutual aid is literally saving lives in disabled communities of color, it also takes a huge toll, especially when so few people outside of the community help support those mutual aid efforts.

Talila Lewis points out that disabled BIPOC already give a disproportionate amount of their money to other community members in crisis in order to make up for the lack of resources and systemic support in the community. "A lot of folks in our families, communities, are not doing well. . . . We pass around the same thousand dollars that we have. You know what I mean? A lot of us don't have a lot, but we're gonna give it out."

"One thing that really kind of breaks my heart, you know, when it comes to mutual aid," Vilissa Thompson says, "is that people get one need satisfied, but then something else—you know—the bottom falls out in another way. So they're having to ask again. And just seeing people be so embarrassed to ask for help. I think that's the really hurtful thing. Like, 'Here I am kind of leaning on the shield, leaning on the community again.' And that's not what people want to do. It's what people are forced to do.

"That does a lot mentally, psychologically. Having to constantly worry how I'm gonna pay for medicine, how I'm gonna pay for my bills, how I'm gonna pay for this, or how I'm gonna pay for that. And that exacerbates some of their health needs, being disabled. I know people complain about mutual aid in general, but they don't understand the psychological and health risks of having to constantly be in need in this way, and having to lean on community that is already short on resources."

It's so important to get funds as closely as possible to the people on the ground doing the work. This means supporting smaller,

BIPOC-led and -focused disability justice groups, and supporting individual mutual aid efforts. It also means challenging the nonprofit–industrial complex to share resources with smaller groups and organizations, and to center disabled BIPOC more in their work and in their leadership.

Disabled people of color have been leaders in anti-racist work for many generations. And the work of disability justice has in it the seeds for all of our liberation in a way no other movement I can think of does. When we boil down issues of bodily autonomy, equitable distribution of resources, freedom from exploitation and violence, the right to safety and care—all of these issues are more clearly articulated and addressed in disabled BIPOC movements than just about anywhere else.

"Imagine a world where all kinds of people can just be their full selves without having to scrape by," says Alice Wong. "Without having to prove their worthiness. Without having to produce. Where they just have inherent value. And that they're cared for, and that they care for others. I mean, that's what I think liberation is. That's what freedom is."

## RACE, LABOR, AND BUSINESS

WHEN WE LOOK BACK on the early years of the COVID-19 pandemic, there will be a lot of stories that likely define the time: the battle over vaccines, the uprising for Black lives, the increase in anti-Asian hate crimes, the storming of the Capitol by Trump-loving white supremacists. And while it hasn't been dominating as many headlines as the rest, I do believe these years will also mark an important turning point in the US labor movement. Labor union participation has been on a decline across the country for decades, successfully weakened by anti-union politicians, with unions increasingly seen as ineffective and disconnected from the average worker. Many younger workers most in need of union protection no longer had confidence that a union could help improve their treatment in their workplaces.

All of that began to change in 2020, as the pandemic brought long-standing issues with worker treatment, benefits, and safety to a head. Workers in warehouses, having been exploited for years with long hours and abusive treatment, were now also being put at increased risk for contracting a potentially deadly virus. Service workers who were often mistreated by both their employers and customers found themselves without any sick pay as they contracted COVID from their peers or the public they still had to interact with every day, while their bosses were able to work from the safety of their own homes. Some of our most underappreciated, underpaid, and vulnerable workers were suddenly deemed "essential" and yet never paid as such. As the death tolls from COVID-19 rose, employers were still hiding employee infection numbers from staff, still reluctant to pay for personal protection equipment, and still reluctant to compensate employees who became sick on the job.

The racial aspects of these labor concerns grew increasingly clear as it became evident that workers of color were overrepresented in these vulnerable and exploitative workplaces. That—coupled with the fact that Black and Hispanic people who contracted COVID were more likely to die of it than white people—spelled disaster for many in our communities.

It's in this context that laborers started organizing. Workers of all ages, workers of color, immigrant workers—they came together to demand better treatment, and in many places those demands turned into calls for a union. Suddenly, places where it had seemed almost impossible for unions to ever get a foothold were facing some of their biggest ever labor organizing threats. Starbucks stores started organizing. Amazon warehouses as well. It wasn't just large companies. Small businesses that thought they would never have to negotiate with collectivized workers were suddenly finding themselves unionized. And many of the faces leading these labor movements looked different than they often had in the past. Black and brown workers were frequently leading the charge. So were women. So were disabled workers. Young workers as well. The demands being made reflected their health and safety needs in the current pandemic but also a newer, more intersectional idea of worker well-being. At a time when millions of people around the world were rising up for Black lives, workers were demanding racial justice as well as economic justice. Workers have come together to change modern businesses that thought their days of having to deal with the demands of their employees were over.

As I write this, we are at an exciting and crucial time for labor organizing. We have an opportunity to revive our labor movements in the image of workers today, but only if we're willing to embrace what workers of all races and ethnicities need now, and face the ways in which labor movements have fallen short of meeting those needs in the past.

## CHRIS SMALLS

As a talented young Black man growing up in Hackensack, New Jersey, Chris Smalls was heavily involved in both sports and music. He played basketball, was on the football team, and ran track. In high school he started performing as a rapper as well. Smalls was raised by a single mother—his father was incarcerated during his childhood—and he learned the value of hard work from watching her raise her two kids on her own.

It was his first job that ended his sports career dreams. He was working at a Target in high school and was struck by a hit-and-run driver in the parking lot. The accident left him with torn ligaments that permanently affected his athletic performance.

Smalls tried college, but after a few semesters, he knew it wasn't for him. So he enrolled in the Institute of Audio Research to focus on his other great love: music.

After some time at the institute, Smalls decided to become a full-time independent artist. He was recording and engineering songs, putting together shows, and performing regularly in New Jersey and New York. "I did bring Meek Mill to New Jersey, but I didn't go on tour with him like they say on my Wikipedia." He laughs.

Smalls loved the hustle and bustle of being an independent artist. He didn't know at the time how widely applicable the skills he was building would be.

"When you're an artist, you're an organizer," he explains when I ask him about his organizing roots. "You gotta organize your own shows. You gotta get people to come out. And at that time, we didn't have the tools that we have now, as far as social media. So it was really word of mouth, face-to-face conversations. I used to do a lot of flyering, going to college campuses. Anywhere I could to really get people to come out. . . . I had to organize every show I did to make ends meet. That was my money, as an independent artist. So I knew how to be a people's person."

Listening to Smalls talk about hip-hop and organizing reminds me of my own partner, Gabriel, who has been both an activist and a hip-hop artist for over twenty years. I've long heard stories from his youth of wheatpasting walls and street poles to get fliers up for shows, or stopping people on the street to try to sell them a CD. It doesn't surprise me that he can now talk to almost anybody about a social issue he's passionate about. After spending your late teens asking strangers if they want to hear a rap you made, and then maybe if they like it would they want to buy this CD for ten dollars, it's not that hard to ask people to show up at a protest.

Smalls got married at twenty-two, and he and his partner welcomed twins later that year. Now a young father of a baby boy and girl, Smalls found that the late nights at clubs and days on the road were no longer possible. So he set his music career aside to get back into hourly work.

He quickly found himself in exploitative work conditions in the temp positions he found through companies like Labor Ready. "They will put people in the worst jobs for minimum wage," he remembers. "We'd get paid by the day, so we'd get, like, thirty, forty dollars a day, for ten hours of labor."

After years of this, Smalls's mom let him know that Amazon was opening their first building in New Jersey. Tired of the poor treatment he was receiving at his current employer, Smalls applied at Amazon. He was so desperate to get out that he even took a pay cut, going from $13.50 to $12.75 an hour.

In 2015, he began work at Amazon in the warehouse at entry level. Having worked a much more labor-intensive job at his previous employers, Smalls worked hard and fast at Amazon, more than doubling the "pick" requirements per day. As his productivity stayed high, he was quickly promoted to supervisor.

After two years in New Jersey, he transferred to another new Amazon building, in Connecticut, and helped open that building. After two years in their role, supervisors are eligible to apply for a manager position.

"I thought I had the best opportunity to come," Smalls remembers. "[I was] one of the best employees, definitely had one of the best teams as a supervisor, number one team in the building all the time. I trained so many hundreds, if not thousands, of new workers and hundreds of their management. And I had already opened up not one but two buildings. So I thought I had a great chance to be promoted."

Smalls put his name in for manager when there was an opening. He had his first interview and that was it. He didn't make it past the first round. As he kept applying, and time and time again he was rejected, he started to pay attention to who *was* getting promoted. He tells me that it was mostly white or Asian employees who were receiving promotions, and very rarely Black or brown employees.

Smalls also noticed that in the rare times when Black and brown supervisors were promoted, they were almost always put on the night shift.

"You wouldn't even see them," he recalls.

If there's one thing about Smalls that Amazon was going to learn the hard way, it's that he doesn't give up easily.

He applied, and applied, and applied for promotion. He was putting in the hours, getting the results, going above and beyond, and again and again he was passed over. I can only imagine how hard it was to show up every day to work in a place so blatant in its disregard and disrespect.

"By the end of my career there," he says with a weary chuckle, "I applied over fifty times to become a manager. I was only interviewed twice in five years."

Smalls didn't take this sitting down. He kept applying for promotions, but he also started filing complaints about how he was being treated. It's easy to begin to feel singled out when you're passed over and over and over for promotion, but the target that was on Smalls's back would've been obvious to anyone as time passed.

In 2017, after he first started speaking out about being passed over for promotion, he was abruptly fired for "stealing company time."

How much time?

"Two minutes," Smalls says, laughing.

He had made an error on his time card and punched in a time that was two minutes off. Instead of asking Smalls about the error so he'd have a chance to explain and correct it, Amazon fired him.

Amazon is infamous for these abrupt firings—and knowing that at any minute you could be escorted out of the building for the smallest infraction adds to the stress and mental health issues that have been well documented in Amazon warehouses (Sainato 2020).

Smalls fought his firing, and this time he prevailed and was reinstated after about six weeks out of work. Once he was back at work, he knew he had to get out of that building. It was obvious that he wasn't going to have any chance of promotion there. So he applied at a new building that was opening up, in his hometown on Staten Island.

Being one of the most tenured employees in the building, Smalls had a friend in Human Resources. She showed him an email with the list of employees who would be moving to the new Staten Island building, and his name was on it. He felt relieved and waited to get his onboarding letter and start date.

As time passed and his onboarding letter never arrived, while many of his coworkers had gotten theirs, Smalls worried that something was up again. He started to ask questions. He wanted to know if he was going to the new building or if his transfer request had been denied.

After his inquiries failed to get any definitive response, Smalls emailed a manager at the new Staten Island building, someone Smalls himself had trained as a new hire. Still he received no response.

Finally, Smalls turned to the nuclear option. He filed an ethics report requesting an investigation into discrimination against him. Within a few days of filing the report, he suddenly had an offer letter to go to the new building.

He was given the worst shift at the building at reduced hours, but he didn't care. He needed to get out of the Connecticut warehouse.

Smalls's fresh start was short-lived. When he arrived, he found that his reputation had preceded him. Warnings that Smalls liked to "escalate things" (that's what his new manager was told by Human Resources) made it so that management was wary to work with him.

But Smalls worked as hard in Staten Island as he had in New Jersey and Connecticut, and won his skeptical manager over.

"He relied on me so much that he didn't even come to work." He laughs. "He would just be out for months, and I'd just be running the floors. Even with our team being the worst shift, I set the building record. You could put me anywhere—it doesn't matter. I know the job."

Eventually, Smalls was moved to the day shift and a team of new hires to supervise. It was against standard practice to not give a supervisor any veteran employees on his team, but Smalls didn't care. He started training up his team to once again be the best in the building.

The relationships he built on the team would become so strong that many members would later become his organizing teammates as well. "The people on my team I actually organize with [now]. Gerald Bryson was on my team. Derrick Palmer was on my team. Jason Anthony was on my team."

Even though Smalls continued to outperform his peers, he still was denied an interview for every application he put in to become manager. After Smalls escalated the issue once again, he was given an interview for a manager position. In the interview, they surprised him with a math test. He asked others who had applied if they were given a math test, and they were not. Even though Smalls passed the test, he wasn't given a second interview.

Smalls had finally had enough and was considering his next steps away from Amazon when the COVID-19 pandemic hit. As soon as he started seeing the working conditions that his team and other workers were being subjected to, he knew he had to do something. It wasn't just about him at this point.

"I couldn't allow what was going on to happen. People were coming in to work sick every day. I'm sending people home. Nobody's getting no real communication from upper management."

Employees were scared and confused. They were watching news stories in the break room about this deadly and highly contagious virus making its way around the country, and it didn't seem like the company they worked for was taking their safety seriously.

"We had no masks. No PPE. No cleaning supplies. No real guidance," Smalls recalls.

Smalls and one of his team members, Derrick Palmer, decided to break the silence that was endangering the lives of workers: "I started to tell the workers the truth. I sat in the cafeteria every day, me and Derrick Palmer, and we told the workers that this is going on. That there's people in there [testing] positive. 'And they told me as a supervisor not to tell y'all.'"

After talking with employees, Smalls would then go to the higher-ups in the building to share worker concerns. He did this every day for about a week when suddenly he was put in quarantine by upper management. He was the only employee quarantined.

"And I was like, *Okay. They're doing this to stop me from organizing the workers*," he recalls.

In response to Amazon's attempts to silence employee concerns,

Smalls and many of his coworkers staged a walkout. On March 30, 2020, employees on the job at the Staten Island warehouse walked out to protest the lack of safety protections provided by Amazon. Two hours into the walkout, Smalls was fired.

Having removed Smalls from the picture, Amazon went on the offense to try to minimize his influence on workers. Jeff Bezos held an employee meeting in which he insulted and belittled Smalls. A move that quickly backfired: "Calling me not smart, inarticulate, ironically making me the face of the whole unionizing efforts against Amazon."

Smalls kept the pressure on Bezos and Amazon. "We continued to protest at his mansions and penthouses for over a year. And then we saw the campaign in Alabama."

In late 2020, employees of the Bessemer, Alabama, Amazon warehouse started organizing to form a union. Amazon's profits soared during the first years of the pandemic, increasing by 84 percent in 2020. The Bessemer warehouse employees, 85 percent of whom were Black, saw very little of that windfall (Perry et al. 2021). The organizers, led by Jennifer Bates and Darryl Richardson, hoped to not only get better pay and better protections and benefits during the COVID-19 pandemic but also address long-standing health, safety, gender discrimination, and racial discrimination issues in the warehouse.

In April 2021, inspired by the Bessemer employees, Smalls and many of his former teammates, including Derrick Palmer, Gerald Bryson, and Jason Anthony, began their own unionizing efforts. Having been so severely let down by jobs and labor unions in the past, Smalls was determined to do things differently.

"I know that forming a union—the way we're forming it—by having Amazon workers in the driver's seat, is gonna be the best way [for employees] to protect themselves." Compared to, Smalls says, other union leaders who come in from outside and assume they know what's best for workers they barely know. "Other unions don't know Amazon as well as we do."

In order to build employee awareness and excitement for their unionizing efforts, Smalls turned to his old hip-hop skills. He was used to reaching out to people, to bringing people together, to getting people excited about something new.

"I'm talking to people every day. Several conversations," Smalls says. "Just . . . being for them as a presence on the ground. At the bus stop. Giving out food. Having barbecues. We had, like, twenty-something barbecues. We had concerts out there. We brought ice cream. It was the little things that mattered. . . . We cared, so we just showed the workers that. Over time, gradually, it grew. The culture that we created was a real thing throughout our campaign."

Many had written off this unionizing effort as nearly impossible, especially after the Bessemer unionizing attempt failed to garner enough votes from workers. But the connections Smalls and other labor organizers were building at the Staten Island warehouse proved genuine and effective, even in the face of reports of rampant interference and retaliation against unionizing efforts by Amazon. On April 1, 2022, workers at the Staten Island warehouse stunned the world by voting to join the Amazon Labor Union by a comfortable margin (Milkman 2022).

Suddenly, everybody concerned with labor politics knew who Chris Smalls was. His face was in magazines and newspapers. He was even invited to visit the White House. Smalls has faced some push-back from older union members who resent his newfound labor celebrity. Some feel that labor leaders shouldn't have celebrity status if they're going to be taken seriously. But he thinks it's actually his ability to relate to the public in a way some older organizers cannot that they resent.

"It's not about being a celebrity," Smalls says. "It's about the fact that I'm able to talk to them. . . . The unionizing percentages are less than 10 percent in the country. How we get that to the other side is by getting to different spaces." He lists various efforts he and his team are engaged in to build upon their momentum across the country. They're using the internet and social media in ways past union leaders have not. "This is a different way of organizing, and a new generation of it."

He's adamant that if labor wants to be relevant today and in the future, it has to make real, meaningful connections with workers—especially younger workers—where they are today, and they have to embrace and support younger union leaders instead of seeing them as a threat.

"A lot of leadership in these unions are outdated. Pass the torch. You gotta allow these younger adults to get up in there and make decisions for the rest of the people. What I've seen, and from my experience of meeting other union representatives, is that there's no real diversity when it comes down to it."

As an example, Smalls recalls a convention he went to recently. When Smalls arrived at the American Federation of Teachers (AFT) convention in Boston, he saw thousands of teachers of various ages, genders, races, and ethnicities. "But the ones at the top, the leadership, there was no real diversity. I saw maybe one Black person—a Black woman—that had this position. But the ratio was just, like, one out of . . . what? Twelve? And then as far as incorporating the younger generation—making it intergenerational—the age difference [between the teachers and union leadership] was huge. Huge. And I was just like, *Wow. How are we talking about shaping the future if y'all not including the people that's making the change right now?*"

Smalls wants more than just surface-level support for his and other younger labor leaders' efforts. He doesn't want to be trotted out for press and then sent away. He says that younger union leaders need older union leadership to support their ideas and stand in solidarity with their goals. When the union refuses to truly embrace the energy and ideas of younger leaders, it alienates younger workers.

So who do younger workers connect with? "Workers want to connect with somebody that they can relate to," Smalls says. "Especially someone from their communities. And for me, when I show up in different spaces as is, I want people to be like, 'He's different. I'm curious. What does he got to offer? Let me go talk to him.'"

A first, historic victory under their belt, the Amazon Labor Union organizers aren't through yet. They've been battling Amazon in court, and now they're ready to get back to the business of building and expanding their Amazon union efforts. Amazon employees are going to get organized all across the country, if Smalls has anything to do with it.

"We're going to be launching a [labor] campaign. We have a campaign in other buildings, so I'm supporting that as well. I have a lot of work ahead with all these [Amazon] buildings now going public. Milwaukee, Kentucky . . . Tennessee, I think, yesterday . . . In California I met some Amazon workers that are ready. So there's just gonna be a lot of buildings that you're gonna start to see organized under the ALU umbrella."

Chris Smalls is someone who, on paper, a lot of people would have written off. A young Black man from the world of hip-hop, with a high school diploma and only a semester or two of college. In person, people tried repeatedly to write Smalls off as well, but he wouldn't let them. The truth is, he shouldn't have had to work so damn hard. He shouldn't have had to work the worst shifts and get the best numbers over and over and over again only to be denied promotion over fifty times. He shouldn't have had to sit in the break room in defiance of his bosses to give important safety information to his team in the middle of a pandemic, and he shouldn't have had to stage walkouts and protests after being fired for doing so. But the incredibly valuable talents that Smalls has and the experience that he has gathered, all of these tools that were dismissed and derided by capitalist white supremacy, are why he was able to take on such a powerful behemoth as Amazon, and it's why he's winning and just may keep on winning.

## Why Labor Matters

It all began with labor. The need to work this large piece of stolen land, the need to expand across a continent, the need to maintain social and political control, the need to preserve as much profit as possible from what was so violently taken, the need to justify that theft. It all created a story of race and a social, economic, and political need for racism.

The United States was built on land stolen from populations of color, with the forced labor of other populations of color. First it was enslaved African peoples, then exploited Chinese and Mexican labor, then it was other, eventually exploited populations coming to the US, desperate for a new start—often leaving behind homelands made unsafe or robbed of their wealth by violent colonialism.

Today, large portions of our industries still rely on exploited, abused, and even forced labor of populations of color, and that abuse and exploitation can take many different forms.

In her book *In a Day's Work: The Fight to End Sexual Violence Against America's Most Vulnerable Workers*, Bernice Yeung documents how immigrants of color are often exploited in their workplaces, and how many women workers in these populations are sexually abused and assaulted:

> *After looking at various industries that hire the most vulnerable workers, I've been forced to conclude that low-wage immigrants laboring in isolation are at unique risk of sexual assault and harassment. While it is not possible to know how often these abuses happen, they are not anomalies. The federal government estimates that about fifty workers are sexually assaulted each day, and in the industries that hire newcomers to*

*the country in exchange for meager paychecks, such assault is*
*a known and familiar workplace hazard. (2018)*

In our country's prisons, slavery is alive and well, as imprisoned people are forced to labor for very little or no pay. And the racism of our carceral systems ensures that a disproportionate amount of those enslaved in our prisons will be Black, brown, and Indigenous.

But the story of labor and race is not just one of abuse and exploitation. Labor has long been at the heart of many of our resistance and abolition movements.

Enslaved Black people often practiced forms of labor protest, from work stoppage to sabotage. Once slavery was legally abolished, the possibility of paid work with more dignity and safety was a driving factor behind the great migration that brought millions of Black Americans out of the South and into the North and West to establish new, vibrant communities across the country.

The Civil Rights Movement was not just about freedom from the violence of racism. It was also about access to good jobs and opportunities for Black people to build and grow their own economic independence. It was clear to many Black organizers how liberation and economic opportunity were tied together. Black union members were helped by the Civil Rights Movement, and in turn, many unions with large numbers of Black membership, like the United Packinghouse Workers of America, were major supporters of civil rights groups and actions (Loomis 2018).

Abusive employers regularly took advantage of racial and ethnic differences in employees of color in order to force them to compete with one another for low paying, dangerous, and exploitative jobs. But just as often employees were able to find common ground on labor issues, which brought entire communities together in struggles for justice.

In *Fight Like Hell: The Untold History of American Labor*, journalist Kim Kelly discusses many of the important actions of solidarity between labor unions and BIPOC liberation movements. One union known for its solidarity work is the International Longshore and Warehouse Union (ILWU). Acts of solidarity by the ILWU have taken many different forms over the years: the union refused to unload cargo from South Africa in protest of their apartheid policies; supported Asian American farmworkers' organization efforts in Hawaii; allowed Native liberation activists who were occupying Alcatraz Island to use one of their piers to move people and supplies to and from the occupied island; shut down the Port of Oakland in demands of justice for Oscar Grant after he was killed by Oakland police officers; and in 2020 shut down ports in protest of the murder of George Floyd. These are just some of the actions this one powerful and fierce union has taken in solidarity with its workers and communities of color (Kelly 2022).

If we want to envision a post-racism world, we must look at labor. We must see the ways in which our common need to be able to provide for ourselves and our communities has been historically used to pit us against one another, to make us complicit in our own harm and the harm of others. And we must look at how we also have been able to come together in the hopes of a political and economic system that doesn't rely on the exploitation of workers. And we must look at different ways to work, to produce, and to provide for ourselves and others.

## TEVITA UHATAFE

Joy radiates off of Tevita Uhatafe. I challenge anyone to spend more than a few minutes with him and not walk away smiling. There's energized love in just about everything the thirty-something first-generation Tongan American does. You can see it when he talks about his family—his wife and two kids—and when he talks about his *other* family: his fellow union members.

Uhatafe is a fleet service clerk with American Airlines and a proud union member. He made headlines in the summer of 2022 as the "Mic Guy" holding the microphone for Bernie Sanders at a Labor Notes conference when the senator's mic stand wasn't working. Pictures of the large Tongan man very stoically holding the microphone out for the labor-championing politician have shone a spotlight on Uhatafe and resulted in a broader curiosity about him and his work.

But in union circles, Uhatafe had already been building a name for himself for a couple of years. If you've been on a union picket line recently, there's a good chance you've seen him. He's the large, smiling Pacific Islander running to grab water for strikers or taking his shift on the picket line in the hot sun. He'll likely be wearing a shirt for his local union (Local 513), even though it's not the union on strike. Wherever there's a labor movement in the US that needs support, Tevita Uhatafe wants to be there—and often he is.

But Uhatafe wasn't always such a staunch supporter of unions, even after having been in unions for years. In fact, for a long time he wasn't really sure what unions *did*. Unions seemed to have no impact on his day-to-day work life, so he paid little attention to what his union was doing.

Public schools in the United States didn't provide Uhatafe and his peers with much of an education about labor or union history, outside of a very broad description of the US Department of Agriculture and the creation of the Department of Labor. But they didn't discuss what the labor movement was or why it was needed.

When Uhatafe was first in a union, he saw it as something you engaged with only when you were in trouble. "I was never in trouble," he explains, "so I didn't even care to learn what it was. And neither were they even offering to show me, like, 'Hey, this is what a union is.'"

This lack of proactive outreach by unions to new and younger workers is a major problem Uhatafe sees across the country: "They don't reach people. With unions, they don't reach out right away and say, 'Hey.'"

But even without engaging with his union, Uhatafe still wanted to help his fellow workers—it was just in his nature. It's, as he describes it, the Pacific Islander way. He became known as the guy to go to with questions, even though that role would typically be a shop steward's. Want to know where the restroom is? Ask Tevita. Want to know how to get to gate 43? Ask Tevita. If you asked him anything he didn't know, he'd happily look it up. Soon Uhatafe's reputation for helpfulness caught the attention of his local union officials and they invited him to become more engaged with his union.

Uhatafe became a regular at union meetings, first just to learn how they work. At the same time, he was getting what he sees as one of the most important educations of his life from his coworkers.

"My real experience into real American history was in the gatehouses at the airport," he says. A lot of his coworkers at the gatehouses were Black men who'd been in the union for decades. Living in the South in the '50s and '60s, these men had lived through a lot of the racist history of this country that is left out of schoolbooks. "They were giving me firsthand accounts of what was going on in the Jim Crow era. This was no schoolbook. This was straight up: 'This is what happened in Memphis. I was there.' And that was my eye opening to the Black experience in America."

For Uhatafe, this history lesson wasn't just about understanding the past; it was about understanding his present and his future: "I—myself, my parents—we benefit from it. Somebody had to go through all this bullshit, and I benefit from it. . . . I will never forget. I would sweat with these guys. We would be working in the heat. The Texas heat. It's a hundred and one, and then you're surrounded by concrete and asphalt and aircraft and fuel."

The bond he formed with his Black coworkers was lasting and life-changing. He considers them his big brothers for how they have taken him under their wing and taught him so many important life lessons. Uhatafe says, "I was working before, but I didn't know what the real world was until they told me their experience. And I finally understood. Everything started making sense."

Uhatafe took this eye-opening experience to the union. He started attending meetings with union coalitions. He started working with the Latine union groups and Black union groups to learn more about what issues were having an impact on his Latine and Black coworkers.

Uhatafe's union involvement would further deepen when the United Auto Workers members at a General Motors plant in Arlington, Texas, went on strike in 2019. Many of the striking workers were Latine and/or Black, and Uhatafe was connected to them though his union work and his work with union affinity groups. So Uhatafe headed to Arlington to support the strike. He was grabbing ice and water bottles for workers on the picket line in the Texas heat. He was picketing during the morning shift. This was the first walkout Uhatafe had ever attended, and he was struck by how strong the feeling of solidarity and cooperation was between workers of widely different backgrounds. "This was the first time I've ever really felt like everybody was on the same page," he remembers. "We didn't even think about race or anything. We were just like, 'Man, it's hot out.'" He laughs. "I felt like we were actually there together, for one reason, and that was the only reason we were there."

Out of the forty days the General Motors employees were on strike, Uhatafe was there for thirty-six of them. He had to work three of those days, and one of the days he missed for his wedding anniversary.

"We just got married, and it was, like, year three or four, so [his fellow strikers] were like, 'You better go home,'" he says with another hearty laugh.

When the pandemic hit, Uhatafe started taking on higher profile work for the union, pushing and promoting the CARES (Coronavirus Aid, Relief, and Economic Security) Act. He started showing up in local news reports and eventually national news.

But even though he was doing good work that his union wanted and needed him to do, it wasn't translating into real respect or recognition from his union, and Uhatafe was getting frustrated as people hired with him were promoted ahead of him in the union ranks.

Some of the workers promoted above him had parents or other family who were already officers in the union, familial access that Uhatafe, a first-generation American, didn't have. But beyond that, he noticed that a lot of the people getting promoted had one thing in common: their race.

"Over time, it just felt like it was the white guys that were getting promoted, you know?" He tells me, "And I was putting in three times the work and going to stuff that nobody went to. They wouldn't put themselves out to go and do that service."

Despite his rising frustrations, Uhatafe continued to show up for unions. As the pandemic persisted, workers became increasingly angry with their working conditions and lack of worker safety, and they started to take more collective action.

"The pandemic had been battling *us*. Our coworkers were dying, and we were trying to figure out, *Should we continue wearing masks? Are we gonna be responsible enough?*" It was disheartening for him to see how little people seemed to care about the health and safety of airline workers.

Uhatafe and his coworkers weren't alone in their fear and frustration. Workers around the country began to go on strike. One of the first national strikes Uhatafe remembers was the Nabisco strike. Union efforts at places like Amazon and Starbucks would soon make headlines, too.

Uhatafe's support of these strikes got him an invitation to the Constitutional Convention for the Transport Workers Union (TWU). Workers usually only get an invitation if they're elected union officials or elected delegates. Uhatafe's invite was an honor, and a sign to him that his union was finally starting to appreciate his work. He shared the proud news with his family, and they became excited for the trip to Vegas for the convention.

But as the date neared and his peers were all sharing their travel plans, Uhatafe still hadn't received any further information about the convention. He reached out to his union to let them know that he hadn't received any accommodation information. No response. Eventually, the deadline to receive credentials for the conference passed. It was clear to Uhatafe that he wasn't going to the convention, and nobody had even bothered to tell him.

"I had already told my family. I told my wife, my kids—they were excited." As he tells me this, I can see the hurt still in his eyes. "It was like a huge slap in the face."

Even though he was hurt by his union's apparent disregard, Uhatafe didn't stay at home to mope. He got on a plane and headed to Chicago, then Portland, where there were active strikes. If he couldn't be with his union members at the convention, he would be with workers on the picket line.

From that moment on Uhatafe decided that he was done waiting for his union to recognize and support his work. He was going to build union solidarity his way. His flight privileges from his airline job helped him get from city to city, and his wife helped cover extra costs by selling leis at graduation ceremonies. Uhatafe kept traveling from city to city, supporting union efforts and championing diversity in the ranks. The sacrifices made to support these labor movements have been difficult for his family, but he feels it's an important practice for them, honoring the history of sacrifice that paved the way for Uhatafe to be able to have a good union job today. Uhatafe tries to educate his children on the history of union solidarity and the struggle they are now a part of, passing down the important lessons he learned from his Black mentors.

"This is a collective American experience for us, right?" He says, "I'm telling them what I heard at the gatehouses, and this is why we're doing that. I'm telling them there was a time where you couldn't even be in the same classroom with your white classmates or maybe your Black classmates. If not for the struggle of another race, the Black race . . . I always make sure that they know that."

Even though Uhatafe believes wholeheartedly in unions, he believes just as strongly that they have to change if they're going to be relevant to younger workers and workers of color.

It's easy for anyone to see that unions have been in decline in recent years. Part of this is due to deliberate anti-union efforts by businesses and big-business-friendly politicians. But unions have done themselves a lot of damage as well.

Throughout the history of American unions, they have often been their own worst enemy. When unions can mobilize to protect the interests of *all* of their workers—especially their most vulnerable workers—they are a revolution unto themselves. Some of the great progress we've made in workers' rights has come because of unions. Union jobs have helped women get a foothold in hostile workspaces. Union jobs have brought prosperity and security to communities of color. But unions are just as susceptible to racism, sexism, ableism, and cronyism as any other system in our society. And it's often those unaddressed biases and bigotries that are easily exploited by those who wish to weaken a union's power, and even without outside interference, these biases keep a lot of valuable workers from being able to actively support their union.

There's a sad irony in this, in that workers of color are some of the most vulnerable to the workplace abuses unions have long fought against. If unions were able to truly become more inclusive and let go of white supremacist tendencies to prefer only white men in their positions of authority, they would have a large and powerful support base in workers of color.

But presently a very visible divide exists between many union leaders and workers. While a large number of workers at the forefront of recent labor organizing efforts (like Amazon and Starbucks) are young and people of color, many of the leaders in established unions remain older white men. This can lead to an important disconnect between up-and-coming labor activists and older union leaders. Uhatafe recalls with astonishment a recent AFL-CIO convention—one of the largest conventions for the largest labor group in the country:

"I get up. I'm wearing an Amazon Labor Union shirt—but the Amazon Labor Union was not invited to the party. Of the largest labor federation in the country. Or Starbucks workers. These are the most media-wise and union-hype [workers]. Like, this is Woodstock people right now. And if you don't let us in, that's the Jimi Hendrix *right there*, bruh."

But Uhatafe knows unions can be so much more than what they often are now. He sees the relationships and solidarity he's been able to build, he sees the efforts that people like Chris Smalls and Jennifer Bates have been leading, and he knows he's working toward something that can be truly great.

"It's a different labor movement. That's what I want to transform it into. Something that transcends these borders and these groups that we put ourselves into."

Uhatafe draws inspiration from his Pacific Islander heritage: "Back in the islands, if something happens to somebody, you get up and you go. You go. You don't ask questions till you get there, right? I've been doing that here with going to pickets, to strikes. Like, *Okay, I'll find out what's going on, what they're fighting for, on the way*. But I'm going. You can just get up and go. You ain't gotta wait on no vote. You wanna show true solidarity, put your money where your mouth is. Just show up."

Strikes are difficult, even traumatic events for workers and their families. This sort of intense collective action requires solidarity that transcends race, gender, ability, sexuality, age, and more. But solidarity requires that we be honest about where we are now and be willing to shake things up. And that can be difficult in such an often patriarchal and hierarchical structure.

"You gonna be alone," Uhatafe says when I ask him what advice he has for younger people of color seeking to become more engaged with their union. "A lot of the time, you will be alone. But don't be afraid. Lean on those allies. If it's one or two, or ten, lean on them. If it's your family or a coworker, a *somebody*, anybody. They don't have to know the work, but just lean on them for support. You're gonna need 'em."

Uhatafe hopes that younger workers will be able to protect them-selves with more awareness of how hostile unions can be to change and to people who represent change while still being willing to call out harmful behavior. And he advises younger workers to open themselves up to fellow union members who may have different backgrounds or perspectives. Build genuine relationships and try to lift up people around you.

Uhatafe also stresses that you don't have to be a part of a particu-lar demographic in order to support and learn from the various union affinity organizations and coalitions.

"I'm not only an APALA [Asian Pacific American Labor Alliance] member, but I'm a dues-paying member for the A. Philip Randolph In-stitute [a Black constituency group of the AFL-CIO], also the Coalition of Labor Union Women. Hey, man, I don't know anything going on with women!" He laughs. "I want to hear from them so they can tell me."

## Racism in Labor Unions

Before Chris Smalls would become famous for fighting to *start* a union, he would find himself *fighting* a union.

Smalls was working the graveyard shift in a large warehouse. It was his first union job. It was a hard job, and almost all of his coworkers were Black, like him, or brown—except for the management, which was all white.

"We were treated like shit. Disrespected every night by the managers," Smalls says. "I'm like, *This doesn't make any sense. Why are we being subjected to this in a union?*"

He didn't know at the time that night-shift labor jobs are notorious for exploiting and abusing workers of color. It's something night warehouse workers, healthcare workers, janitorial workers of color, and more experience. Abusive treatment, stolen pay, even assault, are easier for unscrupulous employers and management to get away with when almost everyone else is asleep.

After three years of putting up with racist treatment from managers, Smalls decided to fight back. He needed to request vacation time off, and knew that his manager would likely not take the request well. So Smalls decided to record the conversation with his manager on his phone. As predicted, the manager replied to his request with racist insults. But this time Smalls had a record of it.

Smalls took the recording to Human Resources and to his union. He went through a union arbitration process, expecting his union to stand up for him. All they did was put the manager through additional "coaching."

Sadly, I regularly hear from BIPOC who are let down by their white-led unions and are not given the protections from abuse, harassment, and discrimination that unions promise. But sometimes I'm still surprised by what I hear. I was recently visiting a middle school, talking with seventh and eighth graders. After a very pleasant morning with students, I was pulled aside by a few Black staff members as I prepared to leave. They were grateful for the time I had given to the children, but they were hoping I might have some time to give them some advice privately.

Often when school staff of color ask for advice, they are asking how to navigate parents who are hostile to education on race and racism or any accurate approaches to teaching history, or they want advice on dealing with administrators who just don't get it.

And as I started to give my usual advice, one of the staff members interrupted me. They weren't asking how to handle parents or administrators—they had actually made a lot of progress on that front. They wanted to know how to handle the educators union.

Every time they made progress in advancing programs or policies that may better serve the needs of students of color, a teacher threatened by those changes would go to their union and then the changes would be canceled or severely weakened. Whenever they got their administration to take a firm stance with teachers who showed repeated patterns of racist behavior toward colleagues or students, the union blocked any real consequences for such behavior, and instead opted for the sort of "coaching" Chris Smalls had witnessed when he brought evidence of racist behavior to his union.

Often when I'm discussing my work, white people will try to sell me labor solidarity as an alternative to anti-racist organizing. Another version of "It's class, not race." They argue that we would have a bigger army in the war against injustice if we set race aside and could unite around labor issues. Populations of color are some of the most affected by labor issues, but so are many poor and working-class whites. Surely organizing for all laborers would be more effective than organizing along racial and ethnic lines.

I grew up in a union household. Unions helped my mother gain a measure of economic stability that she otherwise was unlikely, as a single mother of three, to be able to get. And I know that in our history, union jobs have been one of the most effective pathways to economic and even political power for many communities of color across the country for multiple generations.

But unions have been the foes of workers of color likely as often as they've been friends.

There's nothing inherently anti-racist about unions. A union will be as anti-racist as its policies, practices, and people allow it to be. And since American workspaces have long been dominated by white men, it's easy to see how unions will be very susceptible to the racism and sexism of white male workers and union leadership.

The racism that many unions can't seem to be able to escape has shown itself over and over again throughout the history of labor unions in the United States. And that propensity for racial bigotry and fear has been a particular weakness that employers and politicians have been able to exploit repeatedly, to the detriment of all workers.

One of the most famous Black activists in labor history, A. Philip Randolph, helped organize protest actions aimed at forcing unions to admit Black workers. When the unions capitulated and allowed Black workers to join, often white workers would then follow with their own protests against the presence of Black workers.

In 1943, when three Black workers were promoted at a Detroit Packard plant, twenty-five thousand white workers went on strike (Loomis 2018, 140).

As much as many would like to think of labor and union history as a story of workers coming together for the rights of all, the truth is that white workers have often chosen race and their own positions of racial power over the best interests of their union, whenever it seemed that union goals or union progress threatened to upend racial order.

So powerful and dependable was this loyalty to white supremacy that Nixon even used the desegregation of labor unions to try to drive the white working-class vote to the Republican Party (Loomis 2018, 161).

This long-standing history of racism in our labor movements doesn't mean that we will never be able to truly unify workers, or that the labor movement can't be an important part of the fight for racial justice. It just means that our labor movements have been just as conditioned by systemic white supremacy as almost every other sector of our society, and if we are to make real progress that doesn't harm workers of color, we must be willing to face that and apply anti-racist and abolitionist practices to labor and union organizing. Awareness of how our labor movements have failed workers of color in the past, and how many of them are failing workers of color today, can help keep vibrant new labor movements alive and relevant, and can help improve the lives of all workers.

## LAURA CLISE

My name is Laura Clise. I use she/her pronouns. I am a Korean adoptee, queer woman. I grew up here in Seattle in a biracial family. My dad's side of the family has been in Seattle for generations. And my mom is Japanese American, from the island of Kauai.

My mom's side of the family immigrated to Kauai in the late 1800s as farmers from outside of Hiroshima in Japan. My grandma grew up on a sugarcane plantation. And I mention this, which is going back to the very beginning, because I've come to realize how formative it was for me to grow up in a family where I was very close to both of my grandmothers, who came from very different lived experiences."

Laura Clise's maternal grandmother grew up in hard work. "My grandma went to school until eighth grade," Clise tells me, "and then because she was a girl, that was it. Time to work on the plantation. She hated it."

After working on the plantation, Clise's grandmother found work in housekeeping and domestic services. Her years of work allowed her to save enough money to attend sewing school and become a seamstress. Eventually Clise's grandmother married, and she and her husband were able to purchase an appliance repair business. "Small business ownership was transformational for our family," Clise says.

From her paternal grandmother, born into much more privilege than her maternal grandmother, Clise was able to learn about other important aspects of life. Her paternal grandmother encouraged her love of reading and the arts, and introduced her to new cultural experiences. Her paternal grandmother was also the member of the family Clise first came out to.

Both of Clise's grandmothers are a large part of why we're talking about her work. "In different ways, women that I was blessed to be close to have influenced how I've moved through the world [for] as long as I can remember. And certainly, when I think about Intentionalist."

Laura Clise is the founder of Intentionalist, an online resource and marketplace aimed at providing real consumer connection to local BIPOC-owned, women-owned, and veteran-owned businesses. On Intentionalist, you can find information about each of these businesses as well as purchase gift cards or order from the businesses in Intentionalist's online marketplace. It also often runs discount promotions for the businesses.

"Intentionalist really came about because I couldn't figure out why it was so hard to be intentional about harnessing my consumer spending power in support of people in communities that matter. All of the resources that I felt like I had access to told me what, told me how much, told me how fast. But there was no real acknowledgment of *who*."

Clise wears the inspiration for Intentionalist in her jacket breast pocket. It's a small, colorful pocket square that she pulls out and hands to me, as we sit and drink coffee at Boon Boona, an Eritrean American–owned coffee shop and roaster featured on the Intentionalist site.

"So this, this is not only the amount of color I'm comfortable with in my personal wardrobe," Clise says of the fabric with a chuckle. "This is [from] a scarf that I bought from an artisanal collaborative in Siem Reap in 2012. So the seed for Intentionalist was planted in 2012."

Clise was attending a friend's wedding in Southeast Asia and was excited to shop at local vendors in the area. But she wanted to make sure that the money she was spending benefited people in the local economy she was visiting. It took a fair amount of research, but eventually Clise found an artisanal collaborative that met both her ethical and aesthetic goals. From them, she bought the handwoven scarf she wears every day.

This purchase spoke to a deeper desire Clise had to be more intentional with her spending. She had been happy to pay more for the scarf than she would have for mass-produced items, because the authenticity, craftsmanship, and story attached to the scarf was worth much more to her. She wished there was a way to find and buy more items like this, because it would meet a market need, while also earning more money for those selling the wares.

She notes this moment as the beginning of Intentionalist, even though it wouldn't actually be built until 2017.

Clise had left Seattle for college and career, and moved back in 2015 with her wife. She returned to a city greatly changed. "There was—that continues to this day—this real tension between rapid growth and transformation, and really fundamental questions about who still has a physical place in our communities, as well as who feels a sense of belonging."

Seattle had become much more of a tech city, and much less of the small town that many of us who grew up in the area in the '80s and '90s had known. The impact on communities of color was especially pronounced, with historically Black and Asian neighborhoods being displaced by big tech money and enterprises. Small businesses in these areas were also taking a pretty serious hit.

Clise worked for years with large multinational corporations. At one such corporation, she developed a supplier diversity program to help the company meet their diversity and equity goals. "And as I was developing that program and articulating the business case, articulating why this program created value for us as a company, and for society and diverse communities, what went through my mind was, *Wow, it's really interesting that supplier diversity programs have existed for decades. I might not have billions and spend it like Microsoft, but what if I wanted to spend money in support of women-owned, people-of-color-owned, LGBTQ-owned, veteran-owned small businesses? What resources exist that would make that possible?*"

Clise began meeting with local small businesses to see if there was something she could develop to make this dream a reality.

As she talked with small business owners, she was surprised to discover that many of the "tools" that had been built to make larger businesses more convenient to buyers weren't actually beneficial to small businesses. Clise realized that a lot of these tools and resources had been developed with little concern for the needs of small business owners. This was a revelation for Clise.

"As I started to ask more questions and learn, you look under the hood and you realize that the companies that have been created to cater to your and my transactional convenience aren't centering the benefit and the welfare of the small businesses that we might think and hope we're serving when we are more intentional about, for example, going to an independent coffee shop."

Big tech had appealed to one part of our spending drive, but Clise aims at another important factor. "Tech companies have locked on to the scalability and the profit potential of speaking to the part within each of us that is maybe a little bit busy, a little bit impatient. That values immediate gratification. That's maybe a little bit hedonistic. Maybe a little bit selfish. All of those things that are truths of our shared humanity. What Intentionalist aspires to do is speak to other parts within each of us that care about connection, that care about our community. And would love to do something about it. And so Intentionalist is focused on closing that gap between good intentions that we might have to support diverse small businesses and our ability to easily take action. By hopefully investing in an ecosystem for which the currency really is connection, and the opportunities to build community."

The directory is the heart of Intentionalist, where information can be found about each diverse small business, its owners, and its role in community. Big businesses spend a lot of money and resources to tell a story that can connect with customers in ways that are often inauthentic. Think about all the greenwashing, the queerwashing, the once-a-year claims that "Black lives matter" with no real long-term investment in Black communities or even Black employees. Small businesses may not be as resourced, but Clise believes they have a story to tell, one that's even better because it's authentic.

"Purpose, sustainability, responsibility, ethical sourcing, right? Storytelling emerged as part of brand narratives in a new way," Clise observes. "And yet who can most authentically share a story about local impact? . . . I mean, just the amount of collaboration that happens across POC-owned small businesses, women-of-color-owned small businesses—it's pretty damn cool. But then there weren't the resources. And then we started to think, *Okay, how can we help bring some additional awareness, and instead of just talking about how foodie the food is, what if we talk about the people?*"

In order to tell these stories, Clise had to build trust with local small businesses—not only trust in how they would be represented on Intentionalist but also trust that Intentionalist could actually benefit their businesses. That meant Clise has had to get creative with how she encourages customers to buy from these businesses.

Traditional online marketplaces often rely on deep discounts to entice new customers, and the cost for those discounts is always shouldered by the small business desperate for customers. Where discounts aren't offered, businesses often still have to pay to be featured on these online spaces.

Intentionalist has turned away from that model.

"Part of Intentionalist is an attempt to reimagine an ecosystem that's less extractive, that's intentionally supportive. So that when someone is either engaging with our directory or purchasing something from our platform or participating in some of the promotions that we facilitate, they do so knowing that we are safeguarding benefit to the local businesses that are at the heart of our mission," Clise says.

"And what that means is that our business model isn't predicated on trying to maximize revenue or profit from small business owners, which is often a pretty key ingredient to most platforms, and especially tech businesses out there."

Operation of the Intentionalist website and marketplace is funded by tips that customers can choose to leave. Coupon books offering discounts and free items at local small businesses are funded not by the small businesses themselves but by community members and larger companies and organizations looking to give to businesses owned by members of marginalized communities.

"I remember last year, the first time we tried experimenting with Seattle Storm. Like, okay, we've got this idea. You have a thousand dollars. You could either spend that directly at Black-owned businesses. Nothing wrong with that. Or," Clise says with a smile, "what if we used that thousand dollars as discount money? And then we offer a 20 percent discount on gift cards to fifty Black-owned small businesses, and then the community shows up and does the rest?"

That first collaboration with the Seattle WNBA team may have taken a little convincing, but the team's leadership was down to try something new if it might benefit the local community, and it paid off.

"We were able to underwrite a discount, and then the community showed up. So instead of just receiving a thousand dollars, Black-owned businesses received five thousand dollars," Clise tells me.

That was the start of a new way for Intentionalist to bring revenue into local businesses.

"This year, during AANHPI [Asian American, Native Hawaiian, and Pacific Islander] Heritage Month, our community spent forty thousand dollars on gift cards in a week."

During a recent holiday season I was able to purchase two packets of gift cards from Intentionalist for small businesses in the Central District, our local historically Black neighborhood, to give out to my brothers for Christmas. The coupons for cups of coffee, free appetizers, pastries, and more were a fun way to introduce my brothers to businesses that I knew they would love to be able to support. And it felt great knowing that Intentionalist had designed the gift card program to ensure the small businesses would truly benefit from my purchases. My youngest brother, who had moved to the Seattle area about five years earlier, took a friend and made a day of visiting the businesses in the coupon book, taking an eating tour of his neighborhood. He told me later that every time he brought out a coupon book, the business owner would be excited to see it, knowing that their partnership with Intentionalist had brought another paying customer through their door.

It may seem small, but how we support small businesses is important, even when we're thinking about larger social justice issues. Where we spend our money matters.

"Sometimes it's easier for us to wrap our minds around concepts like pay equity gaps," Clise explains. "So there has been, I think, more and more conversation about . . . how much worse off outcomes, when it comes to pay equity, are for Black and/or Indigenous and/or Latinx and/or other women of color. And I think that sometimes it feels like, 'Well, how are we going to take on the patriarchy? How are we going to address the ways in which systemic injustice permeates everything?' That can feel overwhelming."

Clise argues that we can make a difference right now, in our local businesses: "While you and I might not be in a position to close the gap on corporate pay equity, those same gaps exist for small businesses. So women-owned small businesses make half the revenue of small businesses owned by men. Latina-owned businesses make half the revenue of white women-owned businesses. Not surprisingly, those same gaps exist everywhere, because they're driven by and rooted in the same unjust systems and cultures that have shaped us everywhere.

"But when you choose to purchase a birthday gift from an Afghan refugee woman-owned gift shop, you are putting your thumb on the scales of economic injustice. You are helping to close that gap. And if we all do that, then the gaps close. I mean, I think that's what's cool. Because I think that sometimes institutional policy feels big and slow. And yes, culture feels big and slow. But in terms of something that I can do, just by being a little bit more intentional, you and I—and the other hundred million, one in three Americans that opt in to Small Business Saturday—can decide to be a little bit more intentional a little more often, and we can actually close those gaps for small businesses owned by women and nonbinary folks and people of color."

This is not charity Clise is engaging in. This isn't even about propping up small businesses. It's about her community, and her own well-being, too. She tells me that when small businesses in her community are thriving, she is thriving as well. A strong community is important to her well-being.

"I'm not supporting small businesses insomuch as they are supporting me," Clise adds. "In terms of the quality and the community that I live in. In terms of the way that they look out for people in the community in need. In a world where there does seem to be more and more kind of space between us. So if we're social fabric, we're kind of like this." Clise moves her hands apart, fingers spread. "Where there's all these little gaps. And I feel like my experience has been that small business owners and the communities around local businesses help kind of bring us back together"—she moves her hands back together, interlacing her fingers—"and they help reinforce or reweave that social fabric."

Clise hopes that other people in cities and towns across the country will also look for creative ways to engage with local small businesses.

"I guess what I would want people to recognize is that Intentionalist is an idea. It's a four-and-a-half-years-of-effort idea. But it's an idea. And it's a platform, and it's a resource. But the magic is that diverse stakeholders have shown up around this idea. And together we have been able to demonstrate that there is in fact an alternative to the existing kind of convenient transaction-driven immediate-gratification-prioritizing systems [that] we've become accustomed to. And I think that's really exciting."

Clise adds with pride, "I hope that we can . . . be one of many purpose-driven social enterprises that continue to center people. And, I guess, that also continue to fight for a more relational economy, and that offer busy folks like us bite-size opportunities to close racial wealth gaps, to reinforce the social fabric of our communities. One cup of coffee at a time."

## Can We Build Better Businesses?

Labor issues affecting communities of color aren't just about big businesses. We aren't only talking about how workers are being treated in giant warehouses or on corporate farms.

For millions of people in the US, their economic hopes and dreams lie in small businesses. Small businesses have been the fulfillment of the American dream for many a family of color. Small businesses have lifted families out of poverty, have paid for first homes and first college degrees.

But small businesses have also been sources of the same economic disparities, worker abuses, and exploitation we have seen in larger companies. And in fact, when these abuses occur, there is frequently no Human Resources or other recognized authority within the business to turn to in order to right such wrongs.

Revolution is not just about tearing down what's wrong; it's also about building something right. And often what's "right" is yet to be determined. Therefore, revolution may require daring, big ideas. And those big ideas are usually best tested and built in smaller spaces.

When I sat down to interview Richie Reseda, I thought we were going to be discussing Success Stories, the feminist abolition program he built in prison, as that was how I was first introduced to him and his work. But Reseda quickly informed me that he had, after years at the helm, handed off leadership of day-to-day operations of Success Stories to trusted team members.

His eyes lit up with excitement at the opportunity to talk about his current passion: abolitionist business.

Recent events in larger Black liberation spaces had underlined a key gap in our liberation work that was leading to infighting, distrust, recrimination, and other harm: a seeming lack of focus on how we treat one another in our communities today. Richie wondered, *What are we building together right now that models the world we want to see?* We know what we're fighting against, but what are we fighting *for*?

Reseda is still committed to getting folk free from prison cells, and still serves on the board of Success Stories, but right now, he tells me, "I'm trying to build the world we're trying to see, just within my world."

Reseda is trying to build that world in his businesses. He tells me about two projects he's started. He runs a media company called Question Culture and a clothing group called For Everyone Collective.

For Everyone Collective makes beautiful T-shirts, sweatshirts, and more with powerful messages about abolition. The entire team at For Everyone is made up of people directly affected by the prison–industrial complex.

With For Everyone, Reseda wanted to build a business structure he hadn't seen before. One that was collaborative, consent based, and free from the exploitation we see in so many business enterprises. "I don't own this company outright and now everybody just works for me to boost my pockets," he explains. "We have a community-owned infrastructure where we split up our company between the artists, the employees, and the founders. As long as you're an artist or an employee, you collect quarterly money, like any other owner, from those pots. If you're both, you collect both. And if you're a founder, you collect from that pot, and if you leave the company, you keep your founder pot—so it still encourages people to start businesses and stuff, which is the part that I couldn't figure out when trying to figure out these more socialist, community-based ownership structures."

If the fact that I can't seem to wear one of For Everyone's shirts out of the house without someone recognizing it immediately as a

For Everyone shirt—and informing me that they, too, own one—is a measurement of their success, I'd say that his approach to business is working.

Reseda is hoping more people will give abolitionist business practices a try. "Richie Reseda wants to tell the world: 'You should all make abolitionist companies, or community-based companies,'" he says.

"I'd rather be on the cover of *Inc.*—" Reseda pauses and looks at the tattoos covering his arms and laughs. "I-n-c," he clarifies. "Even though I'd be on I-n-k, too. But on the *Inc.* cover, or the *Entrepreneur* cover or the *Black Enterprise* cover, saying, 'Abolitionist business works! Here, let me tell you how.'"

Reseda isn't alone in finding and creating new spaces of change in the business community. In Laura Clise and DarNesha Weary (next), we see what two women of color have been able to create with their businesses after they decided to set aside what they were told is the "only" way to exist as a business leader and aim for something new, something based in building and supporting our communities and healing some of the harm caused by hyper-capitalist business structures.

You can see the joy in their hard and exciting work, and hopefully it will have you looking at small business as much more than just a way to make money.

"It's different!" Reseda says excitedly. "We over here living abolitionist and it's great! You wanna pull up or not?"

## DARNESHA WEARY

There was quite a bit of buzz when it was announced that a Black-owned coffee shop was going to be opening in the North End of the Seattle area.

Seattle is . . . pretty white just about everywhere you go these days, but the North End neighborhoods are different. The area north of Seattle has little of the tech wealth and comfort of Central Seattle. It's instead a white working-class area, with pockets of Hispanic and Asian communities and almost no Black people. I grew up in this area. It's a tough space to grow up in, in general. There's a grittiness to it that a lot of people who haven't lived in it don't understand. The racism and homophobia are pretty in-your-face, lacking the "Seattle nice" of its neighbors to the south. But there's also a semblance of safety in class solidarity that's missing in much of privileged Seattle, a city that really loves to pretend like its poor people just don't exist.

But back to this coffee shop. I still live in the North End, and I hadn't been able to find a local Black-owned or Black-centered community space in the decades I've lived there. My partner and I were excited to now have a Black-owned coffee shop nearby.

Others were . . . less excited. Before they even opened for business, Black Coffee Northwest had experienced vandalism, broken windows, even an attempted firebombing. That in-your-face racism I just mentioned was really, *really* showing itself.

But once news of the attacks circulated, many people in the community came out to support the new business at their grand opening. The line extended around the block. Inside their spacious coffee shop were tables covered in wares being sold by local Black merchants. Black teens were everywhere, working behind the counter, working at booths, performing with the step team. It was a moment of joy and community in the face of hate and division.

In the months that followed the grand opening, the line was no longer around the block, and the space settled into a more comfortable place in the community. It was still occasionally targeted by vandals, and at least every few months they had to close for the day to deal with a brick or rock thrown through one of their windows. But most days you could come through and a Black teen would take your order and share a list of special drinks they had invented themselves. (Note: They were very much "teen" drinks that they swore were very delicious, but they were often various mixtures of Red Bull and sugar syrup. I usually ordered from the fixed menu.)

There were always kids making their way through from the local high schools. They streamed in at lunchtime and even came in after the coffee shop was closed for business. Just about every weekend there would be a community event happening in their shop or parking lot.

And as much a part of the community as Black Coffee has seemed to have become in just a few years, they are actually so much more than they appear on the surface. And they wouldn't be what they are if their owner and co-founder DarNesha Weary hadn't worked so hard to build something positive from harmful and even traumatic experiences in her life.

DarNesha Weary is a regular fixture at her coffee shop. You can find her leading around a group of teens or walking around saying hi to customers or even working behind the counter. She has lived in the North End for decades now, but she's originally from Rainier Valley, a historically Black neighborhood in Seattle.

"I was born in Seattle to a very big Black Christian community," Weary tells me. "[I] went to Rainier Valley Christian School."

Weary was uprooted in sixth grade when her parents divorced and her mother moved them to Lynnwood, a small working-class suburb north of Seattle. Weary went from an environment that surrounded her in Black community to one where she was an extreme minority.

Her first day of school, Weary dressed up the way she and her Black schoolmates had always done: "I had my overalls on that I got from Mid-K in Seattle, I had the one strap down, Africa medallion—it's like, in the '90s. Oh, it was Kris Kross," Weary remembers with a laugh the fashion trend started by the youth rap duo. "But for me, in my home, the first day of school, you get your hair freshly braided, you put your outfit out. And so I remember getting my hair done. I thought I was fly."

Weary arrived at her new school, and white students immediately questioned her clothing and touched her hair without permission.

"When I came out here," she recalls, "I didn't realize the level of trauma that I was going through at the time, because I was a child. Now that I look back and reflect, I realize what was happening to me."

Weary didn't have other students she could connect to. White students were intimidated by her and assumed that, because she was Black and from the city, she was in a gang. She became withdrawn and depressed. Her grades started to slip. And her mom, fresh out of a divorce, didn't have the emotional capacity to help Weary through this time of painful transition.

One day, while still in middle school, a conversation with her cousin set Weary on a different path. "My cousin told me that they had a Black student union at her school in the South End, and they get all the Black students together, and they have fun. And they have free pizza, and the teacher will pay for you to get pizza. You just gotta get an advisor. And so I was like, 'Oh, *okay!*'"

So Weary started a Black student union in her middle school, and another when she got to high school.

Weary wanted to create a different experience for other Black students at her school than what she had had. She created welcome cards for Black transfer students and asked her school administration to hand them out—they refused, saying that they had no way of knowing which new students were Black because they didn't survey them. She found the new students herself. She started giving out Black hair-care products and giving lessons on hair care. "Cuz a lot of the girls out here were raised by white moms," Weary observes. "For Black women, our hair—it tells our story. It's our pride. And if you don't feel seen or heard at school, the least you can do is come looking fly. So I was like, 'Let's get your hair together.' And I started just trying to help fill those voids."

Weary had worked hard for years to build community in her new home, but when she became pregnant as a young adult, she was shamed by her church and then forced out. She felt like she was once again starting over.

"So I just walked away, had my baby, was in school, and then started working."

Weary wanted to keep helping people, like she had done in middle school and high school.

She decided to enter the nonprofit sector, thinking this would be the best place to be able to help people. "And it was *terrible* for me," she says. "But it wasn't terrible for anyone else that didn't look like me. Like, they're having a great time."

It was very similar to how Weary had felt when she first moved to a white school—she felt hyper-visible on multiple levels. Eyes were always on her and yet refused to fully see her. She was regularly asked to speak on the "Black experience," and her appearance was regularly commented on.

"I changed my hair all the time, still do to this day. My supervisor told me, 'Why do you change your hair? It confuses people. They don't know who they're gonna see day to day.' And I got written up for that!" Weary is still incredulous. She still has the write-up saved as a reminder of that time.

Weary tried to build networks of Black coworkers and industry peers, like she'd had in school, but it couldn't go far enough in countering the toxic work environment she was in.

A lot of these daily microaggressions occurred before diversity, equity, and inclusion (DEI) work became more common in workplaces. But once DEI became a standardized practice, Weary said the situation became even worse for her and other BIPOC employees. There was still no real push for meaningful change in the workplace, but white employees and management now had the vocabulary to *sound* more racially sensitive without having to actually *do* anything. DEI had helped white employees and management gaslight BIPOC employees.

Y'all, when I tell you that I hear this *all the time* from BIPOC in workplaces, I really do mean ALL THE TIME. DEI "efforts" that don't focus on creating real changes to policies and procedures in order to make a measurable difference in the working lives of employees of color can be more harmful than doing nothing at all. They take up time and resources, and retraumatize BIPOC employees, as they have to rehash the harm that has been done to them in their workspaces—only to be told that the painful rehashing they've done is *the* DEI work itself. For those who've never had to battle racism in their day-to-day lives, the uncomfortable act of simply *acknowledging* that racism and hearing about your culpability in it can feel like you've actually done something. And white supremacy will always prioritize its comfort over the safety and well-being of BIPOC, so it's no surprise that DEI efforts are rarely allowed to dive below the surface level.

Eventually it all became too much for Weary and she left her job.

Soon afterward, Weary was trying to figure out her next steps when an ad for a local coffee shop up for sale caught her eye. Weary decided to buy it.

She wasn't sure what she was going to do next, but Weary knew that she was going to have to do some healing in order for her next steps to have a chance of working out.

"I was definitely in therapy, because I knew that I had to heal through my own trauma, so I don't carry that and then put it on others. Because we're human. And when I'm mad, it's going to affect and shift the room, and I know that—2020 forced me to just deal with all that. Even when I didn't have the words, I didn't understand. I was like, 'I have to work through this. I gotta see me.' Because if I don't know who I am, I can't lead other people."

Weary began pulling in young people from the community to take part in the new venture. She wanted the young people to lead this business, in order to make sure it was the type of positive experience that she herself had needed as a youth.

Her first hire was a young Black woman who had just graduated from high school that year. Weary saw leadership potential in her and offered her the opportunity to help build a space that would always work to center young Black voices.

Weary provided resources and support, and together she and the young people she hired figured out how to build a business—in their own way.

"The funny part was that they went on YouTube and they learned everything. And they also went on TikTok. They still go there first," Weary says with a bit of amazement. "They'll, like, *hashtag* something and be like, 'How do we do Canva?' And they'll go there and learn all the news."

Weary learned that when she gave her employees the freedom to forge their own paths, they often found creative solutions to problems and new ways of working. The rigid working hours that Weary thought a business needed went out the window when it became clear that many of the young administrative staff did their best work late at night or wrapped around their school hours. She wanted uniforms, but her frontline employees didn't like them, and Weary discovered that the stress of trying to get young people to remember work uniforms when they already had trouble juggling schoolbooks and sports equipment just wasn't worth the stress.

Weary wanted her employees to feel like they could not only bring their ideas and opinions into the business but also bring their whole selves. "When things are happening in the world, the number one thing I wouldn't want to hear is 'Don't bring politics to work,'" Weary says. "I'm a walking politic. I'm a walking Black person. I can't separate the two, and I cannot ask them to. When things are happening in our community, when things are happening and we're in mourning or we're in joy, we are allowed to be that here. Collectively."

Weary recalls the horrific mass murders in Buffalo, New York, in 2022, when a white supremacist opened fire in a supermarket in a Black neighborhood, murdering ten people, and how it affected her Black staff members. "My staff was just like, 'Those were our elders.' They were mourning." Her staff weren't the only Black youth who needed space to process their grief. "I remember we were in here, and more kids start coming. And we have, like, fifteen teens in here. We were just, like, sad. But it's okay. We can be collectively sad at work."

As Weary has prioritized her healing and mental health, her employees—almost all young Black women—have watched her, and have wanted to do the same for themselves.

"We have free mental health counseling on Tuesdays, Thursdays, and Fridays. Right in our yellow room." Weary gestures to a collection of brightly colored rooms behind the staff break room. "I was taking two sessions a week, and I was always like, 'I'm going to see my therapist.' We made it normal. And my staff were like, 'Well, we want one.' And so we connected with a Black community mental health company that had just started in Shoreline."

Weary quickly realized that some of her employees had different experiences of Blackness and needed different counseling, especially those from the area's sizeable East African immigrant community. "I hired another first-gen immigrant therapist to work with our East African families," Weary tells me. She wanted a therapist who could not only relate to the specific immigrant experiences of some of these young people but could also reassure families who might be reluctant to let their children attend therapy.

Many immigrant parents can be skeptical about therapy and, due to how overwhelmingly white the mental health field is in the US, can also have pretty well-founded fears that the person working with their child may cause harm due to their lack of understanding of the culture that child's family comes from. The therapist Weary hired met with the parents of the youth who wanted therapy, to explain how the therapy would work, and set their minds at ease, so they would feel comfortable with their children attending. Weary says that now many of the parents drive their children to the sessions and sit in the coffee shop and have coffee while the youth meet with the therapist.

Weary is very clear that the investments she's making in her employees are for their futures, not for the future of her business. She wants them to use their experiences at Black Coffee to help them find their paths in life. She's regularly trying to find opportunities for them to expand their skill sets.

"We also built the podcast studio," Weary tells me, pointing at yet another room. "And so we have a podcast that comes out every other Tuesday: *Grounded Conversations*. It's a storytelling platform.

It's a platform for our young girls. They went to Atlanta to learn how to podcast."

Weary sent them to Atlanta because she wanted them to be able to learn from a professional, and she wanted that professional to be another Black woman.

"She's amazing. Taught them the ins and outs of the business. And so now they have their own podcast," Weary says with pride. "They edit it. They invite guests in. It's on all platforms. It's getting downloads. I'm really excited for them, cuz now they're trying to monetize it. Like, 'That's straight-up income for you. Go do that!'"

Weary has built an impressive and growing list of opportunities and spaces for her employees and community members. She tells me about the Sisters Circle they host, which gives high school and college-age Black women and girls a chance to talk with one another in a safe space. The last circle session they had, she tells me, was about setting intentions for the new year while letting go of the past.

They have a music room with instruments for kids to play, and they are planning on offering music lessons.

They have an after-school program every weekday from 3 to 6 p.m. "Although we're closed, we let people just come in and study. And so they'll just be out in the lobby studying away cuz they feel safe, and they feel seen. And no one's gonna look at you weird. No one's gonna make you buy anything. And you can be loud," Weary says with a laugh. The after-school program draws the most diverse crowd. "We know that our young white kids are also tired of their parents' bullshit!" Weary laughs. "They're tired of the system as well. And so they're like, 'This is the only place where I can just come and be.'"

The coffee shop hosts a local step team, too. This team is Weary's baby. She has coached step teams for twenty years and considers step to be her creative outlet. But for the coffee shop, they brought in outside coaches, which has been an adjustment for Weary. "When I'm here, I know my space. It's for them. It's not for me—although I always interrupt," Weary says with another laugh. "I try to join in."

It's not just youth that Weary hopes to help at Black Coffee. Every

Saturday the coffee shop hosts a Black marketplace where small Black-owned businesses and artisans can come sell their wares. "I do a lot of mentoring," Weary says. "I'm helping people sell their brand or, you know . . . I want you to be successful when you come here."

Finally, Weary also runs a social-justice-centered internship program, focused on helping youth navigate social and political systems. "We talk about health. We talk about all areas of justice. We have an attorney come in, we have a doctor come in, we have educators come in, and we have people from the technology world come in."

These are some of the many ways in which Black Coffee is working every day to invest in local community and in Black youth. And yet it's not what people pay attention to when it comes to Black Coffee—and it's certainly not what is covered in local media.

"The news comes here when something bad happens," Weary laments. "We're always saying, like, 'Hey, we had a fall festival last weekend. With, like, a hundred Black and brown teenagers in this space having a great time. We would love to tell that story.' Cuz it was planned by them. The kids planned it—students planned it. I gave them a budget. They were proud. People came. Every time we put out PR, no one pays attention. But when the windows get broken, they [the news media] meet us here. I don't even know how they know."

As Weary struggles to tell the full story of Black Coffee Northwest and what it's doing in the community, she also struggles to get people to understand why it's worth it to invest in the kids she's investing in. "People are like, 'We can't hire now. It's so hard to manage these youngsters—they don't want to work,'" Weary says with a shake of the head. "But have you thought about giving them what they *need*?

"I never had that," Weary reflects. "No one was ever like, 'These are the skills you need to get to the next level.' And 'These are the things you need to change,' and 'Do this better to get to the next level.' And so that's what I've done with this group, and no better group to do it with than young leaders. Because they're now going to be in positions of power one day. They're not going to be young forever. And we're training up a group of young Black women, and there's eight on my leadership team.

"And we have the white girl," Weary adds with a laugh. "She calls herself the cream."

---

## BE A REVOLUTION

In early 2020, many in the Seattle BIPOC community were eagerly awaiting the opening of two new restaurants.

One was Musang, a Filipino restaurant by chef Melissa Miranda, long known in the city's South End for her connections to community and her amazing pop-ups. For years people had been hoping she would open a brick-and-mortar restaurant so diners could indulge in her delicious cuisine more frequently.

And Kristi Brown, longtime owner of the beloved catering company That Brown Girl Cooks!, had announced that she would be opening her first restaurant, Communion, later that year. If you were a part of the Black community in Seattle for any notable length of time, chances are you were served some of her delicious catering at a community event. Often working the tables were other community members, locals who knew they could count on Kristi for a fair day's wage when they were in need of funds.

Then, shortly after Musang opened its doors and before Communion had a chance to hold their big opening, the COVID-19 pandemic hit.

The pandemic was quickly catastrophic for many workers and industries, and in the beginning, restaurants and bars were especially hard-hit. Local spots that had been in business for decades folded, as they couldn't continue to pay high Seattle rents without customers. Others opted for early retirement.

A restaurant is one of the riskier small-business ventures to begin.

A large percentage of new restaurants don't survive past their first few years. Musang and Communion found themselves closed before they could get off the ground. My partner and I, so excited to watch our friends and community members make their longtime dreams a reality, were devastated for what seemed at first to be an early end to those dreams.

Melissa Miranda was the first to turn her restaurant into a community kitchen. She started taking food that was supposed to go to a dining room full of paying customers and turned it into free meals for other community members hard-hit by the pandemic.

Soon Miranda was joined by Kristi Brown and That Brown Girl Cooks!, Feed The People Community Kitchen, Expat Supper Club, and Guerilla Pizza Kitchen.

The chefs of these enterprises had worked together in the past to serve community members in need, and they came together once again to pool their resources and feed their city. They posted menus for the week and what locations and hours they would be serving food on what days.

After a day of working on our own COVID-relief community project, the Seattle Artist Relief Fund, my partner and I stopped by to visit Tarik Abdullah, owner and head chef at Feed The People, as he was serving meals to the community nearby. The small crew was handing meals to people through the open front door, but when he saw Gabriel and me, Abdullah waved us in.

"How many plates can I get you?" he asked with a grin. We offered to pay for them, not wanting to take resources from people in need, but Abdullah explained that everybody eats there, and that he didn't have a register to take our money even if he wanted to. So he made up two plates while my partner quietly sent money to the online fundraiser to support the community kitchen.

We asked Abdullah how the kitchen was doing. It was great, he answered. So busy. The first week alone they had served over five hundred meals, and it didn't seem to have slowed down at all, now a few months later.

As we caught up with Abdullah, he frequently walked over to the door to hand out meals to neighbors. Mid-sentence, he paused to run out the door and flag down a car that was waiting at the stop sign outside of the kitchen.

"Hey! You're gonna want to get a plate today," Abdullah told the woman excitedly. He listed items on the menu that he thought she'd like and took down an order for five plates for her and her family.

Through the dark early months of the pandemic, this small group of chefs and their staff members kept their community fed. Food cooked with the love of communities they had long been a part of. When Musang reopened and Communion finally had their grand opening, the community remembered all that they had done—and also how phenomenal that food had been—and showed up in droves to support their businesses. They are still, as I write this, some of the most sought-after reservations in the city and two of the most critically celebrated new restaurants in the country.

"I'm trying to be like Kristi!" DarNesha Weary tells me. "It gives me hope. It's what I aspire to be."

Weary looks up to Kristi Brown, whom she knew from back when they used to go to the same church. "I saw her back in the day. Catering the church events, being out there in the community."

It is this sort of community-minded success that Weary aspires to and is building with other new BIPOC-owned small businesses in the area. She talks at length about how much they have relied upon one another, especially during the pandemic. "I love that we work with so many other Black businesses, Black and brown businesses. Businesses that just get it. And we can just share with each other, and be up-front and honest, and share resources and information."

Sometimes they share everyday info, like how to manage a glitchy point-of-sale system. Other days they're literally sharing supplies—especially when international supply chain issues were exacerbated by the pandemic.

"When there was a cup shortage, I was able to go get cups," Weary remembers. "We went to Zuri's [Zuri's Gourmet Donutz] because

Davis had cups, and we gave him lids—or 'We got extra blah, blah, blah, blah, blah . . . Come by and get it.' 'We got extra milk. Come grab it.' And I was like, 'I saw all you guys's syrups on sale,' so I bought all of them."

Weary feels a strong kinship with other BIPOC-owned shops, never competition. "I feel safe. I feel good. I'm not competing with nobody. I want The Station [a Black- and Latina-owned coffee shop in the city's Beacon Hill neighborhood] to win. I want Boon Boona to win," she tells me.

These small businesses are caring for their community and one another, and showing us new ways to define business success.

If you aren't planning on starting your own business or your own union, there are still ways every day that you can have an impact on the lives of workers and business owners of color. In fact, as consumers, we have more power to make and support change than just about anywhere else in our lives. Here are some actions to start with:

- **Support unions.** Yes, we have established that unions can be just as racist as the rest of society, but they still are one of our best options for protecting workers that we have today. So support unions, especially unions with high BIPOC membership.

- **Watch out for anti-union legislation and union-busting tactics.** Right-to-work laws and other anti-union legislation seriously undercut unions' abilities to be effective or even financially viable. When that happens, workers become disenchanted with their unions and membership declines even further. This has been a major contributor to decreasing union membership numbers across the country in recent years. In addition, it's important to speak out against union-busting tactics by businesses and try to boycott any businesses that aim to stop their workers from unionizing or that punish workers who do unionize. Pay attention to how union efforts are portrayed in media, and call out any outlets trying to convince people that workers exercising their rights to collective bargaining and collective action are the bad guys. Union wins can change entire industries by setting new standards for compensation, benefits, and employee health and safety. Their efforts can help *all* workers.

➤ **Pay attention to union calls to action.** Follow union and organizing pages on social media and try to support any public asks that a union makes. A unionizing business may request social media shares, may call for a one-day boycott, may ask for donations to support striking workers. Public support for union actions makes it far more likely that workers' demands of their employers will be met.

➤ **Ask your union to do more for racial equity.** If you're in a union, find out how your union has or has not made racial equity a priority in its goals and demands. If your union isn't doing enough to address racial equity, let its leaders know that you consider this an issue that you expect them to prioritize, no matter what your race or ethnicity is.

➤ **Support BIPOC union members.** As we've already established that unions are not exempt from racism, it's important to listen to and support your fellow BIPOC union members when they say they're facing discrimination or bias. Be as public with your support as the person facing the issue wishes you to be. Don't just tell your fellow union member that you support them; show that you do.

➤ **Support BIPOC union cohorts and affinity groups.** As Tevita Uhatafe has shown, you don't have to be a member of a particular demographic in order to advocate for BIPOC union groups. Listen to them, learn from them, and support them in whatever ways you can.

➤ **Support small businesses of color.** If you really want to know that your money is going directly into the hands of workers and smaller entrepreneurs and creators of color, and helping to close racial wealth gaps, support your local small businesses of color. This will not only more directly help people of color than any campaign a large white-run business could ever come up with; it will also strengthen your own community.

➤ **Try not to support businesses that make money from the oppression or exploitation of populations of color.** Look, I know that if we tried to make sure every business we spent money at was ethically operated and didn't cause harm, we'd quickly be exhausted, and we'd be left with very few viable options. I think many of us would love to always make the perfect ethical spending choice, but often that choice doesn't exist. Most of us have very definite budget constraints, time constraints, and more that will dictate a lot of our spending choices. But when we can take a little time to become more aware, and make a better spending choice when available, we should. Try to prioritize avoiding businesses that exploit workers of color, are causing environmental harm where populations of color live, or make money from prison contracts or prison labor.

➤ **Support BIPOC business dreams.** BIPOCs who want to start their own small businesses often find it harder to get funding for those businesses. They are typically less likely to have family funds or large savings to dip into, and less likely to be financed by banks or financed to the same degree as white business owners. So when you see a fundraising campaign for a local BIPOC-owned business, give a few dollars if you can. In addition, push for and support government programs that fund new businesses and affordable rents in underrepresented communities. Then, when these new businesses open, you'll have a particular sense of pride or connection when you visit them.

Every day we wake up and begin making decisions, big and small, that interact with the systems that run our world. We can go through a lot of our days completely unaware of how these systems affect our communities. Or we can take a little time and see the multitude of opportunities we have every day to make real change right where we live. How we spend our money and how we make our money matters, whether or not we choose to take advantage of these opportunities. Some of these solutions will require us to get together and vote differently or support a strike or boycott a business. Others will be as simple as walking into a local BIPOC-owned coffee shop and ordering a tall latte. But every time we make a choice that supports the ability for people of color to work in safe environments at a living wage, free from exploitation, our communities become stronger and we all benefit.

## RACE, THE ENVIRONMENT, AND ENVIRONMENTAL JUSTICE

ATLANTA IS KNOWN FOR many things, among them its history in the Civil Rights Movement, its peaches, and its status as the birthplace of Coca-Cola. And if you've been to Atlanta, one thing you will likely remember is its forests.

The hundreds of acres of lush forest that surround the city center are known as "The Lungs of Atlanta." Yet one of its main areas, the South River Forest, has been facing environmental disaster for years.

The residential neighborhoods around DeKalb County, where South River Forest is located, are predominantly Black. It's an area long neglected by state government, with some of the nation's highest rates of poverty (Desai 2023).

Even though high amounts of sewage have been polluting South River for years, leading to it being called one of the US' "most endangered rivers" in 2021, it has not been prioritized for cleanup (Kiernan 2021).

Still, even with the pollution and neglect, these forests are essential to the well-being of the majority Black residents who live around them, as the trees clean the air and reduce urban temperatures in the rapidly expanding city.

In the summer of 2021, the people of DeKalb County were speaking up in defense of their forest, as the Atlanta City Council was considering an ordinance to move forward with the building of a ninety-million-dollar police training facility in the middle of South River Forest. Residents, abolitionists, and environmental activists came together in opposition to the proposed facility, which would drastically alter their forest.

At the city council meeting to vote on the ordinance, more than 1,100 Atlanta residents submitted recorded comments, 70 percent of them urging the council to vote against the facility, often referred to as Cop City (Herskind 2022).

The plans for Cop City will make it the largest police training facility in the United States, razing 85 acres of the vital forest. It will contain a mock city, where police can train in tactical assaults on urban neighborhoods, along with shooting ranges and other training spaces. It will bring an increased presence of heavily militarized police to a majority Black area that is already one of the most over-policed in the country.

Cop City will have a direct impact on the safety of Black residents throughout the Atlanta area, and it will be placed right in the backyard of those who will be harmed by it the most. It also will directly threaten the health of nearby residents with possible further contamination of the water, and threaten the environment of the region with the destruction of forest canopy.

Despite overwhelming opposition by Atlanta residents, the Atlanta City Council voted to approve the ordinance to build Cop City 10-4.

Since then, a loose coalition of activists known as forest defenders have been camping in South River Forest to try to stop the construction. Yet despite the risk to the local Black population, despite the risk to the environment, and despite the overwhelming opposition to the project, those fighting the building of Cop City struggled to get much nationwide attention.

Journalist David Peisner, who visited the forest defenders, was drawn to one defender in particular. Their name was Manuel Terán, but they were known to the other forest defenders as Tortuguita, which means "little turtle" in Spanish.

Peisner was drawn to Tortuguita because "they were great company: curious, engaging, earnest, educated, self-aware, well-read, and very funny. They loved to talk, to connect, to debate, and did so joyfully and passionately, without malice" (Peisner 2023).

Tortuguita loved the forest and had been defending it for months at the time Peisner talked with them. They spoke often about the peacefulness of their mission, and how vital that peacefulness was. "The right kind of resistance is peaceful, because that's where we win," Tortuguita told their interviewer. "We're not going to beat them at violence. They're very, very good at violence. We're not. We win through nonviolence. That's really the only way we can win" (Peisner 2023).

On January 18, 2023, Georgia State Troopers shot and killed Tortuguita during a morning raid of the forest defender encampments.

Law enforcement claims that Tortuguita opened fire on the officers unprovoked, shooting a state trooper in the abdomen. They have not yet—months later as I write this—released further evidence supporting that claim.

The Atlanta Police Department, who was also on the scene, released their body-cam footage of the morning's deadly events. The shooting can be heard, but it's not caught on camera. What is caught on camera is an Atlanta PD officer insinuating that the state trooper may have been shot by one of their own fellow officers.

"Man . . . you fucked your own officer up?" he asks.

He then walks up to two other officers and asks, "They shoot their own man?"

This alone is not nearly enough to have a clear picture of what happened that morning. And little more has been made public by authorities.

What we do know is that Tortuguita, only twenty-six years old and referred to by those who knew them as kind and gentle, was shot at least thirteen times by officers. And we know that since the killing of Tortuguita, officers have ramped up their raids of the forest defender encampments, calling the forest defenders terrorists, and often charging them as such.

Cop City is a prime example of how environmental injustice, racism, capitalism, and colonialism often go hand in hand. As Atlanta has been increasingly expanding, known more and more as a city of industry and wealth, it has been pushing its poor Black residents farther and farther out of the city. The wealthy white minority and white-owned businesses have been demanding "law and order" in Atlanta, long a code phrase for control of the Black population that they have been taught to fear and that stands in the way of their lily-white vision for a prosperous future.

Whatever collateral environmental damage from efforts to expand wealth for elites and control and marginalize the Black population will be concentrated on areas into which the Black population has been pushed.

Those who seek to defend their communities and the land that nurtures them are labeled terrorists. This is a continuation of the colonial project that forced the Muscogee people off the same land hundreds of years ago.

What happened in South River Forest is not an anomaly. So much of what we call "progress" in this country has been built off the destruction of the environment and BIPOC communities.

Environmental issues are racial justice issues. BIPOC communities are often the first affected, and almost always the worst affected, by environmental injustice—and that's by design. If we all shared an equal burden for our ravages to the environment, people might be compelled to do something about them.

Further, environmental injustice is often perpetrated by the same powers behind racial and economic injustice, and these injustices often serve to compound and defend one another.

And yet this is not typically how our environmental crisis has been discussed in society. It's a story dominated by white voices, focusing on the harm that will eventually come to white communities, not the harm that has already been wreaking havoc on communities of color for centuries.

## JILL MANGALIMAN

I never really considered myself an environmentalist growing up," Jill Mangaliman tells me. "And even in my adulthood, until I started to really get involved with Got Green. Then the definition of what it meant to be an environmentalist became broader to me. Before it was like, 'Oh, environmentalists are people who, you know, are vegan or who drive a nice car and have solar panels.' But for Got Green, the community is saving the planet in our own way."

Mangaliman is an environmental justice and racial justice movement worker and the former executive director of Got Green.

Their journey toward activism started before they were born, when their parents fled the Philippines in the 1970s, seeking to escape the repression, violence, and poverty of the Marcos regime. The family landed in Seattle, a place that Mangaliman's father had visited once as a child. He had always imagined that it would be a nice place to raise a family, and he also longed for cooler weather.

"It's an interesting thing to be a Filipino American in the Northwest, which is a very white area of the country," Mangaliman reflects. They didn't fit in at school, being one of the few students of color in the private Catholic school Mangaliman's parents had enrolled them in.

Mangaliman was further ostracized due to the fact that they had to work at the school as well, in order to help cover the cost of tuition. Mangaliman remembers the embarrassment of feeling their white classmates watch them work.

Their parents didn't find Seattle as welcoming as they had hoped either. This cold reception, combined with their trauma from the violence and instability they had experienced in the Philippines, led them to distrust their neighbors. Mangaliman's parents isolated themselves and their family in order to protect themselves. They didn't socialize with neighbors and didn't have many local friends. "They were just scared of being in a country that didn't seem to want them there," Mangaliman explains.

As Mangaliman talks with me about their childhood isolation, it stands in stark contrast to the open way they're talking with me and the welcoming smile on their face. Connection seems easy for them.

But as a child, the isolation they experienced led to depression.

"I wasn't sure if there was a future in store for me," Mangaliman remembers. "Cuz it was just like: *Okay, just get a job. Just work for the rest of your life and try to get by.*"

After a few years of feeling adrift and depressed as a young adult, Mangaliman decided they had nothing left to lose. They left their dead-end job and joined a political action organization working in support of universal healthcare.

Mangaliman's mother had struggled with health issues throughout Mangaliman's childhood, so the issue was very close to their heart. But they admit with a smile that one of the main attractions to the job was that it gave them opportunities to talk with people and break free from their isolation.

Mangaliman's work quickly expanded to "Get out the vote" work, which connected them to immigrants' rights work and helped them see how immigrant communities were made particularly vulnerable to social issues, and how immigrants were being targeted by ICE and police forces.

"For me that was like, *Oh dang, I'm getting an education here!*" Mangaliman says with a laugh. "This was not the kind of education I got in schools."

While working on these healthcare access and immigrants' rights issues, Mangaliman met longtime Seattle organizer Michael Woo. He took a special interest in their work.

After the 2008 elections, the majority of canvassers were laid off, Mangaliman included. They were trying to figure out their next steps when Michael Woo called. "He said, 'I have a project. I'm asking young people of color to help me talk to people about the green economy.' And I'm like, 'What is that? I have no idea what you're talking about. But yeah, sure. I'll come along.'" Mangaliman laughs.

That project was a door-knocking campaign in South Seattle. They were to knock on doors, share information about energy efficient practices that people use in their homes to save on energy bills, and ask if they wanted further information on climate change.

For Mangaliman, who had grown up in the majority white neighborhood of West Seattle, this experience in much more diverse South Seattle revolutionized their relationship with the city.

"I was like, *Wow, there's actually a lot of brown people here in Seattle that I didn't know about.*"

That project became a part of Got Green, which Woo founded that same summer. Got Green is an organization that aims to activate young BIPOC to educate their communities around climate change and the green economy as well as to advocate for environmental protections and opportunities for their communities.

In Got Green, Mangaliman was supported by a community of elders of color, who had decided to invest their time and expertise in the young people working there.

"I would say I grew in leadership. I had elders who supported me," Mangaliman says as they remember leaders like Michael Woo and Kristyn Joy, who invested so much in them. "All these folks who were just supporting the young folks, saying, 'This is your generation. This is your time. We did a lot of work in the '70s and '80s.' And the way that Michael framed it is like, he founded Got Green as a gift to young people of color to take on."

Over the years, Got Green grew and found its particular niche of environmental justice and economic justice work. Work that focused on how environmental issues affected communities of color, and sought out community centered solutions.

In 2013, Michael Woo decided it was time to retire, and he told Mangaliman that he wanted them to take over as executive director.

"I was like, 'No. No thank you.'" Mangaliman laughs. They wanted to keep up their on-the-ground organizing work and didn't want to be in the spotlight. But the board was confident that Mangaliman was the right person for the job. "I finally gave in and I was like, 'Okay, I'll do it.' . . . It was very daunting to go from someone who didn't really see themselves as having a future to [having] all these people rooting for me."

Under Mangaliman's leadership, Got Green continued to grow. It now works in three main areas: food access, climate justice, and leadership development.

The food access program focuses on closing food security gaps in Seattle. One of its biggest achievements was organizing working-class women of color to fight for greater access to fresh fruits and vegetables. The program they were able to win for the city, called Fresh Bucks, provides a spending card for low-income people to use to purchase fresh fruits and vegetables at farmers' markets, independent grocers, and supermarkets. The program has since been instituted statewide.

When the City of Seattle sought to pass a sugary beverage tax, Got Green fought to ensure that the revenue from that tax would be invested in closing the food gap in Black and brown communities.

Their Young Leaders committee helps young people learn how to organize for climate, racial, and economic justice. In 2016, members of the Young Leaders successfully pushed for and won a resolution with the City of Seattle to create living-wage green-job internships for young people of color, improving access for communities of color to the green economy.

Got Green's Climate Justice program co-authored *Our People, Our Planet, Our Power*, a report outlining a pathway to climate resistance. They have also been organizing against the displacement of communities of color by land developers.

While Got Green is a local organization, they recognize that environmental justice is an issue that connects many communities of color in struggle. "It's totally a racial issue," Mangaliman says. "If you think about the places where extraction of resources happens, it's in our brown folks' and Indigenous folks' communities. Extraction and digging and dumping and burning. The stuff that people don't tend to see. For example, where do minerals come from, where do the resources come from? They're from the land[s] of Indigenous folks."

Mangaliman adds, "Even here in Washington State, places where they've done uranium mining, it's right by Native reservations in Yakima. The Hanford nuclear site is in that area as well. Think about the placement of airports and highways: it's basically where migrant, poor communities are. If you think about old maps, redlining—the red can also symbolize the most toxic places in the city."

Larger environmental organizations often fail to fully consider these racial justice intersections and the needs of the communities most affected by and most vulnerable to environmental issues. "I think the struggles with the big greens, the big environmental groups, is they think they already have the answer," Mangaliman says. "So they come into our communities like, 'Hey, here's our campaign. Sign on and take our solutions.' And really, that doesn't work. You can't just impose solutions on folks."

As an example, Mangaliman points to a tree-planting program in Seattle a few years back. "It was well-intentioned. They went around and dropped off trees in Chinatown—the International District.

Didn't give explanation. There was a pamphlet in English. They left the trees in front of people's houses. People had no idea. They were like, 'Why the hell is this tree here?'" Mangaliman laughs. "Some even threw them away or uprooted them. It's all well-intentioned, knowing that there's a lot of pollution in the ID, but without properly involving and engaging the community, it just didn't work. In fact, it wasted a lot of people's time. And it wasted a lot of trees."

Real environmental solutions have to work with communities most affected and mitigate any potential negative impacts on already vulnerable communities, especially when those changes might negatively affect existing jobs or ways of life for communities of color.

Mangaliman discusses the concept of "just transition" that came from efforts of atomic workers and Indigenous communities to try, together, to move away from environmental harm while also protecting vulnerable workers. Mangaliman says that people seeking to transition industries away from environmentally harmful practices have to ask some important questions. "How do we be intentional and move away from fossil fuels without creating more injustices or further marginalizing our people? The transition is inevitable. Change needs to happen. But how do we ensure it's just? You can't do that without really engaging the people most impacted."

Over the years, Mangaliman became more and more involved in environmental justice battles being fought by Indigenous people in the Philippines. While working to support Indigenous land protectors there, Mangaliman was also supporting their Got Green teammates who had traveled to stand alongside Indigenous land protectors at Standing Rock. This helped underscore for Mangaliman how connected the global fight for environmental justice is.

"My view around environmental justice really broadened during that time," Mangaliman remembers. "It's not just about the climate or the temperature or how many trees we plant or carbon net-zero or something. It's about the health of our people, the health of their community and the land. . . . Time and time again I learn from Indigenous folks how sacred [land] is, that we have to protect it. There's a saying among peasant farmers: 'Land is life.' Without the land, people will die. And then if people aren't there to protect the land, the land will also be destroyed."

After seven years as executive director, Mangaliman made the difficult decision to leave Got Green in 2021. The COVID pandemic had been hard on everyone. But for many BIPOC, the pandemic not only disproportionately affected our communities but also compounded many of the other traumas and hardships caused by systemic oppression. For movement workers, these unprecedented crises in the communities they serve placed an untenable amount of work on their shoulders as well. And sadly, the rest and care that movement workers need in order to make their work sustainable became even more difficult to prioritize. Mangaliman was certainly affected in this way. But they also had the additional heartbreak of losing their mother in 2020, only a few years after they had lost their father. Deep in grief, they needed to step away from the high demands of organizational leadership.

"I needed time to heal and regroup," Mangaliman says. "I still have fight in me. I'm still organizing via BAYAN-USA, which is a Filipino national democratic organization. I'm still involved with Front and Centered, the statewide climate justice coalition. I'm just not doing the day-to-day leading of an organization. I don't know how people do it for so many years."

Having transitioned into a different phase of their movement work, Mangaliman is grateful for the years they spent at Got Green and how this work has helped them build relationships with such a beautiful activist community.

"For anyone who has interest in doing change work, whether it's changing systems, environmental justice, food justice, land defense—all of these things," Mangaliman says, "know that you can't do it alone. Organize with other people. Lean on other people. Work with other groups. That's how we'll win."

## Race, Environment, and Environmental Apartheid

My partner and I go to Palm Springs for vacations at least once a year. It started with our first anniversary. We had only a few days to get away, but it was December and we really wanted some sunshine. We decided on that desert oasis: a quick flight, chill vibes, a warm climate, private pools, all at fairly reasonable prices. From then on we were hooked, going to the California desert for a few days in the fall and winter months in order to escape the cold, wet darkness of Seattle. It's not the *perfect* place for us. It's very white, and most people there are a few decades older than us, but the advantages for a quick trip have far outweighed the disadvantages. We need the vitamin D and love a nice pool. And the quiet, more elderly population lends a sleepy, relaxed vibe to the area. I also absolutely love midcentury modern design and architecture, which Palm Springs has an abundance of.

During recent trips, my partner and I have taken to driving farther and farther out of the city to explore. You don't have to go far to find yourself in a vastly different environment.

About thirty minutes outside of Palm Springs is the city of Thermal. In Thermal you won't find wide boulevards where middle-aged white people comfortably stroll from air-conditioned shop to air-conditioned shop. You won't find private pools next to beautifully restored midcentury homes. What you will find are trailer parks, some home to over a thousand people. These are the homes of Palm Springs' Latine workers and their families. They are the people who keep Palm Springs' hotels clean, who pick the fruits and vegetables that end up on fancy restaurant china.

What you will also find is heat. Unbearable, oppressive heat.

Temperatures in Thermal are 6 to 7 degrees hotter on average than they are in Palm Springs. That may not sound like a lot, but there is a pretty big difference between 95 and 101°F, and Thermal already has 139 days a year when the weather is over 95°F. Many are far higher than that (Weil and Pons 2021). The mobile homes that people in Thermal live in tend to lack proper insulation or air-conditioning. Typically they aren't hooked up to municipal water systems. And landlords often refuse to pay for upkeep of the crumbling homes.

It's not by chance that Thermal's 99 percent Latine population is living in these conditions. Agricultural and hospitality workers—especially undocumented workers—aren't paid enough to live in wealthier and more hospitable areas like Palm Springs. And the high percentages of undocumented residents in Thermal seems to make issues like the poisonous arsenic increasingly leaching into water sources less of a priority for the California government than it might be elsewhere.

The differences between Palm Springs and its neighbor Thermal are not anomalies. Across the United States, people of color and poor people are more likely to live in areas that are hotter than where wealthier whites live. As the alarm continues to be raised over the future impacts of global warming, it's evident that the nightmare has been here for poor people of color for decades already.

On the other side of the country, in places like Florida's Pahokee, Belle Glade, and South Bay, residents in these lower-income Black and Hispanic communities are struggling to breathe. Sugar companies in the area burn the cane fields almost daily in spring and winter, a cheap way to prepare the cane for harvest. These daily eruptions of smoke filled with harmful particulates are visible in the air and coat the grass of nearby homes. Residents in these towns complain of asthma, breathing issues, and coughing when the burns are happening.

The United States is the fourth largest sugar producer in the world. Of the top five countries producing sugar, only the US and China haven't taken steps to end the practice of burning cane.

When residents in whiter and wealthier communities east of the sugarcane fields complained of the smoke from the burning, sugar growers were prohibited from burning when the wind blows in the direction of those areas (Ramadan, Ngu, and Miller 2021). No restrictions were put in place for when the wind blows west, toward communities of color.

Environmental racism plays out in many ways across the United States. It could be the highways that cut through Black neighborhoods, bringing asthma and groundwater pollution, and killing local economies. It could be the nuclear plants built near Native reservations. No matter how it shows up, it will pretty much always involve money. Corporations and governments that don't want to pay workers a living wage often don't want to pay for responsible environmental practices either. They end up cutting corners on the backs of populations that the public is less likely to care about, and populations already overwhelmed with other daily impacts of systemic racism.

When I was younger, I thought white people became environmental activists because they had the privilege to care about issues "to come" and they could ignore the issues that already exist for communities of color. Now I understand it differently. Communities of color are fighting environmental injustice every day, because it's racism. It has the same root capitalist causes, and it has the same violent, devastating impacts. They can't be separated. If you think "environmentalism" is your issue and somehow racism isn't, you need to ask yourself if the future you're trying to save has people of color in it at all.

## CÉLINE SEMAAN

When you look at environmentalism, it's very white. It's very Nordic. It's very purist. It's very perfectionist. And it's a lot about doom and gloom, about what we have already done to the planet, and 'We humans collectively killed the planet.' When that statement in and of itself is false. It's a false narrative," Céline Semaan tells me. "Doom-and-gloom philosophies lead to apathy, lead to policy change that is impacting the Global South with sanctions that end up hurting the Global South."

Semaan is the founder of Slow Factory, an environmental and social justice organization based in New York. Her journey to Slow Factory started in Lebanon, where she was born. Semaan fled war-torn Lebanon with her family to Montreal, Canada, when she was a small child. They lived in Montreal until Semaan was thirteen, when the family moved back to Lebanon after the civil war.

Taken from Montreal, where she had lived since she was small, to postwar Lebanon was a shock. "The last cease-fire had just occurred," Semaan remembers. "There were no roads. It was apocalyptic. It was a shocker for me but so instrumental in who I am today. I'm so grateful, so grateful they took me from the Global North. Even though in the first year I was like, *Oh my god! What am I doing here? This is apocalyptic!*"

It was in Lebanon that Semaan started to learn from her teachers, her grandparents, and her lived experiences about the global harm of colonialism. She was able to see the lasting impacts of colonialism on Lebanon and on her family.

"One of the things that kept coming back to me was—and I've heard it a million times—the colonizers are afraid of two things: love and ideas. They suppress love, and they suppress ideas. Because if they can control those two, they got you. They got your people. They got the future of your people."

When Semaan returned to North America as an adult, she took those lessons with her as she began her activism work. If colonizers were afraid of ideas, she was going to make sure that people had access to as much information and new ideas as possible.

After years of working as a user-experience designer in tech, Semaan moved into more direct activism work. She became heavily involved in digital literacy in support of resistance movements—work that combined her tech experience with her belief in open access to information. In the lead-up to the Arab Spring, she helped to secure internet access in countries like Lebanon. The internet was a vital tool in the Arab Spring, allowing resistance workers to communicate with one another and with the rest of the world. The internet was also vital for recruitment to the cause, and as a check on state power, with its ability to make state abuses visible to the world.

"Every revolution has begun because there was access to information," Semaan says. "Access to digital literacy is also access to information. Sharing information, sharing resources. Organizing, communicating. All of these things allowed for that to accelerate once the internet was connected. So that was my work before I entered the climate space. But in that work, there was always a climate awareness to what we were doing."

Issues around access to natural resources, especially clean water, access to energy, and the effects of pollution were exacerbated by conflict and in turn exacerbated conflict. Semaan was able to see more clearly how colonialism, climate injustice, and conflict were intertwined.

After the Arab Spring, Semaan wanted to combine her digital literacy and information access work with climate justice. "Everything is connected. Our lives, human rights, climate justice. I started writing down the thesis of it, that climate justice and human rights are one issue."

Semaan began her climate work with outer space. NASA had added images of Earth to Creative Commons, a nonprofit organization that hosts a vast amount of publicly accessible content in a digital library. "I was looking at these images that showed changes on the planet," Semaan says. "There was a slider where you could look at 2000 and scroll to 2012 and see the changes on the planet. Like, drought, deforestation, the impact of light pollution in cities where we can't even see the stars. The rivers turning red and blue across different areas on the planet that are producing garments for the world."

Using NASA's data, Semaan started charting the flow of resources around the world, mapping the modern-day production and distribution routes of goods that are considered "daily necessities" in the Global North, like sugar, cotton, chocolate, coffee, and leather. Then she superimposed it over the environmental changes. The flow of raw materials followed routes set up hundreds of years earlier with violent colonization. The comparison showed not only that colonialism was still alive and well but also that it was still leaving vast environmental destruction in its wake.

"Colonialism is not a thing of the past; it's an economic reality," Semaan says. "And colonialism is tied to climate change."

From this project, Slow Factory was born.

Slow Factory operates from a core belief that climate injustice and the climate crisis are colonial projects. That the violent extraction of resources from the Global South and Indigenous communities to fuel the capitalist needs of the Global North is a primary driver of racial, economic, and environmental injustice.

"The ten richest countries in the world are actually the most responsible for carbon emissions," Semaan observes, "causing climate disaster in the Global South. Communities that are frontline communities are oftentimes Black, brown, Indigenous communities of the Global South, that are faced with this climate disaster that is being caused by Global North countries."

These connections are invisible to a lot of people affected by these issues, because information on how these systems operate is often denied to the general public.

When we voice concern about the climate crisis, we're often given simple, individualistic tasks to make us feel like we're making a difference—reusable straws, anyone?—while the main perpetrators of climate injustice continue to operate freely.

Slow Factory hopes to combat climate injustice by making information about it widely accessible.

This work is done through multiple programs, like their Landfills as Museums tours, which take design students to landfills to make them more aware of the life cycles of the products they are designing, and to help them understand the importance of designing products that have more environmentally responsible life cycles.

Deep Ecology is their global coalition-building initiative that seeks to unite communities of color and Indigenous communities in decolonial climate justice work. This program began in Oahu, where Slow Factory was invited to join water protectors at Red Hill Bulk Fuel Storage Facility in their fight against the water pollution caused by the US Navy.

Slow Factory is well known for their Open Edu, which is their climate education program. Open Edu classes focus on three main areas of study: human rights, collective liberation, and climate justice.

Semaan and her team strive to make these courses as intersectional and inclusive as possible. They're free to attend and available online, plus they're captioned.

The majority of classes are taught by BIPOC instructors. Some examples of past courses include: Challenging Anti-Blackness for Collective Liberation, taught by maya finoh; Equity-Centered Community Design, by Antionette Carroll; and Fashion and Prison Labor, by Teju Adisa-Farrar.

Thousands of people have attended Open Edu classes online or have watched the archived videos of them.

These are just a few of Slow Factory's programs, and now, in their eleventh year, they're aiming to do even more with the Slow Factory

Institute, an in-person climate school and lab in New York, currently in the advanced planning stages.

Semaan wants to empower people to be able to effectively tackle environmental justice issues within industries and help design solutions that center those most affected.

"When you look at the supply chain of any material, oftentimes at the very end of this production line there are people who are being exploited," Semaan says. "Oftentimes they're in the Global South, and oftentimes they don't have any means to communicate what is happening, or no one really cares to know. And that's what we're trying to change. Pollution reduction, material science, human rights, and climate justice."

Semaan stresses that these are systemic issues, and they will need systemic solutions, but those solutions will not be universal or easy to implement.

"When we are talking about abolition, about justice, about revolution, these are systems that we are asked to redesign, to rethink. And when we are asked to evolve or innovate on these systems, we need time and space to pace ourselves, to think together, to collectively have grace to make mistakes, to design something. When we put [redesigned systems] into practice, it's messy. It's chaotic. And that's the kind of creative energy that creates transformation."

Semaan and Slow Factory hope to be a large part of that messy, chaotic process by providing the information and creating the spaces needed for that to happen. Semaan draws on the work of psychoanalyst and philosopher Frantz Fanon as she looks toward the future:

"What happens when the last white policeman leaves? Let's observe that for a moment. Can we project ourselves into this near future that is very conducive to ideas and innovation? It's very important for us to be able to be there."

## Environmentalist Colonialism

In the face of genocidal colonialism, the Makah people made a deal with the United States government to try to preserve what they could of their way of life. In exchange for giving up over 90 percent of their land, the Makah would retain their right to fish and hunt whales and seals, according to their long-held customs.

The Treaty of Neah Bay, signed in 1855, was a series of promises that, like so many of the promises made to Indigenous nations, the United States swiftly began breaking.

Commercial fishermen and whaling boats quickly converged upon the Pacific Northwest waters the Makah had long hunted in.

Between the years of 1856 and 1876, colonizers decimated the gray whale population, reducing it from thirty thousand to between eight and ten thousand (Last Real Indians 2020). With the creatures that were so vital to the Makah at risk of extinction, the Makah voluntarily suspended their whale hunt, beginning in the 1930s. Whale hunting is not sport for the Makah people. It has, for two thousand years, been an important part of Makah life. The Makah have long depended on the whale hunts for food and fuel, and the hunt itself is full of important ceremony for the tribe. It is even important to their language.

"There are things in whaling you can only say in Makah—they don't translate to English. It's an important stepping stone to keeping our language alive," explained Makah member Chris Martinez, one of only eight Makah language instructors remaining, in an interview with the Sierra Club (Robinson 2021).

In 1998, after the gray whale population had recovered, the Makah sought to resume their traditional whale hunt.

The Makah had deeply felt the loss of this important tradition. But they also missed the food and fuel the hunt provided. Like

many Native areas around the US, colonialism and white supremacy have led to widespread poverty.

"If you go out to Neah Bay, there are not a lot of grocery stores
around, so a lot of people still live off of subsistence living," Matt
Remle explains.

Even though their plan was to hunt only up to five whales a
year, white-led environmental organizations showed up in protest, led by the activist group Sea Shepherd. They took the Makah
to court to try to block the hunts. They showed up to protest at
Makah practices for the hunt.

"They set their stupid freaking boats out there to try to capsize
the hunters who were out there in their canoes," Remle recalls.
"They'd get really violent, racist. They'd put these signs out about
'Save a whale, harpoon a Makah.'"

The racism went beyond hateful signs. Sea Shepherd's founder,
Paul Watson, has led the anti-Makah charge. Watson was reported
to have yelled at a group of Makah, "Just because you were born
stupid doesn't give you any right to be stupid" (Hatch 1999).

In their efforts to stop the hunts, Sea Shepherd teamed up with
Jack Metcalf, a far-right Washington State representative who was
long connected with anti-treaty groups and has reportedly stated
that "Black people are genetically incapable of controlling themselves" (Hatch 1999).

In the run-up to the hunt, Makah people received bomb
threats and their homes were broken into. When the tribe successfully hunted one whale in 1999, the first in almost seventy
years, Makah celebrations were drowned out by the air horns of
angry Sea Shepherd members (Ahtone et al. 2020).

After that one hunt, environmentalist groups doubled down
on their efforts to block the Makah from being able to hold any
more hunts. For over twenty years, the Makah have been battling
in court for their right to resume hunting.

In September 2021, the Makah cleared an important legal hurdle when a state judge recommended, after new environmental impact studies showed negligible risk from the hunts, that the Makah be allowed to resume their ceremonial hunts.

A final decision on the hunt is expected from the National Oceanic and Atmospheric Administration in the summer of 2023, but as of September 2023 no decision had been announced. But for many, it will be too late. Some Makah spent the last decades of their lives in this fight.

"I can't help but reflect on the people we've lost over the years trying to get to this point," said vice-chairman of the Makah Tribal Council Patrick DePoe after the judge's recommendation. "There are people who have passed on. There are people who have aged to the point where they might not be able to jump into a canoe and take part in something so dangerous" (Wilkinson 2021).

Indigenous peoples make up just 5 percent of the global population, yet they protect 80 percent of the world's biodiversity (Fleck 2022).

Many of the environmental problems that we face today and have faced over the years are the result of colonial powers abandoning Indigenous land stewardship practices. Sustainable uses of resources, crop rotation, preventative burning, rotational grazing practices, and more are long-standing Indigenous methods of ensuring that the land can provide for all its creatures. But these practices come into direct conflict with Western capitalism and the idea that wealth and power is about individually owning a fixed piece of land and squeezing every drop of resources you can out of it as quickly as possible. To act as if the Makah don't care about the health of the whales that have been a central part of their culture for two thousand years and that they've responsibly cared for is anti-Indigenous, racist, and frankly ridiculous. This is but one example of environmentalism as colonialism.

As an example, Matt Remle talks about white-led environmental efforts to preserve land that end up harming Indigenous people. "They'll purchase these areas up in the Cascade Mountains or whatever. Tribes still have the right to hunt and gather and fish and stuff like that, in these areas that are off-reservation. But they purchase these lands and make it private property, and so now there's these legal fights that tribes are having to engage in just to exercise their treaty rights."

Environmental activists who target factories that pollute in ways that put low-paid workers at risk, without consulting those often exploited (and often BIPOC) workers, can cause more harm than good. Those workers may be treated as part of "the problem" and not as exploited people who typically have few other options for income, and in many ways they may be far more concerned by the environmental impacts of the work they have to do—work that could be poisoning them and their families—than are the activists swooping in to shut the factories down.

External solutions forced upon locals by people with no first-hand experience with a specific situation frequently result in poor communities of color having to choose between watching their families starve or continuing to be slowly poisoned.

The ways in which environmental injustice affects communities of color aren't usually addressed by mainstream environmental movements. Communities of color are being harmed by contaminants leaking into their ground and water sources due to crumbling infrastructure that governments refuse to invest in. Communities of color are being poisoned by industrial waste being dumped in their backyards. None of this elicits the outcry, or the funding, that future environmental catastrophes threatening more privileged populations do.

A large part of mainstream environmental activism is aimed at preventing disasters from landing on the doorsteps of white communities that are already occurring in poor communities of color, or trying to protect wildlife in ways that are often racist and anti-Indigenous, and ways that neglect to center the peoples who have been responsibly stewarding the environment and its creatures for centuries.

Many of the "solutions" peddled today to people concerned about the environment are very individualistic in nature and sold to us as products—products that often lead to more harmful consumption. This commodification of environmentalism and sustainability erases the long-standing sustainability practices of communities of color and Indigenous communities and instead creates an environmental industry that white people are the main beneficiaries of.

Aja Barber, author of *Consumed: The Need for Collective Change: Colonialism, Climate Change, and Consumerism*, finds bitter irony in this. "In the United States Black people were stewards of the land against our will. We know how to make things grow," she tells me. "I think of my grandmother in Alabama who captures the rainwater to water her yard. While we also have places where people are banned from catching rainwater."

It's going to take courage and cultural humility to shift our focus to the real causes of environmental injustice, and how we contribute to that by upholding harmful systems. It will require us to challenge capitalist ideas of wealth and abundance that are based on individual ownership and the accumulation of resources. We live in a society that has defined freedom as the ability to individually acquire and hoard land and wealth, and any focus on collective resources and collective care is an enemy of that freedom. We live in a society where even the water that flows through our rivers can be "owned" and sold as a commodity. To break away from these environmentally devastating beliefs and practices will take a lot of systemic change as well as shifts in personal mindsets. This is not a quick fix. But while we work toward much larger changes, we can still start to make important smaller changes today, in our homes, our cities and towns, our states. We can start by listening to those who have long practiced alternative systems and practices of land stewardship—people and practices that have been as under attack and often as endangered as our climate, if not more so.

## MATT REMLE

I don't really look at myself as an organizer-activist at all," Matt Remle tells me. "I think you'd find this is a common statement among Native communities, that we have responsibilities that are toward our communities but also toward our non-human relatives as well. So a lot of the work that I've been involved with—whether it's fighting pipelines or fracking, energy extraction, stuff like that—it's all centered back on the relationship we have with our non-human relatives. They provide for us every single day, and they've fulfilled their responsibilities towards life. And we also have a responsibility in there, because we are a part of creation."

Remle introduces himself in Lakota. It's a long introduction, which he then translates for me:

"My Lakota name is Wakínyaŋ Waánataŋ. It loosely translates to 'He Charges with Thunder.' It's a family name that was passed down a number of years ago. My English name is Matt Remle. My parents are Donna Harrison and Charles Remle. I also let you know who my grandparents are, on both sides of my family. I'm from Standing Rock but live here in Seattle. I'm Hunkpapa Lakota. And then I'm just thanking you, acknowledging you for the good work that you do, and that I look forward to our conversation here today."

Remle explains to me that introductions are very important to the

Lakota people. These introductions not only share your name but also tell people where you're from, who your family is, and whom you're accountable to. This is vital in building trustful relationships.

The "where" and "who" that Remle is from—the Hunkpapa Lakota people—is important to the work he does as an educator and movement worker.

*Húŋkpapȟa* translates to "Those who camp on the edge," Remle tells me. This name for his people references the traditional responsibility of the Hunkpapa within the Lakota Nation. "When we gathered together, the Hunkpapa band would pitch our camps on the outer edge, as a frontline protection against any attacks. And that's a responsibility that we continue to carry to this day. It isn't just a traditional role. When the fight against the Dakota Access Pipeline happened, all those very first tepees that went up, the frontline protectors, the vast majority were Hunkpapa placing themselves at that front line. That is also a role and responsibility that I have to fulfill with my family."

Remle has fulfilled this role in many ways throughout his life. To list a few: He was an organizer in the fight to raise the minimum wage in Washington State in the '90s. He was the lead organizer for the Community Coalition for Environmental Justice, which battled the contamination of land and water in BIPOC and low-income communities by hazardous waste facilities. He authored Seattle's Indigenous Peoples' Day resolution in 2014, which replaced Columbus Day, and he helped write numerous other resolutions for municipalities across the US.

Remle is also the editor of Last Real Indians, which is a Native news site that sheds light on issues faced by Indigenous peoples around the world. *And* he co-founded Mazaska Talks, an organization that works to stop industrial and government projects from harming Native lands and violating Native sovereignty.

On top of all of this, Remle has for decades been the Indian Education Program coordinator for a Seattle-area school district.

We could talk about Remle's work for days, but as we sit down, we focus on his work with Mazaska Talks.

This discussion takes us back to 2016 and 2017, when protests against construction of the Dakota Access Pipeline through Native lands were heating up. When Energy Transfer Partners started to build their pipeline through Native lands, threatening vital water sources, the Standing Rock Sioux Tribe and other Indigenous organizers used various methods to try to stop the construction.

The water protectors engaged in direct action, placing their bodies in front of construction equipment. They tried to raise awareness to gain support for their efforts and to show people how the pipeline violated treaties and posed great environmental risk to the region. They also fought in the courts.

And time and time again, Energy Transfer Partners showed that they felt they were accountable to no one, in sometimes shocking displays of violence.

Tim Mentz, the Standing Rock Sioux Tribe's historic preservation officer, had been able to map out exactly where the pipeline would run through burial sites, important Native cultural sites, and sacred sites. The tribe brought this documentation to a judge, in the hopes that Energy Transfer Partners would then avoid digging in those areas.

"Literally the next day, they brought in those private military people and their attack dogs and bulldozers and bulldozed those exact sites," Remle remembers. "They released their dogs on folks."

It's easy to see how the outrage and heartbreak of this still affects Remle.

"If a bulldozer showed up at your church, your mosque, your synagogue, temple, and just started bulldozing it, you'd probably be pretty pissed off." But Remle points out that it probably wouldn't happen to those spaces in the US, just to Native spaces.

After these brazen attacks by Energy Transfer Partners, Remle and his fellow water protectors realized that they were going to need to add a new mode of attack.

"In our thinking, we've tried multiple routes with direct actions," Remle recalls. "None of the arguments, none of the conversations, were stopping this corporation. So we figured: Money's really behind everything. So we might as well go after the financial institutions that are giving the money and the loans and backing and profiting off of financing these pipelines. Because up to that point, they really hadn't been held accountable."

*Mázaska* means "money" in Lakota, and Mazaska Talks aimed to hurt those behind the Dakota Access Pipeline where it could really be felt: their pocketbooks.

The story Remle tells me next is a master class in organizing strategy.

Mazaska Talks started with the Seattle City Council—more specifically, they started with Councilmember Kshama Sawant. Remle had worked with Sawant, the city's lone socialist city council member, on the Indigenous Peoples' Day resolution and on a resolution condemning the atrocities against Native peoples at Indian boarding schools, and both efforts had been successful.

Tribal governments across the country had written resolutions condemning the violations of treaties and tribal sovereignty that Energy Transfer Partners had been carrying out with the pipeline. "But no non-tribal governments at that point had taken a stand," Remle tells me. "My thought was, *Seattle claims to be a human rights city, so they should be speaking out against human rights abuses.*"

Remle brought the idea to Sawant, and she agreed to sponsor the resolution condemning the actions around the building of the pipeline. The rest of the council was happy to agree to the resolution. It was easy for them to do, as the resolution was not binding; it was more symbolic in nature.

But now that Seattle had gone on record condemning the pipeline, Mazaska Talks had what they needed for the next phase of their plan. They would ask the City of Seattle to put their money where their mouth is.

Wells Fargo was identified as one of the major funders of the Dakota Access Pipeline, and they became a prime target of Mazaska Talks' efforts. Seattle did a lot of financial business with Wells Fargo—about three billion dollars a year—and Mazaska Talks wanted to target that business in order to increase pressure on funders of the pipeline. As they were researching Wells Fargo, they found an opportunity to broaden their fight beyond Standing Rock.

"It's our job as people who are organizing these different campaigns to draw these connections and try to build stronger coalitions in these larger fights," Remle says.

While protesters were battling the construction of the pipeline in Standing Rock, Black youth were battling the construction of a massive new youth jail in Seattle. Mazaska Talks discovered that Wells Fargo was also a major funder of the new jail.

Remle reached out to Nikkita Oliver, who worked with the youth who were running the No New Youth Jail campaign. "We have a pipeline in our homeland that's bringing death and destruction to our communities," Remle explains. "And then you have another sort of pipeline happening here with the school-to-prison pipeline. And they're really kind of the same thing. They play out in different ways, but they're really the same thing, with the harms that they're causing—especially in Black and Native communities."

Having established these shared causes, Mazaska Talks and other water defenders started showing up with No New Youth Jail. "We brought a lot of Native folks out to the actions they were holding at the construction site. We held a joint concert together," Remle says. And in turn, many of the youth from the No New Youth Jail campaign supported the protests against the pipeline, some even traveling to Standing Rock to join protests there.

In their research, Mazaska Talks also discovered that Wells Fargo was a funder of the immigration detention center in Tacoma, just south of Seattle. Mazaska Talks reached out to immigrants' rights protestors who were organizing against the actions of ICE and the detention center, just as they had reached out to No New Youth Jail. Soon Native people were showing up at the detention center protests in solidarity with immigrants' rights activists.

With these relationships established, and a clearer picture of how these different issues were connected, Mazaska Talks went back to the Seattle City Council with a proposal for a socially responsible banking ordinance targeting institutions like Wells Fargo.

The ordinance established criteria for banks that were bidding on city contracts, such as not investing in projects that violated Native treaty rights or threatened the environment, and favored BIPOC-owned and local banks and credit unions in the bidding process. The ordinance also obligated the city to end its contracts with Wells Fargo, listing its funding of the Dakota Access Pipeline, its fraudulent and unethical business practices, and its funding of the Northwest ICE Processing Center and other private prisons in its justification for ending the contracts.

Sawant agreed, again, to sponsor the ordinance. When she brought it before the council, there was a large multiracial and multiethnic coalition of people at city hall to support it.

The Seattle City Council passed the resolution in 2017, pledging to not renew their contracts with Wells Fargo, ending a three-billion-dollar-a-year relationship.

But Remle and Mazaska Talks did not stop there.

"We were also organizing with other cities," Remle says. "We used Seattle as a larger media market to hold our actions and draw attention. But we were also working with folks in San Francisco, LA, Chicago—who have even greater banking contracts with these same banks."

Mazaska Talks worked with water protectors and organizers across the country and put together a strategy guide for those who were looking to get similar legislation passed in their municipalities. Cities like San Francisco, Davis, and Santa Monica joined Seattle in severing ties with Wells Fargo shortly thereafter.

This sent a strong message to those who would back such projects, forcing banks to weigh the potential profit from destructive energy projects versus their proven financial relationships with cities. But the wording of the ordinances also provides precedents for other BIPOC who seek to target financial backers of harm to their communities.

Remle's belief in coalition building comes from his auntie LaDonna Brave Bull Allard, a Native historian and matriarch who in 2016 established Sacred Stone Camp, the first resistance camp in the Standing Rock protests. "When I was younger, she told me something that really stuck with me," Remle shares. "She said everybody has their own responsibility within the community. And it looks different. No one responsibility is more important or elevated than the other. You might have some people whose passions lie within addressing Indian mascots. Some might be passionate about the substance-abuse problem that plagues our communities. Some are about the language. Others are about police violence. And our family is more centered on protecting the land and culture sites. They're all equally important. Because ultimately, it's about protecting the community and the land."

While many activist groups are often pitted against one another, forced to compete for resources and attention, Remle stresses that these colonial mindsets will only lead to further destruction.

Remle's role as a Native land and water defender requires him to stay connected to others.

"*Lakota* itself translates to 'being a good relative,'" Remle tells me. "We're taught to be in good relationship, not only with our immediate families or even with our tribes but a good relative to all of creation."

This family is one that Remle stresses we all are a part of.

"It's our responsibility as relatives of this earth to work together. I'll support your movements in the different ways that I can, and you can come along and support the work that we're doing in different ways as well."

## BE A REVOLUTION

When it became widely known in the late 1970s that polychlorinated biphenyls (PCBs), used in things like paint, plastic, and adhesives, caused birth defects and cancer when absorbed through the skin or inhaled, Robert Burns saw dollar signs.

As companies discarded their toxic PCBs, which had now fallen out of favor, Burns, who owned a trucking company, snatched them up and sold them to companies who still needed them (Fears and Dennis 2021).

Burns partnered with his friend Robert Ward Jr., who stored the PCBs in a warehouse.

Things didn't go according to plan. It was far more difficult and expensive to transport and store the toxic chemicals than Burns and Ward Jr. had expected. So the duo, with thousands of gallons of PCBs on their hands, decided to go out at night and spray them along North Carolina roads.

Once the EPA discovered what Burns and Ward Jr. were doing, the men were arrested and sentenced to prison. But now what to do with ten thousand truckloads of PCB-soaked soil?

North Carolina governor James B. Hunt Jr. settled on a solution: they would dump the contaminated soil in a soybean field in rural Warren County.

The community living around the dump site was predominantly poor and Black, factors that likely contributed to the appeal of the location. Black and brown communities have often been dumping grounds for the toxic trash white companies and governments want to get rid of. It had been done before with little fuss—at least not from people who mattered. Why would anyone care this time?

But the inhabitants of Warren County were not going to be poisoned in silence. For six weeks in 1982 Warren County was the site of a massive Black-led protest. People of all ages took to the streets to fight this blatant pollution of their community. Some laid their bodies in front of the dump trucks that were trying to bring the poisoned soil in. Over five hundred protestors were arrested, and yet hundreds more still came (Office of Legacy Management, n.d.). But in the end, the protesters were unable to stop the dumping of the poison in their communities.

It would take more than twenty years for the land in Warren County to be cleaned. But the protests in Warren County sparked the first nationwide conversation about the intersection of race and environmental harm. People of color across the country who had long decried the pollution and destruction of their communities by governments and businesses started to come together to discuss their shared experiences and identify patterns in them.

Chinese American researcher Charles Lee was inspired by the Warren County protests to look deeper at patterns of pollution in communities of color. He found in his research that three out of every five Black and Hispanic people lived in communities surrounding toxic waste sites, and that race was *the most* predictive factor in the placement of those sites (Office of Legacy Management, n.d.).

Convinced that this correlation was intentional—that it was the result of systemic discrimination—Lee reached out to some of the hundreds of activists of color he had worked with in his research to develop the First National People of Color Environmental Leadership Summit. Lee told *The Washington Post* that at the time he had thought, "Let's do something that really kind of makes a statement about the leadership that already exists in people across color communities on these environmental issues . . . and use it as a way to coalesce a movement" (Fears and Dennis 2021).

They hoped for three hundred attendees, but one thousand BIPOC community and organization leaders showed up.

In September 2022 in Warren County, forty years after protestors had taken to the streets to defend their community, hundreds of people gathered to commemorate the protests that are now known as the beginning of the environmental justice movement, a movement that specifically battles racist environmental harm against communities of color.

People who were there at protests, who had laid their bodies in the road in front of trucks to protect their community, who had been dragged off to jail by police officers for defending their homes, shared stories with younger generations of environmental justice activists they had paved the way for.

At the celebration, Edgardo Colón-Emeric, dean of the Duke

Divinity School, said that hope has two daughters: courage and anger (Atwater 2022). And it is those daughters of hope that fuel the environmental justice movement to protect communities of color and the land they live on.

We need hope, and its daughters, courage and anger, if we're going to be able to save our communities from environmental injustice and the climate crisis. The protestors in Warren County took on a system that seemed much more powerful than them, and at first, it seemed like they had lost. But they gave birth to a movement more powerful than anyone could have imagined.

If you want to be a part of this movement, here are some places you can start:

➤ **Support free, prior, and informed consent (FPIC) for Indigenous peoples.** Indigenous communities around the world are fighting to have a say in what happens on their lands.

"What it really means," Matt Remle explains, "is that any sort of project that is taking place in, on, or near traditional Indigenous communities—no matter where that Indigenous community is at globally—that they have to engage in a whole process of meaningful consultation with all the impacted Indigenous communities and obtain consent. If they don't, the projects don't happen."

Around the world, movements are aiming to get governments to sign on to these agreements, and where governments have refused to sign (like in the United States), they have been trying to get banks and insurance companies to sign on, so projects that violate Indigenous sovereignty don't receive funding or underwriting.

In addition, all communities should have the right of informed consent for development and dumping projects that may have adverse impacts on health, well-being, or the environment. This is a right often afforded middle-class and wealthy white communities but rarely given to poor communities and communities of color.

- **Demand the repair and maintenance of infrastructure in BIPOC communities.** Decaying and neglected infrastructure in BIPOC communities is not just about inconvenience; it's an environmental justice issue. These structures can lead to contaminated drinking water (like we saw in Flint), sewage contamination (like we see in South River), and more. Further, the neglect of infrastructure makes BIPOC communities more vulnerable to climate disasters, which will only increase in frequency with the climate crisis.

- **Demand the cleanup of toxic sites near residential areas, the creation of safer disposal practices, an end to disposal sites placed in the backyards of communities of color, and more responsibility from manufacturers for the end life of their products.** "At the start of your product a Black or brown person is being exploited, and at the end of your product a Black or brown person is being exploited," Aja Barber points out. And at the end of a product's life, it's Black, brown, and Indigenous communities in the US and throughout the rest of the world who are often forced to live near the waste that's left over. Dump sites should never be approved near people's homes if there is any risk to community health. For those that already exist, cleanup of those sites should be made a priority. Waste that we don't want here should not be shipped overseas to poison the environment of communities of color in other countries. We have to demand responsible care of the waste we have now, but we can go a long way toward not needing dump sites at all if we demand that manufacturers integrate considerations for the end life of their products in their product designs. The most environmentally friendly products are those that have a life cycle instead of a life span.

- **Demand stricter air pollution guidelines for facilities that are near residential areas.** Part of how sugar producers in Florida are able to get away with poisoning local residents with toxic smoke are the lax guidelines around air pollution as well as a lack of resources to enforce said guidelines. Current guidelines do not accurately measure how much particulate from air pollution is actually being inhaled by people near these plants, and that needs to change.

- **Honor treaties.** We should support Indigenous nations who are fighting for the sovereignty promised them in treaties. If you aren't aware of whose ancestral land you currently reside on, now is a good time to find out, and see how you can add support to that nation.

- **Support the creation of green jobs for communities of color.** As they have by many emerging industries, communities of color have largely been left out of green job opportunities. Advocate for the creation of green jobs in communities of color, and for viable paths to those jobs through entry-level positions and paid internship and training programs.

- **Support legal funds for BIPOC communities fighting to protect their land and water.** Communities of color who are in these battles often go up against businesses or state entities with millions of dollars at their disposal. Since these issues are predominantly decided in court, it's vital that our communities have the funds to pay for the legal expertise they need. In addition, protestors who are targeted by police will need legal representation, so it's important to support legal defense funds.

- **Support land-back efforts.** California made headlines in 2020 when Governor Gavin Newsom announced a state policy that worked to return ancestral lands to Indigenous tribes. There was a lot of excitement around this policy, but in reality, the pace of the return of land actually slowed after Newsom's announcement. California is home to the largest number of Native people in the country, and yet tribes own just 1 percent of the land there. It's vital that states return more ancestral lands to Native tribes, but businesses, organizations, and individuals can transfer ownership of privately owned land to tribes as well. Giving land back to Indigenous people is important not only for helping in a small way to acknowledge and atone for the great theft of land and resources that created the United States; returning land to its traditional stewards also can help protect that land from over-development and degradation as well as help preserve traditional hunting and fishing practices (Plachta 2022).

➤ **Demand accountability from racist and anti-Indigenous environmental groups.** Strong ties exist between white-led environmentalism and racism, xenophobia, and anti-Indigeneity. Many early conservation movements in the US were based on the idea that lands needed to be taken from Native peoples and preserved for white heritage. John Muir, founder of the Sierra Club, is widely acknowledged as having been racist, and he referred to Black and Native people as dirty, lazy, and uncivilized (Kashwan 2020). Conservation movements often targeted "overpopulation" as the largest threat to the environment, and therefore targeted communities of color with higher birth rates as well as immigration policies in order to keep populations of predominantly white countries down. All of this and more has shaped how our mainstream environmental movements look today, and is likely a large contributor to why these organizations are still overwhelmingly white in membership, staff, and ethos. These organizations should be held responsible for the harm they have created and should be asked to make amends for that harm by directly supporting environmental justice and Indigenous sovereignty efforts in whatever ways those populations prefer.

➤ **Support environmental justice groups.** Of the eight billion dollars that goes to environmental groups each year, only 0.5 percent of those funds goes to environmental justice groups (Thomas, n.d.). The future of our communities and our environment is in environmental justice, and our support should be going there first and foremost.

## RACE, EDUCATION, AND THE
## PEDAGOGY OF OUR OPPRESSORS

M Y WORK HAS ME spending a lot of time in schools, especially predominantly white institutions. Every time I visit a school I'm confronted with the ways in which students and faculty of color are being harmed every single day by racist policies, racist peers, racist parents, and racist administrations.

This is not because schools and educators aren't trying. There are educators, administrators, and students trying hard to create more inclusive and anti-racist classrooms. But this work has always been hard. Educators—especially those in public or more "mainstream" schools—are by the nature of their work tied to deeply racist institutions in ways they can't extricate themselves from and are often not fully aware of. It's a battle that even for the best of educators has often been one step forward, two steps back.

I was surprised to find that of all the conversations I had with people for this book, it was the educators I found to be the most weary, most pessimistic, even fearful. I struggled with this chapter, in a book that I hope to be uplifting for people seeking to make change. Because it's clear from my conversations with educators, and from looking into the current state of public education in general, that the situation our students and educators are facing with regards to issues of anti-racism and equity are more dire than what many of us have seen before in our lifetimes.

There is little to feel optimistic about—due to the rapid speed with which ignorance, fear, and bigotry have been able to tear apart what little progress students, families, and educators have made in recent decades to create safer and more equitable education for all students. I genuinely fear for our children, as an activist and as a mother. I fear what the long-term ramifications of the destruction of our education system will have for all students in the years to come, but especially for our most vulnerable students.

Recently I was invited to speak at a conference for people working in diversity and equity in higher education. I was to give the opening keynote address. The organizers of the event had asked me to give the attendees some hope. "They really need hope right now," I was told. It felt like a tall order, especially as I wasn't feeling particularly hopeful myself.

In the morning, before my talk, conference leaders reminded the audience repeatedly to check in with attendees from states where their work was being especially targeted. "Check in with your peers trying to work in Florida, in Texas, in North Carolina, South Carolina, Utah, Iowa, Oklahoma . . ." They continued, listing an alarming number of states.

Emotions were high in the room as I took the stage. I was looking out at hundreds of people who had dedicated their careers to creating safe and equitable environments for students and faculty in their schools. The majority of attendees were BIPOC, and the majority of them worked in predominantly white institutions and had had to fight hard to create opportunities for BIPOC and other marginalized students on their campuses. And all of that progress they had worked so hard for, often at great personal cost, was being torn down in front of their eyes. They found their budgets slashed, their movements monitored, their work attacked. Many feared their departments would be cut altogether. Some had already moved to different institutions earlier in the year due to their employers deciding that equity was no longer politically viable in the current climate.

One attendee had told me over lunch that the stories he was hearing from his colleagues in states that had been most heavily attacking equity work in education were heartbreaking and terrifying. "Their emails and text messages are being monitored to make sure they aren't practicing any 'critical race theory,'" he said. They're afraid not only of losing their jobs but also of legal consequences, simply for trying to make sure that marginalized students and staff feel safe and included on campus.

In recent years, conservative politicians and political operatives have been able to mobilize a very vocal and powerful minority, stirring up white fear and outrage over inclusivity efforts in schools. Across the country, white parents are being told that their children are being taught to hate their whiteness, to hate their history, to even hate themselves and their families. To hate their assigned gender, to eschew heterosexuality, to reject patriotism. That white people are inherently evil and that POC are always victims. That children who believe in "traditional" American values are being actively discriminated against.

These coordinated campaigns to strike fear into the hearts of white Americans have drawn angry parents to school board meetings, demanding the removal of "wokeness" from their schools. Equity-minded school board members have been replaced with conservative activists promising to rid classrooms of the ever feared and never defined "critical race theory."

Schools have made a remarkably easy target for conservative operatives. Part of this is because of the racism that was already embedded within the education system itself. The overwhelmingly white-led power structure, the carceral systems already in place within, and the preexisting disempowerment of BIPOC parents and caregivers has eased the takeovers of school boards and the passage of anti-equity education legislation.

Across the country, whole states have banned the teaching of "critical race theory" in state schools and organizations. (Note: I'm putting critical race theory in quotes here not because it isn't real but because those putting in place these bans have no actual idea what it is, and they really don't care to know.) Since 2021, forty-four states have taken steps to try to limit teaching around race and racism (Schwartz 2023). There were 1,269 attempts to ban library books in 2022 alone. Of those bans, 58 percent of them were in school libraries and classrooms (American Library Association, n.d.). It's not only books like mine being targeted or those from other writers covering issues of race and racism, patriarchy, ableism, or queer- and transphobia. Children's books featuring protagonists of color, or queer or trans protagonists just being everyday kids–books that have helped kids feel seen, heard, and safe in schools–are being removed.

What little autonomy teachers have had to create inclusive classrooms has been stripped away in many states and many school districts. This is not just in Southern conservative areas, lest you try to rest in the idea that you live in an area "safe" from these attacks. One in four teachers have reported that they have felt compelled to change their lesson plans to comply with anti-CRT rules and laws (Lehrer-Small 2023).

Florida has taken this even further with the Individual Freedom Act, otherwise known as the Stop W.O.K.E. Act. This law is both devastatingly vague and far-reaching, and was designed to make it impossible to effectively teach on issues of race or systemic oppression, or to advance any equity efforts in education or employment sectors. Bans on education that cause "discomfort, guilt, anguish, or any other form of psychological distress on account of his or her race, color, sex, or national origin" make it pretty much impossible to teach accurate US history or about any topic that might touch on discrimination or oppression (Kevin Kelly 2022). Of course, the very real harmful impacts of being BIPOC, queer, or trans in classrooms that have effectively erased your identity and your history are not considered in this legislation.

The effects of this legislation have been pretty immediate in Florida. The state has been scouring school textbooks, removing mention of "prohibited topics" that try to address racism or discrimination. One elementary school textbook had to change its section on Rosa Parks in order to not risk running afoul of Florida rules. Instead of explaining to students that Rosa Parks was told to move to a different seat on the bus because of the color of her skin and she refused, it was rewritten to say this:

"One day, she rode the bus. She was told to move to a different seat. She did not."

In Florida, Rosa Parks is no longer a Black woman who stood up to racial segregation and oppression and helped change history; she's now a woman who was told to move bus seats for some unnamed reason, and she just didn't want to (Mervosh 2023). Not only has Rosa Parks been erased from our children's schools, not only has the reality of the racism that Black people endured during the civil rights era been erased, but so has the beautiful story of how we were able to come together as Black people to fight for our rights and our dignity. The story of what we've overcome and what we've been able to accomplish in the face of so much hardship, the story that our love for ourselves was bigger than the hate of white supremacy—that's a story not only Black children need to hear.

And yet educators are still trying, and where they can, they're making very important pockets of progress and safety for students of color. As I looked out over my podium to give my keynote, I saw hundreds of educators and equity and diversity professionals who had been so under attack in recent years. But they were still in the room, gathered together, trying to find a way to still do whatever they could to create some measure of safety and inclusivity in their institutions. I was struck by the love they must have for their work and for the students who are most at risk from these attacks on our education system. They are, once again, proof that our love for our communities is bigger than the hate of white supremacy. I asked them to focus on every little win, on every little bit of safety, joy, or opportunity they are able to create for students and faculty. I asked them to not let our white supremacist systems tell them that their work doesn't count, that it doesn't matter. It does matter, because every single student of color in our school systems deserves to be fought for, and every opportunity we can create for them deserves to be recognized and celebrated.

## ZHARINA ANGELES LUNA

Right now, December, all educators are feeling this sort of low. So that's where I am right now," Zharina Angeles Luna explains with a small laugh.

When I sat down with Luna, a young Filipina American educator in a Seattle-area school, I was expecting an energy to match her youth. The stereotype of a young educator is one of abundant, if not reality-defying, optimism. But the educator I'm talking with is carrying a weariness beyond her years. Yes, it's December, and my own son's teachers seem a little more exhausted than usual, but what I'm seeing in Luna seems deeper than that.

Luna didn't always feel this way. She was once the cheerful and optimistic educator one would expect. Luna became an educator because she loved learning—especially literature. It had brought so much to her life, and she was excited to be able to bring similar enrichment to other students, especially students of color, who are often overlooked by our school systems.

Luna was born on occupied Kānaka Maoli land, also known as Hawaii, where her parents had emigrated from the Philippines. Her early childhood was spent on Oahu in an agricultural community.

"I think that my upbringing in Hawaii is unique," Luna says, "in that I had teachers that looked like me. And I was in a community where most people came from a similar background."

Luna didn't know that this was unique for people of color in the US until her family moved to Seattle when she was twelve and the demographics of her classrooms significantly changed. "I didn't have another teacher of color until college after that," she says.

By the time Luna had graduated from high school, she was thoroughly in love with literature and learning. But she didn't enter college with plans to study in the fields she loved. "I'm a first-generation college graduate," Luna explains, "and so my parents thought, *Okay, you went to college, so that means you should get a job that makes money.*"

Luna planned to major in biology, to fulfill her parents' wishes for her, wishes that many immigrant parents have for their children, in the hopes these paths will lead to security they themselves may not have had or had struggled to obtain. (As someone whose Nigerian uncle was *deeply* disappointed I wouldn't add pharmacy to my political science degree, I can relate to Luna's experience.)

But Luna moved away from her original biology plans and shifted to literature and education. Her parents were concerned about her financial prospects, as teaching is not known as a lucrative field. "They came around to the idea of me teaching later," Luna recalls, "probably after I started sharing stories of my experience in schools, and how much good it was doing for the community. And that's when they started to realize, *Oh, okay. Maybe this is something to be proud of for my child.*"

Teaching is at times a very difficult profession. Having raised two children, I'm often in awe of how one teacher can not only handle the varying and rapidly changing moods, energies, and interests of twenty or thirty children at once but also actually manage to follow a lesson plan at the same time. Being a teacher of color trying to advocate for students of color, especially in predominantly white school systems, can make it much more difficult on both professional and personal levels. It's a very particular type of pain to love and believe in your profession so deeply, and to feel it pulling you apart piece by piece.

"I go to therapy," Luna tells me. "I go to therapy every other week. And I don't know how I would get through this, this profession, without it."

She compares her struggle in teaching to that of a fish constantly trying to swim upstream.

"I'm exhausted. And I don't know how much longer I can do it. But it's been the same feeling I've had since I entered education. I've wanted to quit teaching every year since I started. I've wanted to quit admin every year since I started. And I have to constantly root myself in why I chose to do this."

Luna was identified as a troublemaker early on in her teaching career. She entered the field determined to make sure that all of her students saw themselves, their lives and their histories, in their studies. "I explicitly taught critical race theory alongside books that are probably banned in other states," she tells me. "And yes, there were complaints. But for the most part, students loved it. And so as a high school teacher, I loved it."

Then Luna moved on to other grades: "In middle school, I thought, *Yeah, they're younger, but why not?*"

Luna's middle school language arts students responded positively to this diverse curriculum as well.

"And then when I got to elementary, it was a whole new world.

Because my kids are learning to read. Which is magical, by the way," Luna says with a smile, "and they are learning their identity and, sort of like, where they fit in the world."

Luna says that this sort of education isn't nearly as controversial as many make it out to be. Giving children a real sense of identity is almost always a positive experience for them. "And I've seen teachers teach race effectively and without ruffling feathers of some parents, through identity," she adds. "That is part of it. Like, a student should know who they are. Or actually just start the journey . . . I mean, even adults don't know who they are. But to start the journey of finding their identity at an elementary school level."

When I'm talking with white parents and teachers, they often balk at the idea of talking with young children about race. They're too young for that, is the argument. But the truth is that this world racializes children even in the womb. Our children are living in a reality shaped in a large part by the color of their skin, and they deserve to be given the age-appropriate tools to understand that. Further, kids of color know they're kids of color, *especially* in majority white schools. And they wonder why the adults around them keep pretending like they don't exist.

Luna is now a parent and has seen that this process of learning about your identity can begin even before school. "I have a two-year-old, and to see him figure out his identity is beautiful. Anti-racist curriculum can be taught the minute a child comes into the world. My son knows the color of his skin. He figured that out as soon as he learned what colors were. And he knows that Mommy and Daddy identify as Filipino. And he made the connection that that means he's Filipino, too. He's figuring out that our dog is not Filipino, which is adorable," Luna adds with a smile.

She knows that not all teachers are willing or able to take the same risks she takes in teaching her students. It's difficult, and often unsustainable, to be constantly battling parents and skittish administrators in order to just teach kids in a way that helps all students feel seen.

Luna's commitment to this work stems from her strong belief in what education can do for society: "I do think that the most proactive way of combating injustices is through education. And so I truly believe in it, and want to give that to the students and families. When I first entered education, I would probably not describe myself as political. But I soon found out that being in education is political. There's no way around it."

Luna's frustrations with the seeming lack of support from school administrations led her to seek out administrative roles herself, in the hope that she could enable greater change at that level. If administration had the power to dictate what change was or was not allowed, she was going to become administration. She began working toward an administrative role and, in her training, got to see deeper into some of the more harmful areas of public education.

During her administrative internship, Luna was placed in the role of an "in-school suspension specialist" for a school year. She tells me the name of the role with a wry smile. "The name was changed to 'in-school restoration specialist,'" she explains. "And the reason I smiled is because I truly believed in restoration."

But restoration was not what Luna found in the role.

"What I was being asked to push did not look like restoration. What it was is a pipeline to prison," she says frankly. "It's the same thing: You're put in a room all day. You're given a meal. But you can't go get your meal with the other kids. And then, after your time is served, you go back."

Luna found herself steeped in the carceral side of education, the part of education that tells students that their right to education and to community is conditional, and that there are things they can do—as growing and learning children—to no longer deserve those rights. As difficult and disheartening as the role was, it helped give Luna greater focus for her future role in school administration. She was getting a clearer picture of what she wanted to change.

"I did learn a lot about the position in what ways an admin, like in my position, can change it. So when I entered admin, my goal was, 'Yep, we're gonna look at discipline.'"

In trying to create change at the administrative level, Luna found that her fellow administrators kept demanding the data to back up what she and so many other educators of color see happening every day. Luna has the data, she tells me, and the data shows over and over again that students of color—especially Black boys—are being labeled as "aggressive" or "defiant" and are being over-disciplined in schools. A 2022 double-blind study by Jayanti Owens (2022) had 1,339 US teachers watch videos of children misbehaving. Some videos had Black boys misbehaving, some had Latino boys misbehaving, and some had white boys misbehaving. In the videos, the misbehaving boys all exhibited identical behaviors, and yet teachers who were asked to watch the videos of Black or Latino boys were more likely to hold those children directly responsible for their misbehavior and to refer them for further discipline than they would white boys. The study also found that the larger the population of Black or Hispanic kids in a school, the more likely those children are to be found personally responsible for routine misbehavior and punished for that behavior to an extent that white children are less likely to be.

Even though Luna doesn't look back on her time as a "restoration specialist" fondly, it isn't because she no longer believes in restorative practices. It's because she has found that schools themselves don't actually seem interested in restorative practices. "Restorative practices do work. They do," she argues. "But they don't produce what, I guess, the grown-ups want to see. But when a student enter[ed] in-school suspension, what the grown-ups wanted to see was that the behavior would stop."

Luna believes that actual restorative practices do, in the end, lead to changed behavior, but not as quickly as schools expect. "It is a slow, long process and there's a lot of deep wounds that cause a student to look that way in the public. And, I mean, schools are a microcosm for society, for American society." She found that students were exhibiting the same effects of systemic oppression and trauma in class as we see in wider society, and schools were responding in the same carceral ways that we see in our systems outside of school.

She has tried hard to use what power she has now as an assistant principal to create change for her students. "I almost have to be sneaky about it," she confides, "but essentially my position allows me to be a gatekeeper in some ways. And I decide who is written up for a referral—a discipline referral. I decide if the student is suspended or expelled. And I'm okay with that. I feel like I know enough about my own biases and all of the historical contexts with school discipline that I feel confident in taking on this role as a gatekeeper. And I do not feel confident in other people taking that role. Unfortunately I'm not in every school, so it feels like my impact is small and only to the students in my school."

And at times, Luna feels like her efforts fall devastatingly short. Heavy on her heart as we talk is a student she tried and failed to keep in her school. A young Black disabled student was brought to her repeatedly as he struggled with school faculty.

This student's disability had been caused by traumatic brain injury, which can cause behavioral changes and can make impulse control more difficult, especially in times of stress. In children, those impulses can be physical in nature, and those physical responses can be seen as more deliberate and threatening to those who are predisposed to seeing Black boys as violent. But Luna saw this student's actions differently than her peers did: "That's how he survives," she explains. "But what the grown-ups see in schools is aggression, violence, yelling."

As much as she tried to get fellow staff members to see the student's behavior in the context of his age and disability, Luna says, "a lot of adults use the word 'assault.' Like, they were assaulted by him."

As we saw in the Owens study, educators are more likely to hold Black boys personally responsible for misbehavior, and Luna saw that with her student. They kept insisting that he could control his behavior more than Luna thought he could, she tells me.

In the end, Luna lost the battle.

"The student was pushed out," she says. "The grown-ups in this building do not agree with using the language of being 'pushed out.' But no—he was pushed out. He was pushed out by the grown-ups."

I can hear the bitterness, sadness, and guilt that Luna carries over this incident still.

"And ultimately, I'm part of it. And that's hard to admit. Like, I feel like I could have fought harder."

After eleven years in education, Luna seems worn down by so many battles and heartbreaking losses. But she insists that she's not ready to give up the fight yet.

"I'm in a pretty cynical place right now. But the thing is, I wake up every day to continue doing it. And the reason is because I really do have hope that things can change, and that my own child will have a better experience in schools than what I had in schools, and that the students being pushed out have in schools. So . . . my last word . . . is that I truly believe there's still hope."

---

# Racism in Our Schools

Our school system is racist. It was racist in its founding, it is racist in its practice, and it is racist in its outcome.

Early formal education in the US was reserved primarily for elite whites, providing schooling in subjects designed to allow privileged white people (usually men) to be able to better pursue endeavors open only to them and to make the connections necessary to take their place in ruling society.

Many poor whites were given a rudimentary education, if any at all. And it was not unusual for those in the white laboring class to be unable to read or write.

But for enslaved Black people, education was not only often denied but also forbidden under the threat of physical violence. As education became more available to populations of color, it was still very different from the education made available to whites. Black schools were underfunded and under-resourced, and limited in scope of education. And many white-run schools were more interested in obtaining the obedience of Black students than in their education. White-run Native schools were often implements of genocide, forcing the erasure of Native cultural practices, understanding, and identity. Black, Native, and Hispanic students were banned from the majority of colleges and universities for much of this country's history.

K–12 schools were legally segregated across large portions of the country until 1954. After legal desegregation, the quiet practice of segregation continued in school districts across the country, using the histories of redlining methods and very imaginative drawing of school district boundaries to keep white students—and their families' income—away from students of color.

Today, majority Black, brown, and Native K–12 schools remain under-resourced compared to white schools, even when you control for an area's income.

Today, test scores and graduation rates show that Black, brown, and Native students are still being horribly underserved by our public school system.

Today, Black, Native, and Hispanic students are targeted by their schools for suspension, expulsion, and even arrest at school in ways that white students are not. For Black students, and especially Black disabled students, our school system is often their first introduction to the prison–industrial complex.

Even if our students of color manage to stay in school despite all of the efforts to push them out, they still largely receive a white supremacist education that erases their history and their vision of their future.

You can love learning and love education while still recognizing how deeply racist our education system is.

In fact, you must.

If we love education, and want it to be the enriching and liberating endeavor it has the potential to be, we must educate ourselves about it. We must seek out the truth about how our education system is serving, or failing to serve, students of color. We must learn about who benefits from our education system operating as is, we must learn the ways in which racist oppression has been built into the system, we must seek out different ways of learning, and we must embrace different definitions of academic success.

## SAARA KAMAL

Saara Kamal is working to make sure that more young, talented educators like Zharina Angeles Luna don't encounter as many hardships in their teaching career.

"Our programming centers a lot on identity development and growth, and really what is each person's personal definition of 'liberation'—and how they can have a community of support to actualize it themself, and actually be transformational in their work."

Kamal is the program manager for the Martinez Fellowship, a program for teachers of color. They work with new teachers and teachers working toward their certification to equip them with the tools needed for long-term success. The fellowship program is rooted in what it calls its "Liberation Pedagogy," in which "fellows co-create spaces by and for BIPOC stories, experiences, and learning that center heartwork, headwork, and community" (Technology Access Foundation, n.d.).

The Martinez Fellowship was created by former professional baseball player Edgar Martinez and his wife, Holli Martinez. "As a result of them also recognizing that the teacher workforce did not represent the student population here in Washington at all, and was failing our kids," Kamal explains.

Eventually the fellowship was passed on to the Technology Access Foundation (TAF) to run, and it became a part of the equity work that TAF has been doing in schools in Washington State for years. "We are going into year fifteen—we're welcoming our fifteenth cohort this year," Kamal tells me.

Kamal comes from a family of educators. Both of her paternal grandparents were longtime educators in Iran, and many members of her mom's family worked in education as well. Kamal was taught to cherish both teaching and learning.

She spent her early childhood years in East Los Angeles before moving to the Pacific Northwest with her family. The difference in experience between the predominantly Black and brown East LA she had known and the predominately white Seattle area she had moved to was stark. "Coming up to the Pacific Northwest, which was very, very white, and not seeing any families that really looked like mine—that were multiracial and multicultural. And having both a proximity to whiteness with having a white mom and then having a brown dad." Kamal reflects on the complicated dynamic she found herself in, in this space that prioritized whiteness. "So you have access to that privilege, but then also the othering as well, going through K through 12."

That othering was increased by the fact that Kamal couldn't see herself in any of her teachers. "I didn't have an educator that looked like me until I was in college," Kamal recalls.

The differences in her experiences between East LA and the Pacific Northwest, coupled with the isolation she experienced in school, motivated Kamal to become a teacher.

"I remember the feeling that I got when we had shared cultural understanding," Kamal says, and in those experiences, she was able to see what could have been. She says she found herself reflecting on "what would little Saara have gained from having a teacher that looked like me in school?"

This desire to be the teacher she never had took her first overseas to teach in Rwanda and Beijing. When she returned to the United States, Kamal taught refugees and worked in community outreach.

When the opportunity to work with the Martinez Fellowship Program opened up, she jumped at the chance. "Because I saw myself in it. You know, going to grad school as a person of color and not really having the community, and it being a predominantly white community as well—what that would have been like for me ten years ago—and to be able to shape professional developments that really centered that experience specifically."

The teachers Kamal serves face a lot of issues that white teachers don't have to face to the same degree. While these new teachers are taking on the daunting task of figuring out what it means to be a teacher, they're also faced with what it means to deal with how they're perceived and treated because of their racial identity.

"The microaggressions that they encounter from their colleagues, from their students, from parents, from their administrators. And really not feeling like they are in a position of power to speak back to some of those instances . . ." All that adds to the burden on new teachers of color, Kamal explains.

Another large part of the extra burden these new teachers carry is from often being one of the only teachers of color in the building. K–12 teaching is overwhelmingly white, with BIPOC making up only 21 percent of teachers nationwide, and in areas like the Pacific Northwest, the disparity can be even greater (Teach.com 2022). Kamal explains, "So you have a lot of kids of color who will see [this teacher and think,] *Hey, this person I think would be a safer space for me to talk about and process what is going on for me.*"

While it's vital for students of color to have adults in their school whom they can safely confide in, BIPOC teachers in majority white schools often find themselves outnumbered and under-resourced to be able to handle the emotional needs of all of the students of color.

"There is an additional weight of caring for these children in these schools, that is only placed most exclusively on BIPOC folks," Kamal says. "And then additionally, they are either tokenized or they are seen as the expert on issues of diversity, equity, and inclusion when they are within their first year, and they are put in positions of some extra responsibilities, I would say."

This all can add up to an immensely stressful, even traumatic teaching experience for new teachers.

Kamal explains that often BIPOC teachers have to face the trauma of their own past experiences with racist school systems when they were students while also dealing with the further harmful reality of working in majority white spaces. And they have to do this in front of diverse student groups watching them and learning from their example. "It's a very high burden," Kamal observes, "and they burn out way too quickly."

Added to this are the pressures of capitalism and the knowledge that many BIPOC have to work harder than their white peers in order to be valued nearly as much as them. This creates a situation in which new teachers of color don't feel like they can afford to enforce boundaries that would protect their mental and emotional health.

And also, to state the obvious, teaching doesn't pay very well— especially in its first years.

The notoriously low rate of pay for public school teachers can be felt especially hard by teachers of color, who are less likely to have financial buffers or safety nets to get them through lean early years. "I know so many educators who have multiple sources of income just to survive and take care of their own needs and their security," Kamal says.

It's in this reality that Kamal aims to build spaces of connection, restoration, and empowerment for new teachers of color.

I ask Kamal about how she would reflect on her time working with teachers in the fellowship.

"I think the bright spots consistently over the past four years have been being able to cultivate and, as best I can, create spaces through our events that are modeling liberatory practices," Kamal answers. "So that comes to the types of speakers that we have, and bringing them into the space. And the approach for how we go about defining what is professional development and personal development. Really decolonizing those constructs."

She adds, "Focusing on the heartwork, the headwork, and the community for a holistic approach, being able to create spaces like that, that really center BIPOC story, BIPOC narrative, BIPOC experience, has been amazing."

Kamal has been able to integrate traditional restorative practices into the fellowship program, in places that one might not expect. She talks about the fellowship interview process, and how she's been able to reformat the recruiting and interview structure for the fellowship. She has structured the interview process in a way she hopes will create opportunities for candidates to shine from their own personal identities, strengths, and interests, "and not to perform in a way that they've been expected to," she explains.

Kamal is regularly working on new ways to bring liberatory and restorative practices to the Martinez Fellowship, with the hope that in the fellowship the teachers will find the career-long connections and support they need to be able to have long and happy teaching lives.

The teachers in her program inspire her in her work, and she's motivated by the future she wants for the next generation of students. "I think when I've been reflecting on kind of my story and the 'why' for how I go about doing this work, I reflect a lot on a speaker that we had come into our space, Dr. Anthony Craig." Dr. Craig is an Indigenous scholar and a professor at the University of Washington. "He was talking about this driving question of: When liberation comes, are we gonna be ready?"

Kamal wants to do her part to make the world ready for liberation.

"I have a little niece and nephew right now that are seven and nine, navigating a very complicated, complex, very harmful world at times," Kamal says. She tells me that she wants to do the best with the influence that she has "so that the world is deserving of them and their stories and their gifts."

## Is Revolution Possible in Our Schools?

"I transitioned to admin in 2016, which is also the year I consistently started going to therapy as well," Zharina Angeles Luna tells me. "Donald Trump was elected into office, and the overt hate that students of color were feeling and experiencing immediately after the election results was . . . I don't even know what the word for it is. It was horrible. And the lack of support I got from admin in trying to support students and their emotional well-being was nonexistent. And so that was my call to enter admin. Because I thought, *Okay, well, if I'm experiencing this, and I think it's coming from admin, why not enter that sector and then change things myself?*"

Luna entered school administration excited to make change for students and for educators like her, who felt unsupported in their efforts to serve students of color. But becoming a part of school administration was not nearly as empowering as Luna had expected. "Now that I'm in it, now that I'm in admin, that is very difficult. It is not as easy as I thought it would be," Luna admits. "And now I'm in a place where I'm starting to feel it's not admin. And it's not the district. A lot of people like to say it's the district. Like, who is the district? This being is not a being. It's a system. And it's not even the district, it's the system of education."

Luna is battling increasing frustration as she continues to encounter barriers in her efforts to create change for students.

"I was definitely in a place—I think I'm still working through it—in a place where I'm like, *I don't know how much longer I can do this.*"

I've found that this sentiment is not unusual for educators of color. I've found them to be uniquely dedicated to their jobs, and uniquely aware of the importance of education and their roles as educators of color—and yet many are feeling beaten down every day by the seeming futility of their constant battles with the system of education they're in.

In recent years, the stress teachers of color have had to endure has been increased by the manufactured outrage over critical race theory, that has made targets out of teachers who aim to provide inclusive education for their students.

"It's been a hard few years," Saara Kamal tells me. "There are so many more obstacles for teachers wanting to center care and see all of their students. That is just leading to so much emotional exhaustion, I think, that they are not supported to overcome." Kamal tells me that teachers are trying to balance their need to create inclusive educational environments for their students with the pressure they get from administration to avoid any communication with students or parents that might be construed as teaching "critical race theory." Teachers want to do what they feel is right for themselves and their students as they build their careers, but they also don't want to lose their jobs. "And so the toll that takes on building relationships with students and creating environments where they feel safe and they feel like they can explore and they can learn and they can grow—it's just made that much more difficult by these external things," Kamal says.

In recent years, discussion and debate around defunding the police has been in the spotlight like never before. And in those discussions, the question of whether or not an institution so deeply harmful to so many populations can be reformed at all has been at its core.

I, and many others who have studied the history of systemic racism in this country, believe that our police and court systems cannot be reformed. I believe that there is no room for healing or growth in carceral systems, and that our particular carceral systems have been founded and built on the idea that large swaths of our society are beyond care or redemption. I believe that a system like that must be torn down if we are ever to have liberation.

When we look at the history of the US education system, and the way in which it fails to serve students of color—and often harms them—a similar question arises:

Can this system be reformed?

I'm not saying that our education system is the same as our prison-industrial complex. Although, for young people like Richie Reseda, who shared his story of how he was first sent into the prison system by the California school system as a Black child, and other kids of color who have been targeted and thrown into our prison systems by the schools meant to nurture and educate them, the comparison would not be unfair.

Black students account for 46 percent of students who have been suspended from school more than once. An astounding one in four Black disabled students will be suspended from school at least once, almost three times more often than white disabled students (Elias 2013). In the 2015-2016 school year, 290,600 students in the US were referred to law enforcement or arrested. Of those 290,600, 36 percent were Black and 26 percent were Hispanic or Latine, even though they made up only 15 percent and 13 percent of school populations, respectively (American University 2021).

Our existing education system—when students of color are given full access to it—is still the most reliable path to economic security in communities of color. A college degree will bring higher incomes and more job access to all workers, and for Black and brown workers, who face economic discrimination at all levels of employment, a college degree may be all that can keep a family out of extreme poverty even while racial wage gaps remain fixed for workers of color at all education levels (Wilson and Darity Jr. 2022). While those with economic privilege can use education to find their passion, or to build community and connections, for many BIPOC education is first and foremost about survival. And yet with what BIPOC—especially Black and brown people—risk economically without education, they are also made to pay more for their higher education. I'm not just talking about teacher discrimination, the school-to-prison pipeline, or the harm of racist curriculum. School for Black and brown students *costs more*. Not only are Black and brown families less likely to have the funds to pay for the rising costs of higher education, but also what economic assets they do have are more likely to be used against the amount of financial aid they receive than the assets of white families. Black and brown families will pay more out of pocket for their children's education than white families of the same income level will, and their children will graduate with more student loan debt than white graduates (Levine and Ritter 2022).

But education has existed in this country in a myriad of ways, and has at many times been what it is in its purest form: a tool of access, enrichment, and enlightenment that connects us to one another, ourselves, and our history. Education is powerful and capable of powerful good. And it is because of this that white supremacy has worked so hard to keep it out of our hands. I really want to stress here that education can be, and should be, more than just about preparing people to take their place in capitalist systems. Education can show us who we are, who we can be, how to be in community with one another, and what is possible in our communities. Real education, that freely gives knowledge and recognizes the inherent knowledge of all communities, is profoundly liberatory.

The war over education—who gets to use it for personal enrichment, who has to use it for basic survival, and who can only access it as a tool of control and conformity—has been raging throughout the entire history of this nation and is a testament to how very important education is.

I think there are elements of our education system that can't be reformed. I think the system itself is deeply broken in important ways. But even within this broken system, there are pockets of hope and pockets of potential that can make a vital difference in the lives of students of color.

Education is needed. Accessible, public education is a necessity for our society. And it's also the only option for many to gain an education at all.

Within our education system we have educators fighting every day to reduce harm to students of color and to create the safety needed to nurture true learning. These educators do this work while knowing that there will always be limits on what they can accomplish, and that there will likely always be a steep price to pay for their efforts.

And so while we look at the important issues around race and education, we have to find a way to be able to support educators and students of color who have to work within this deeply flawed system, while also recognizing that our most revolutionary change in education will likely have to happen outside of that system.

## JENNIFER WHITE-JOHNSON

While many of the people I talk to came into their change-making work in their young adult or even childhood years, Jennifer White-Johnson found her voice and her space in the disability justice community well into adulthood, after the birth of her son, Knox.

When White-Johnson's son was diagnosed with autism, she went searching for information to help her better understand her son and his needs. Her family was able to provide support in this journey, but she needed more community support, and that was initially hard to find.

"We come from a very supportive family of educators and folks that are just like, 'Well, let's go ahead and start on this journey.' When I was looking for that support outside of just my family unit, I really didn't like what I was seeing, in terms of how autism was being discussed and talked about within our own people, our own community. It bothered me a lot," she recalls. "There was a lot of blaming and shaming and a lot of sorrow-filled family narratives. Or they were just very comfortable putting the child's business out there."

Outside of her Black and Afro-Latine community, White-Johnson found what many in the Autistic community disdainfully refer to as the "autism moms"—the parents (often mothers, but certainly not always) who make their child's diagnosis all about themselves, and who often seem to only be able to talk about their child from a place of struggle.

For decades, a diagnosis of autism has been more concerned with how this neurodivergence will affect parents and the rest of neurotypical society and how to get Autistic kids to mimic neurotypical people, than how to help Autistic kids thrive by their own definitions of happiness, autonomy, and success.

White-Johnson is emphatic. "Autism moms are very much not what I want to be. And I've worked really hard to destigmatize what that means for me."

As a neurodivergent mother of an Autistic kid myself, I also try very hard to find a space of support and advocacy for my son in a world that can be very hostile to Black and brown kids who are neurodivergent, without speaking for him or violating his autonomy or privacy. It's a tricky balance, and whatever balance I've found has come from the helpful guidance of other Autistic and neurodivergent people.

White-Johnson wanted to parent from a place of joy. She wanted parenting rooted in her connection with her child. She also found that in the wider Autistic community.

In approaching Autistic groups both online and in person with honesty and humility, White-Johnson was welcomed in and given insight into what support and needs many Autistic adults had bene-fited from, or would have benefited from, as children.

But she found much more than support for her son in these groups; she also found a thriving community dedicated to creating change and diverse representation through art.

White-Johnson had long had a passion for design, but as a dis-abled, neurodivergent Afro-Latine woman, she found that main-stream design and arts communities often weren't welcoming or reflective of the imagery she wanted to bring to the world.

In this new community, she saw inspiration and greater possibili-ties in art and design. And she saw an opportunity to address an issue that had long been bothering her.

Many parents read to their young children. Before children can even understand the words, we tell them stories that can nurture their imagination and their ideas of who they can be in the world. But if your child can never see themselves in the stories they're be-ing told, what impact does that have on the possibilities they see for themselves in the world?

This is the problem White-Johnson had long struggled with as a parent: "I always go back to this one statistic that was released in 2019 by Diversebooks.org, where they say that main characters in US children's lit—it was, like, 41 percent white. And then you have 29 percent animals. So it's, like, white folks and animals represent-ing more main characters than the 11 percent of Black and African American kids. When we're looking at disability and queer culture, it's only 3.4 percent of what is being represented of kids within those spaces."

As Knox became older and would excitedly go to school book fairs, only to leave without any choices that truly reflected his ex-periences in the world, White-Johnson decided to create a photo zine that reflected the neurodiverse community that she and her son were a part of.

The publishing industry can be as limited in representation for dis-abled people and people of color as any other—if not more so—and

White-Johnson struggled to find a home for her zine. She eventually sought out a small independent press run by two femmes: Homie House Press. The press was known for publishing work with queer, disabled, and immigrant narratives, and White-Johnson saw them as her best chance for a successful publishing partnership.

"I kind of stalked them and hunted them down at a book fair," she remembers, "and I was like, 'Yeah, I really love what y'all are publishing.'"

This kind of initiative is a common trait in many creatives who exist outside of the "mainstream," and I've found it's quite common in disabled writers—especially disabled writers of color, who can have some of the most difficult time breaking into a very white, male, non-disabled field.

"I love when disabled authors say, 'I'm not going to let anything stop me, even if I have to publish little mini-zines or free digital resources that talk about my story, or if I'm kind of dispersing my narratives in a blog to kind of just be the overall authority on what we're going through.'"

Homie House Press partnered with White-Johnson, and she began to take her zine to festivals and art book fairs. She was able to see firsthand the impact of her work on other disabled and neurodiverse people, as they got to hold her zine in their hands.

Inspired by the success and impact of her zine, she saw a way to turn her work into an avenue for disabled and neurodiverse children to have even more personalized representation. White-Johnson saw her zines as a potential way for disabled children to not only see themselves represented in print, but to help those who care for them to better understand them and their needs.

She used her design skills to put together a vehicle for Knox to represent and advocate for himself at school—a zine all about him. The first zines were filled in by White-Johnson, using Knox's words. For his most recent fourth grade zine, her design skills were in the template, but many of the words are filled in by Knox's own hand.

There's a picture of a smiling Knox on the cover. "Hi!" Knox says in a voice bubble above his picture. The zine introduces itself as a "zine about me," with Knox's name written in his own hand below his smiling picture. Inside, Knox has filled out information that can help his teachers and school staff members better understand him and meet his needs. He gets to talk about things he likes and how he likes to interact with the world. He lists how he soothes himself when he's anxious and how he wants to be supported by school staff. The zine is colorful and beautiful, and puts Knox—his needs and his personality—first.

As White-Johnson made these zines with her son over the years, she shared them with her disabled and neurodivergent community. Other parents and caregivers of disabled and neurodivergent kids have made their own versions of the zine, much to White-Johnson's delight. It has fostered new connections for her and Knox that have spanned across many racial and social lines.

"Other families have been able to adopt the template that I've made," she proudly tells me. "There's a white family in North Carolina who took the template and adapted it for their own Autistic son. . . . It's beautiful because she just saw my post on Instagram and was like, 'Jen, I just wanted to reach out to you and let you know that I took your template and made my own. I was inspired by seeing what you did for your son, and I decided to create something for my son, too.'"

White-Johnson now works with that parent who first adopted her template, in order to make the zines accessible to more families. "And look at that really beautiful relationship that was formed between two completely different parents who are raising Autistic kids, but we share that same voice about wanting our kids to be accepted and loved and celebrated. It's an example of shifting that narrative." She beams. "This is about creating and sharing resources, and building spaces of liberation. We just want these to be in schools everywhere."

In 2022, White-Johnson was able to make her zine template even more accessible, making it available for download and customization, so parents and caregivers can have this great tool for their children, no design skills needed.

For disabled and neurodivergent kids of color, a tool like this can be especially important. Traditional pathways for getting support for disabled students can cost families a lot—in both money and time. The individualized education program (IEP) is notoriously labor-intensive and expensive—and often once a family is able to go through the process of professional diagnosis and school documentation of a student's disabilities and needs, the IEP is denied.

But even when they have the time and resources, many families of color are reluctant to embark upon a formal diagnosis process. Especially Black and Native families, who have long been targeted by the same social services organizations they would be expected to turn to for a diagnosis. Further, the combination of racism and ableism in many schools can keep a lot of parents of color from seeking a diagnosis as they fear their child will come out of the process with little more than a label and a stigma that will make it even harder for them to find success in schools. Many kids of color are already seen as disposable in our schools. Some parents have little hope that their disabled kids of color will fare any better.

This fear is not at all irrational. Disabled students of color are far more likely to be suspended, expelled, referred to law enforcement, or arrested than white disabled students and non-disabled students (Resendes 2020).

This is why we absolutely need systemic change. The ways in which our schools and other social systems treat disabled kids of color are unacceptable. This change is something that parents like White-Johnson fight for in different parent and caregiver advocacy groups. But while pushing for that change, students need accommodation and understanding now. And something as simple and accessible as a zine outlining a child's personality traits and needs can go far in bridging some of those gaps.

"I showed this to one student the other day and they were like, 'Yeah, you're essentially hacking the IEP.'" White-Johnson laughs. "And that's exactly what I'm doing."

As White-Johnson's work has become more well known, she has

been spending more time speaking about and presenting her work at disability justice events, arts conferences, educational conferences, and colleges and universities across the United States. She has become a sought-after voice on issues of disability and racial justice for students. She has also collaborated with other disability justice workers, using her art and design skills to create stunning visuals on projects highlighting BIPOC disability justice leaders, and shining a light on issues that the BIPOC disabled community faces. She's proud to have joined the ranks of many disabled people of color in creating tools and resources where systems have failed to provide them.

"If we're not really seeing it, then what do we need to do to form our own spaces of liberation? That's what a lot of disabled people have had to do. We create our own resources, our own avenues of cross-disability solidarity. Exchanges. Whether it's resources, info-dumping sessions, parties, food, clothes . . . We've been building spaces of access for quite some time."

It's this connection and collaboration that is at the core of White-Johnson's work, even as white supremacy and ableism try to make us feel alone.

"I'm realizing that you can't create collective liberation in this little small silo," Jennifer tells me, "and oftentimes, Black mamas—they feel isolated. They feel like they're the only ones that exist in this bubble and it's—no: there is a big spate of folks that are doing the work . . . We want to be able to provide the resources and show, 'Hey, this is how it works, this is how we're living. Come on the ride with us so that we can save lives.'"

## Working Outside of the School System

By the time Nikkita Oliver was finished with law school, they knew they didn't want to be a lawyer.

They had deepened their activism work while in law school, and that work combined with their studies had helped Oliver realize that there was no justice to be found in the criminal justice system.

"I finally convinced myself I would take the bar, just so that I could have my bar card and go into jails to visit folks when needed," Oliver remembers. "But for the most part, it was just like, 'I don't really want to be a lawyer.' Because everything I had been taught made me feel like we were just a cog in the system."

As Oliver was trying to figure out what came next after the bar, multiple people sent them a listing for a job opening at an arts diversion program called Creative Justice. Creative Justice aims to build "community with youth most impacted by the school-to-prison-(to-deportation) pipeline." In Creative Justice, "Participants and mentor artists work together to examine the root causes of incarceration, like systemic racism and other forms of oppression, creating art that articulates the power and potential of our communities" (Creative Justice, n.d.).

They applied to be a mentor artist, teaching art to twelve to fifteen young people who had been charged with crimes and referred to the program. "And they would get to spend time making art with me. They'd get paid for their time, and then at the end we'd do a community action project, where community but also court folks would be invited to see the work the young people created."

Oliver was surprised to be selected for the position but excited to begin work.

"My first session was wild," Oliver remembers with a laugh.

"I had almost all girls in my session, which as you can imagine, sometimes things got a little interesting in my room."

At the end of the program, Oliver came up with a group project for the students to do for their community and the court representatives that were responsible for the kids' fate. "In the end," Oliver says, "they did a photo project and they made a poetry book. And the photo project—it was a simple photo voice project. They were to pick two pictures and then write a poem about the pictures. And they read their poems at this event, where everyone sat in a circle around them."

They used the traditional restorative justice circle practice in the presentation, which usually has a physical object to indicate who is speaking and when someone is done speaking, as a way of centering attention on the speaker and creating space for respectful sharing. "And so," Oliver continues, "thinking about RJ [restorative justice] and circle practice, there was a vase in the middle of it, filled with these blue strips that all the folks that had come in had put into the vase. And after a youth would read a poem, they'd put a rose in the water."

At the end of the presentation, attendees were in tears, so touched by the power of these young people's words.

"And that was a moment when I realized, yes, this is a diversion program, but it has been set up in a way that we really can speak truth to power. We can put money in these young people's pockets. And they can start generating safer spaces with each other. And young folks who never viewed themselves as artists or creative started to view themselves that way."

Oliver was asked to become Creative Justice's advocacy director after their first year, and eventually would become executive director.

As much as Oliver believed in what Creative Justice could do, it became clear that being tied to the court system caused serious problems for the program—like the fact that only kids who were caught up in the criminal justice system could participate, but at-risk kids not yet caught up couldn't participate. Students who were benefiting from the program wanted to bring in community members who needed that space as well. "We're not gonna tell them you have to catch a court case before you can join," Oliver says.

So Creative Justice decided to move away from the court system in order to more fully realize their abolitionist vision for the program. Oliver and then Creative Justice director Aaron Counts began work to make the program, as Oliver says, "an arts space, healing engaged space, for youth."

Creative Justice teaches more than just art. It is now a youth-led arts and restorative justice program. "Youth-led" is a term increasingly used in organizations that work with youth, and it can mean a lot of things as far as the level of involvement that youth have in the program. But the youth at Creative Justice really do take strong leadership roles. The youth leadership team makes funding and spending decisions as well as organizational decisions. They even interview the Creative Justice teachers and adult leadership team. They are learning how to lead, and how to lead and work as a team.

"What I love most about Creative Justice is, I do think the youth feel a strong sense of agency and ownership over the program. Yes, it provides some economic access and opportunity to create art," Oliver explains. But they are also learning how to be in relationship with one another. "Even when we're having issues—we've had young people from different sects in the space, and they will deescalate each other and say, 'Hey, homie, this is the one safe space in the city. Can we keep it that way?' That to me has always been the most powerful thing. That I'm not out here playing authority with them or telling them how to be. They literally are negotiating safer space with each other. And they're using art, and they're using RJ tools. They're facilitating mediations with each other."

Oliver works hard to nurture a safe and empowering space for learning and self-discovery.

If you've ever raised or worked with teenagers, you know that they can be hard to engage on a good day. But for young people who have been targeted by authority figures for much of their lives, the trust needed to fully benefit from a space like Creative Justice can be even more of a challenge. This is a challenge Oliver tries to meet with patience and understanding.

"A story really sticks with me from my first year in Creative Justice," Oliver shares. "We had a youth, a Native young person. Who, their first session with us, they only came to class and slept. Their second session with us, they would come to class, they would eat, then sleep, and then usually do a check-in. Their third session with us, they were finally engaged in the class. And so we really try to think about building relationship with young people on the long haul, and on their terms. So if it takes me letting you come here and take a nap every day for three months before you want to engage, cool."

But that trust is powerful, once it's won.

"That same young person also brought five of their siblings to Creative Justice," Oliver recalls. "And as more of their community was in the space, they were more engaged."

Oliver has found that the young people in the program shine because it's one of the few places in their life where they're allowed to, and one of the few places in their life where adults actually think they're capable of doing so.

"I think young people are brilliant," Oliver tells me. "And they're observing and thinking about more than they often get credit for. And just cuz they don't voice it, doesn't mean they're not thinking about it. It probably just means you're not a safe space to share it.

"And I really challenge, especially educators, to consider that.

If a young person is not doing something in your classroom, have you considered it's your classroom that's the problem? Have you considered that maybe there's a million things going on, that your classroom isn't a safe space to bring up, and as a result, they can't think about whatever the fuck is on your agenda for the day?"

For many students of color in the US, our education has come in spite of our racist education systems that did not want us to learn about our history, our identities, or our potential. Many of us have come through public education systems deeply scarred. And many of us have managed to survive due to the amazing educators working outside of these harmful systems.

It's vital that we do what we can to reduce harm in public education and support educators in that system who want our young people to learn in a safe and healthy environment. But we must also honor our long traditions of teaching our people outside of these systems. From the enslaved teachers secretly helping other enslaved people learn to read, to Native elders keeping languages alive for future generations, to Black elders giving their young people books on Black history and culture that have been banned from their school libraries. We cannot hope to ever approach real education in our public schools if the keepers of the flame of our revolutionary knowledge are not respected and supported.

## FEMINISTA JONES

Education is the key, but not the key that we thought it was," Feminista Jones tells me. "So the indoctrination that we get from public schools is not really what's working. What we need is education that is empowering. To that, with getting the PhD and founding the school and doing the research and stuff that I'm doing around these things, I'm like, *All right, this is a lane that I can shift to.*"

Feminista Jones is, among other things, an activist, author, social worker, organizer, and educator. Many know her from her online activism work around race and gender. She's the mind behind #YouOkSis, an online movement aimed at raising awareness about the abuse and harassment of Black women. She was also the main organizer of the National Moment of Silence, a national protest against the murders of Black people at the hands of police. She's organized conferences on Black feminism, she's written books on Black women's movement work and Black women's sexuality, and she has helped raise tens of thousands of dollars for the families of Black people killed by police.

But her work goes back much further and reaches far wider than that.

Jones was raised by her mom, in the sort of poverty that makes one very aware of how systems work as a matter of survival. "My journey started in these streets. I'm from New York City, born and raised. The Bronx really made me who I am, and most of my professional career was in the Bronx."

Jones made movement work her career. She got her master's in social work in organizational leadership and management. She has additional certification in social impact strategies, and she is working toward her PhD.

By many measures, she has been very successful in her work. She's helped raise national consciousness around issues of racism and misogynoir. She's developed successful conferences around race, gender, and sexuality, and she's helped individual Black people and Black neighborhoods obtain much-needed resources. Her large online audience learns regularly from her work and words. I first looked toward her for guidance when I began working in online spaces. She tells me she was dedicated to this work. It was all she wanted to do, from the moment she woke up in the morning to the moment she went to bed in the evening.

But as the years added up, the work started to take its toll. Not just the inherent difficulties and hardships of doing movement work and battling powerful systems but also the price that Black women are often made to pay for daring to shine a little too brightly.

I myself have been targeted for my work as a Black woman. So have many other Black women I know. In fact, I can't think of a single one of my Black women peers that I know who *hasn't* experienced harassment or abuse for their work. But I know few Black women doing this work who have been targeted with the same level of vitriol that Feminista Jones has been, both from white supremacists and from Black men, who feel threatened by her work to protect Black women from interpersonal violence. This is something I could clearly see just from how she has been treated online over the years. But for Jones, these attacks, insults, and threats happen in person as well.

After seventeen years, Jones decided to retire from the work she was doing. "I turned forty, actually. I think when I turned forty, I was just like, *You're gonna die out here if you don't do something different.*"

Jones still has to keep an online presence, because for many Black women (myself included), social media is still one of the only ways we have to bypass white media gatekeepers. We need to exist in these spaces in order to do our work, and we are made to pay for that existence every day with regular insults, threats, and harassment.

"I still need this to promote my work that I'm doing," Jones explains, "and to connect with folks that are in the same spaces. From all the doxing, the threats, the violence, the nasty words, people projecting their own hate onto me and their own issues and things like that. Over time, if I did not set up ways to protect myself, I would not survive this."

But online filters can only do so much. Regularly interacting and trying to work in spaces so vitriolic can be very harmful to both one's physical and one's mental health.

"And I definitely would admit that it's had its impact on me,"

Jones confides. "I mean, my depressive episodes significantly have increased in the last decade. The impact on my sleep—I've developed insomnia. I struggle with that every day. I take supplements and things like that, just to be able to get five hours of sleep. All of that stuff is coming from this idea that I can step outside of my house and someone could have found out where I live and want to take me out."

So Jones took a step back to reevaluate her needs and goals for herself and her work, and focus on her PhD. As she did so, and as she analyzed the interactions she was having with people online, she started to identify a new path for her work.

Jones started to focus on the gaps between academic discussions on race, Blackness, and Africana, and discussions being had in the broader community—especially online.

Academia itself is highly problematic in the way it looks at race, Blackness, and Africana—especially in predominantly white institutions (PWIs), but historically Black colleges or universities (HBCUs) are not immune from white supremacist educational ideals either. That's something Jones has experienced personally. But Black academics have been able to access history and information around Blackness that has been deliberately kept out of public schools and away from the general public. Jones had been in this academic space for over a decade, and hadn't realized how very different this access to history and information was for Black people outside of these circles. Jones puts it succinctly: "I gotta say, I definitely realized I was living in a bubble."

Jones noticed that often white supremacy was able to weaponize this lack of information in order to turn some Black people against liberation work, making them think that such work was not in their best interests.

Jones wanted to see education that avoided the elitism, gatekeeping, and white centering of academia, while also avoiding the suppression and propaganda of public K–12 education. So she decided to create such a space herself: Sankofa Summer School.

An adult education program, Sankofa Summer School is aimed at filling the wide gaps in knowledge about Blackness across many fields, and at countering the years of harmful propaganda and anti-Blackness that public school students have been indoctrinated with.

"I'm operating under the premise that K–12 education is indoctrination into the United States capitalist society," Jones explains. "So everything that you learn there, even when you get cool electives, is still focused on making you this productive member of society and working within this machine. Afrocentric education is going to provide you with the opportunity to actually learn for learning's sake. But also obtain knowledge that could be used towards education. So you're gonna learn things that you haven't learned before. You're gonna be introduced to ideas that you'd never be introduced to outside of this."

Afrocentric education is key to the school, but before the classes could even be developed, the teachers all had to be on the same page about what Afrocentric education was.

"A big part of this is teaching people what Afrocentricity is, which many people—I would say most people—do not know. We throw around the term, and they don't understand that it means centering African people and people of African diaspora in their own narratives, in their own stories. Literally: Afro. Centric. So much of how we think about ourselves is from a Eurocentric perspective," Jones explains. "And so I said to the instructors, 'You have to be teaching something that is centering us, that is making us the subject, not the object.'"

Eurocentric education has been the norm in "mainstream" educational spaces in the United States for this country's entire history. It has used white perspectives to teach not only white history and culture but the history and culture of communities of color as well. White scholars have taught our history and our culture through their lens and to suit their needs. This not only has been incredibly harmful to BIPOC and to our sense of self but also is an inaccurate and incomplete education. Afrocentric education insists that we are capable of telling our own stories and educating ourselves to serve our own educational goals, and that those stories and that education are valid and vital.

Its first year, Sankofa Summer School offered nine courses taught by Black women selected by Jones herself.

"It started last summer, and it was such a success," she tells me with a wide smile.

The feedback from students was glowing, with requests for even more classes.

So for the following year, Jones opened up the teaching to proposals. Half of the teachers were handpicked by Jones, and the other half were chosen from those submissions.

As we talk, this second year of Sankofa Summer School is wrapping up. This year offered classes like Memorializing Blackness: Artistic Interventions That Challenge Memory Within Public Space; African Womanism: Historical Role of Patriarchy and Race in Undermining the Power of the Black Woman; and Forty Acres and a Mule, Ante Up!: Eminent Domain and Theft of Black Land in America. The school expanded to fourteen classes this year, all taught by Black instructors.

Having experienced poverty herself, it's important to Jones that her work remain as accessible as possible. Classes were offered for twenty-five dollars apiece, but Jones and others also donated to the school to help cover admission for those who couldn't afford the fee.

After the school ended for the year, the recordings of the classes were made available for purchase online. "Half of it will go towards the school, and half of it will go back to the instructors," she explains.

Jones is working toward further expansion next year, with in-person classes, instead of just online. She also hopes to be able to make the classes free for all one day.

"My goal is that nobody has to pay," she says. "So my ultimate goal is that people can sign up and go for free, and I can just pay instructors a fee based on what funding I get."

The Sankofa Summer School has helped Jones find a new pathway in her work, rooted in her love of Black community. And it is making vital, liberating education more accessible.

Jones wants this for Black people, but she hopes that others who see education projects like Sankofa Summer School will be inspired to embark on similar work in their communities.

"We need an Asian-centric. Afrocentricity and Afrocentric education is trying to inspire others," Jones explains. "There needs to be an Indigenous-centric. There needs to be a Latine-centric. Everything that centers you and your people in your own stories and your own narratives. And so that is where we need to go."

Jones advises other BIPOC, "Start reading more authors that look like you. That come from the same spaces as you. Start reading more of them—but also making sure that what they're writing about is not upholding white supremacy."

To Jones, Afrocentric education is center to liberation work.

"That's what Afrocentrism is really about—disrupting European universality and this idea that whatever they say applies to everybody," Jones says. "Y'all have been telling our stories for so long and making it up as you go, and telling stories about us that serve you. We need to tell our own stories. And the only way we gonna tell our stories is when we go back and fetch it. That's what Sankofa Summer School is about. To go back and fetch it."

## BE A REVOLUTION

I was almost always the only Black girl in my class. I was treated like a sort of unicorn. I was a Black girl with potential. I loved reading and writing. I loved learning. I loved making my teachers happy.

Education was one of the few areas where I could shine, where an awkward Black girl with no friends could be special.

By the time I started sixth grade, things started to fall apart. My home life was a shambles. Structurally, emotionally, financially, we were a complete mess. I became more and more isolated, due to anxiety and depression but also due to not having a phone and often not even electricity. My grades plummeted. I couldn't remember my lessons, and I never turned in homework.

My teacher turned to "tough love," isolating me further by keeping me in on recess until I turned in the quality of work that she knew I was "capable of."

I desperately wanted my teacher to approve of me. I wanted my one safe place to remain safe. That was the year I learned to ignore what my brain and body needed and just produce. That was the year I learned that my well-being didn't matter.

I was talking with my therapist about this moment, identified as the beginning of a time when I learned to ignore my own trauma in order to remain useful to others. My therapist asked me what I would say to that teacher right now, if I could.

I wasn't really prepared for that question or how emotional it would make me. I'd long considered myself "lucky" for how I was treated by teachers. It has taken me decades to realize how little I was seen as a human being, as a child in need of care, by so many of them. So I took a deep breath and tried to answer as best I could.

"I guess I would ask why she wasn't more curious," I said.

I was a child suddenly struggling. A child who loved school and yet couldn't turn in assignments, couldn't engage with her peers. Why didn't that make my teacher curious? Why didn't it make her want to ask what was going on?

In seventh grade I moved to middle school and had six teachers to disappoint, instead of just one. My self-esteem took a nosedive, as I couldn't seem to be able to do the assignments for classes and subjects that I knew I loved. I was in the advanced program, and I was the only Black girl in my class. And I felt sure that I was the only person in my class getting Cs and Ds. On top of that, my situation at home had become even worse. I felt isolated on just about every level.

The only class I excelled in was art. There was no homework; there were no deadlines. Any way that I chose to show up was enough for my teacher. I'm pretty sure my art teacher, Ms. Dickenson, saw how lost I was, and how much sanctuary that one class was able to give me. For eighth grade, she decided to give up her planning period to me and another kid who was also an art-loving misfit.

Every morning, at the start of our day, the two of us would spend the hour in her classroom. She would find a way, with her meager teacher's salary, to procure for us any art supplies we needed. I remember showing up one day to a brand-new high-quality drawing pad and brand-new colored pencils. The other kid in the class, who said he'd always wanted to work with leather, showed up to what looked like an entire cowhide.

I remember trying to find a way to express through my art how lost I was feeling in the world. Collage seemed to work best for me. I remember watching Ms. Dickenson as she looked at a jewelry box I had repainted and covered in words I had cut out of various magazines to express my state of mind, along with a self-portrait painted in blue. She inspected it carefully for a while, then told me that I felt alone because my world was very small right now, as it was for most young people. All I had was within the walls of my home or my classrooms. But every year that I got older, my world would get larger, and one day my world would be big enough that I would find my people. That nobody would ever be too different to not have people out there somewhere.

We moved halfway through the school year and my sanctuary was gone. But the words that Ms. Dickenson said to me in the months we quietly worked together stayed with me, and helped me get through the hard years to come.

I remember, in a world that felt so unsafe for a young Black girl, how badly I needed school to be a safe place. I know how badly other kids of color need school to be safe for them as well.

But it so very rarely is.

But I know it can be. And I know how much that safety can mean to a child who has been made a target by the rest of the world due to the color of their skin.

As broken and harmful as the system of education can be, because it can also be so vital to the lives of people of color, I can't give up on it. I love our young people too much to give up on the chance that they can have more.

You don't have to be a parent or a student to care about what's happening in our schools. It affects all of us on so many levels. All of us had some sort of schooling at some point. The people we interact with every day likely did as well. The norms for how we treat one another are set in school. Our social and political identities are formed at school. Many of us find our lifelong passions at school. Most of us go through our most formative years in school.

There is no way we can hope to tackle systemic racism and think we can leave schools out of the equation. Creating more anti-racist schools and finding ways to bridge the gaps in our current education system for our young people today should be of top priority.

If you want to make schools an area of focus in your anti-racist journey, here are some starting points:

➤ **Learn about and engage with your local school board.** School board and superintendent elections are some of the most powerful votes we can cast. Further, our school board members are easier to reach and in many ways made more accountable to their constituents than most other elected officials. Who is elected to your school board matters. And the wrong board can make any change that individual teachers or even principals want to make nearly impossible.

This is something that those who wish to protect white supremacy in our schools know well. These parents and community members are showing up at school board meetings demanding that equity programs be dismantled, that all mentions of race and racism be removed from textbooks and lesson plans, that teachers who try to support students of color be fired. They are voting in school board members who promise all of this and more. And they are, in many school districts across the country, getting what they ask for. If we want to protect our students of color, we have to show up in these spaces to protect equitable education for our students and to protect educators who are trying to provide that education. So please, vote in school board elections, engage with your school boards, go to meetings. We have to show that our children's right to education won't be taken away without a fight.

➤ **Get police officers out of schools.** Police officers in schools endanger students of color and disabled students. Full stop. The strongest correlations to be drawn when trying to determine which schools will have the most students arrested in school has nothing to do with truancy or violence and everything to do with how many Black students are in a school and if the school has police officers. Schools with police officers are criminalizing our children, terrifying our children, and abusing our children.

➤ **Ask about school policies.** If you have children or are responsible for children in school, it's important to know about that school's policies and insist on changes where those policies could be harmful. Of special note are disciplinary policies: Who has to sign off on suspensions or expulsions? What reviews do they have to guard against bias? What are their policies for dealing with racist faculty and staff? What are their policies for dealing with racism among students? What is the school dress code and are students penalized for dressing in styles that are associated with people of color? How would a student report harassment, bullying, or discrimination?

➤ **Support PTA, booster, and school-supply fundraising drives for majority Black and brown schools.** There are many ways in which wealth is hoarded in white schools and kept from Black and brown schools. Levies and property-tax-based funding puts many BIPOC-majority schools at an economic disadvantage. But that disadvantage is greatly magnified by how much money white neighborhoods are able to pour into their schools, due to more disposable income and more free time to fundraise. This is also magnified by the tendencies of white families in mixed-race neighborhoods to put their kids into private schools without contributing financially to public schools in their area. While the ways in which our schools are funded desperately need a systemic overhaul, we can help bridge some of the gaps right now by giving financial support to underfunded schools.

➤ **Support HBCUs.** The funding gaps we see in K–12 education are magnified at the college level. While almost all universities have absorbed harmful racist and anti-Black ideas of our education system, HBCUs are the best chance for Black college students to learn in a more inclusive and Black-centered institution. And many of these institutions are at grave risk. HBCUs are deeply underfunded in comparison to predominantly white schools. This is an issue that dates back to the founding of land-grant colleges and the limited areas that HBCUs were able to focus on.

➤ **Fight against truancy laws.** Laws that criminalize children for missing school are cruel and inhumane, and disproportionately affect children of color. We should not be incarcerating children ever and certainly not for missing school, the circumstances of which are often out of a child's control.

➤ **Talk with other parents and caregivers.** If you have a child in school, talk with other parents and caregivers—especially those of children of color. It's important to know what's happening with kids at school. If you're a parent of color, this can help you identify patterns in treatment that may need to be addressed and can combat the gaslighting many schools employ, telling you that your child is the only one having problems. If you're a parent of a white student, it's vital to know about the experiences children of color are having in your child's school to be able to identify differences in treatment and issues that families of color are facing that you can stand in solidarity with.

➤ **Demand ethnic study programs.** All children of all races and ethnicities need diverse education because they live in a diverse world. Any school that fails to provide that education is failing your student.

➤ **Support independent education programs for students of color.** Independent arts programs, cultural programs, tutoring programs, and more fill important gaps for children of color who are not being properly served by public education programs. It's important that these programs stay vibrant and viable, even as we work to ensure that public schools do better by our children. Support these programs whenever you can.

➤ **Support diverse books.** Buy books by authors of color to fill your own gaps in education and for your family. Request books by authors of color from your local public library. Those library purchases not only support the authors who wrote them but also increase accessibility of those books for readers who may not be able to purchase them from a store.

➤ **Support affordable housing initiatives.** Affordable housing, both in rentals and through affordable home-buying programs, is important in the battle for reducing racism in education. Why? Because mixed-income neighborhoods help share resources and reduce the wealth hoarding that happens in white schools in more segregated districts. In addition, students do far better in schools that they can afford to stay in. They are healthier, happier, and better able to learn when they don't have to move every few years in a search for more affordable rent. This basic level of economic security helps all children in poor and working-class families, of which children of color are more likely to be a part.

There's a lot we can do right now to make our schools more equitable for all students, and there's a lot we can do outside of our education system to get and support diverse, anti-racist education.

This is one of the most actionable and quickly rewarded areas of anti-racist work we can do. But our US education system is also in a state of emergency. Our young people are only young once. We don't get to give these important years back to them once they've passed. Safe, healthy, robust, and racially informed education is vital to the well-being of our young people, and our society. Let this year be the one when the most important lesson students of color learn is that they matter.

## ARTS, RACE, AND THE CREATIVE FORCES OF REVOLUTION

IN JANUARY 2020, WHEN COVID-19 hit the United States, it hit Washington State, where I live, first. By March, all of my speaking engagements for the rest of the year had been canceled. Having grown up in poverty and having struggled for years to pay bills as a writer, I had, with the success of *So You Want to Talk About Race*, found myself in the position of having a healthy savings account for the first time in my life.

My assistant, Ebony, and I looked over our financial needs for our small business. I looked at my savings. My partner, Gabriel, and I had just broken ground on building our forever home, but the money I had saved for that would now need to cover our bills and pay my small team as well as help any family members who found themselves in need. The house would just have to wait.

I went upstairs in our rental to talk with my partner, who was in his studio. I updated him on the conversation I'd had with my assistant and marveled at how lucky we were to be able to weather this storm, at least financially. Had it been a few years earlier, I'm not sure what we would have done.

We realized that this pandemic was going to hit the arts community hard—especially BIPOC artists. Musicians lost gigs as venues closed. Teaching artists found their classes canceled. And the bars and restaurants where many artists worked to help cover their bills had also closed. BIPOC artists were less likely to have savings or wealthy relations to turn to for help in these times.

In the past, I had been able to leverage my local network to get resources to neighbors in need. My community had been generous, and I was wondering if we might be able to do something like that again.

This was the beginning of the pandemic. We thought we needed to help people get through a month or two, at most. We set a goal to raise twenty thousand dollars.

Gabriel, Ebony, and I put together a fundraising campaign. The application process was a simple form. We asked people for their basic contact info, what work had been canceled, how much they had expected to make from that work and what they would need to meet immediate financial needs. We also asked demographic information: Were they in the BIPOC or LGBTQIA+ community? Were they disabled?

We wanted it to be simple for people to apply. Having grown up in government systems that make you jump through laborious and often demeaning hoops in order to get even the most minor financial assistance, I didn't want to do that to people. We wanted to trust people. The demographics information would be used by us to ensure we were doing enough outreach to the communities we knew would be most hard-hit by the shutdowns.

Within a week we were in over our heads. We were unprepared for the hundreds of applications that came in. But we were even more unprepared for the hundreds of donations. We had raised a hundred thousand dollars in the time we had hoped to reach twenty thousand dollars.

Tim Lennon reached out to offer help administering the fund. He was the director of Langston, an arts organization dedicated to supporting Black artists in the Seattle area. He and the Langston team took on fiscal sponsorship of the fund. We worked out a mathematical formula to distribute funds as equitably as possible. Nobody who applied was turned away. We went from sitting in a daze, wondering what we were going to do while locked in our homes, to working ten-hour days running the fund.

Ebony and Tim managed the distribution of the funds to artists. I managed the publicity and communications. Gabriel worked with dozens of people from across the country who had heard about our fund and were trying to set up their own.

Amid all of the heartache, loss, and fear of those early pandemic days, working on the fund kept us going. We couldn't send out much. An average of a few hundred dollars a person. But we were able to get money directly into the hands of thousands of people who had been left out of a lot of state-run COVID relief programs.

Most of our funds came from individuals. We got a few donations larger than ten thousand dollars, but not many. Most of the donations to the fund came from individuals within our arts community. People who I knew personally were suffering from these closures themselves were sending a spare twenty dollars, even if they weren't sure if they would need that twenty dollars in a few days. Sometimes we would send artists funds only to receive them back in the mail a few days later, with the artist explaining that they had been able to book a gig in the time since they had applied, so they wanted to make sure the money went back into the pool for other artists.

We noticed how much BIPOC artists who had received funds from us worked to try to support the fund for other artists in whatever way they could. Many artists of all races and ethnicities tried to show their appreciation for our work and support us. But BIPOC artists especially showed up and out. They held benefit performances online; they sold art, with the proceeds going to our funds; they participated in our fundraising videos.

When we closed the fund, a year after starting it, we had disbursed over a million dollars to Seattle-area artists, becoming the biggest provider of artist relief in the region.

The next year, as in-person events started up again, I had my first in-person speaking gig. It was in Langston's theater, and it meant so much to see people return to a venue that is so vital to the Seattle Black arts community. As we were setting up, one of the crew members walked up to me. He was a Black man, appearing to be in his twenties. He wanted to tell me that he hadn't thought he was going to be able to stay in Seattle when the pandemic hit. As a Black artist, he had felt forgotten and left behind. But then he received a check from our Artist Relief Fund, and he knew that he hadn't been forgotten. It was enough for him to be able to stay a little while longer. And then he had found his job at Langston and he was hopeful that he'd be able to stay for good.

Less than six months after starting the fund, the house we were renting was destroyed in a fire. We escaped with the clothes on our backs and little more. After the fire, I was able to pull out three paintings that were heavily smoke damaged. Everything else was gone. It was the same BIPOC arts community we had helped with the relief fund who surrounded us in love. We were overwhelmed with handmade gifts that somehow found us in the hotels we were staying in, with the songs people sent us, with the prayers and poems, with the healing herbs sent to clear our lungs. My partner and I hadn't really cried the night of the fire. We'd been in shock. But the next day, as we listened to a song sung by an elder in our community, a song of love and loss recorded for us, we both were able to cry and release some of the pain and fear that had been squeezing our hearts.

I had bought, just a few months earlier, a beautiful painting from one of the artists who had applied to our fund. It was a vibrant painting of multicolored blocks that represented community. I snuck into the house after the fire, before the fire marshal had declared it safe to enter, to grab the painting off the soot-blackened wall. It was almost completely unrecognizable.

The original artist took it back and lovingly restored it. It took her months. She returned it to me, gorgeous and vibrant, and carrying an even deeper story of community.

I have loved art my entire life. But even more important, I've loved artists my entire life. I don't know who I would be if it weren't for the writers, poets, painters, and musicians who have been able to give voice to my experiences as a Black queer woman at times when I could not. I have never been alone as long as I've had art, as long as artists in my community were making art. I have never been lost as long as I was able to look to our arts community to show the way.

It has been an honor to be a part of this community. And it was an honor to be a part of the support network for our community. But I will never be able to put into words how beautiful it was to be lifted by that same community at our most difficult times.

The arts are the heart and soul of our communities. Art is a part of us; it is in our blood. It has told our stories, it has sung us to freedom, it has remembered our dead, it has shown our outrage, it has reminded us of what we are fighting for.

And yet when we think about how to support our movements, and how to maintain healthy cultures, protected against the ravages of white supremacy, we rarely talk about art. Not at least with any focus on how to support and maintain arts and artists in our communities.

It is through art that we understand the world, that we know our history. Yet, just as in our history textbooks, we run the risk of it being written by white men. Our movements cannot survive without art, and our culture cannot either. The revolution may not be televised, but it will be painted. It will be sung.

## COMPLEX MOVEMENTS

In every city that Complex Movements arrives in to hold their performances, they put a lot of effort into facilitating connections between movement workers and community groups. Often those connections lead to collaborations in art and justice work. Complex Movements' visit to Seattle in 2014 left a lasting impression on me. One that has influenced how I work to this day.

Reading from their bio, ill Weaver tells me that Complex Movements are "a Detroit-based artist and organizer collective supporting the transformation of communities by exploring the connections of complex science and social justice movements through multimedia interactive performance and installation work."

Their members are Wes Taylor, Sage Crump, ill Weaver, Carlos Garcia, and Waajeed. They are musicians, writers, filmmakers, organizers, and visual artists. The members come together and move apart at various times. They are all very active in arts and movement workspaces and are often working on multiple projects as individuals and with different groups at the same time.

Complex Movements' largest project to date is *Beware of the Dandelions*, a multidiscipline hip-hop experiential art installation and performance. And still, it's even more than that.

A Complex Movements show doesn't feel like your typical hip-hop show, and it doesn't feel like your typical art installation, and it doesn't feel like your typical activist gathering, although it has elements of all three. It's something different and new, and each performance is unique to the space that Complex Movements is performing in.

The seeds of Complex Movements were sown in conversations in the early 2000s between Weaver and the legendary organizer and movement leader Grace Lee Boggs. Boggs was telling Weaver about her earlier participation in women's liberation movements and how they had inspired her. "Because it taught her to move away from singular charismatic leaders and towards being more like the midwives that support the birth of movements that are already emerging," Weaver explains to me. "And I was like, 'That is dope, that's beautiful, that's what I want to aspire to.' To help doula and midwife the liberation that's already emerging. That's not top-down, 'We're gonna impose liberation on people.' People are liberating themselves, and we're gonna accompany them in that process."

As Weaver brought these ideas back to Wes Taylor and Waajeed, it was this focus on emerging movements that stuck with them. They were just starting their media company and record label. "And I was like, *That would be a dope name: Emergence*," Weaver says.

As they started looking into the scientific theories around emergence and emergent properties, Weaver started finding striking similarities between how smaller entities interacting with one another in nature can have much larger, and surprising, outcomes, and what they saw in decentralized global movement work. People and movements interacting with one another in hyperlocal fights for justice can, unexpectedly, also have much larger and broader outcomes.

As the collective continued to work with these theories in mind, the frustration of one of their members provided them with the opportunity to apply these theories even further.

"The origin of Complex Movements, as we exist now," Taylor explains, "came from an ultimatum from Waajeed—in some ways to not perform hip-hop in the traditional way, as an MC, as ill was doing as Invincible, and on the stage with a DJ. And so Waajeed was like, 'I'm not down with that format anymore. It's old. It's stale. Let's try something new. And if we don't try anything new, then have fun doing it—but I'm not doing it anymore.'"

The rest of the members took in this ultimatum and thought about what they could do with their performances that was new for both them and their audiences. The collective looked for ways to more completely embody their belief in the importance of emerging movements.

All of the members of Complex Movements were veteran performers and had a lot of experience with more traditional touring. The touring life of artists—especially independent artists—can be quite grueling and isolating. You're often hustling as hard as possible to get the resources you need in order to make the tour financially feasible, but you're unable to stay in any particular place long enough to make real connections or give back to the communities you're working in. Complex Movements aimed to create something different. Something that would be positive and nurturing of the movement work in the cities they traveled to.

"Because of the scale of our work, for it to move around and to have life in different communities, it required a certain level of infrastructure," Sage Crump explains. "And we know that touring in this country is—has always been—inherently capitalistic, inherently extractive. For the artist and the communities it comes to. And so we're like, 'How do we be inside this?'—because the infrastructure was necessary. 'How do we do that with our values intact? How do we do that in a way that supports local organizing? How do we do that in a way that doesn't pull resources from the communities that we come to but leaves something as we move through?'"

This started with input and permission from movement workers and community leaders.

"Some of our early conversations," Weaver recalls, "were just, like, meeting with movement organizers in Detroit and in other cities and asking them, 'If we were to use these really nerdy abstract poetic concepts from emergence theory and complex systems and, like, all these metaphors about fractals and ferns . . . you know, ant and other insect societies, and starling murmurations, and wave particle duality—are they useful to you? Or are we just going down some weird bunny hole that's not serving anybody except for our creative whims?'"

The response from community members in those early conversations was overwhelmingly positive, and so Complex Movements began developing their shows. But this process is one they've repeated in every city they've gone to. They've always entered into conversation with movement folk and community leaders to make sure their presence is both needed and desired, before agreeing to any performances with venues.

I got to witness this long and detailed process firsthand in Seattle back in 2014.

By the time I met with Complex Movements, working with the venue they would be performing in, they had already held meetings with community members and movement workers. But in the months leading up to those performances, those meetings continued.

They listened to the stories of our communities. They asked about our movement priorities. They asked about the current social and political environment in the area. They asked about the community relationship to the venue they would be performing in. They searched for opportunities to amplify community messages.

In these meetings, people from different movement organizations got to connect for the first time. Complex Movements helped facilitate conversation and collaboration over other arts projects outside of their own in the community.

When we came back weeks later for the performances, we were walked through an immersive arts experience. We entered a structure filled with lights and video, sharing messages about collective struggle, and collective liberation, rooted in emergence theory. While we were taking in the visual information, Weaver rapped to the collective's music.

The messaging of the music and visual art tied into broader racial and economic justice issues but was also distinctly local—influenced by the conversations the collective had had with community members.

After the show, we were led through a room lined with tables that were manned by representatives of local activist groups and organizations. Attendees were encouraged to engage with the representatives, take information, and give them their support.

This process fostered connections between different people and groups that are still influencing Seattle movement work today, and some of the movement workers profiled in this book were first introduced to me in that room.

"It's never just an artistic piece," Crump explains. "It's designed to support. We were thinking, *How is this a tool, as well, to support local movement?* And that was part of our intention."

Complex Movements' approach to their artistic activism highlights the need for work that is both universal and hyperlocal at the same time, because the issues we face are both universal and hyperlocal.

Weaver compares it to how we look at the climate crisis. If climate change is the overall harm, and we can all recognize that the overall issue is climate injustice, that doesn't mean it's going to look the same all over the world. "Those weather systems are gonna show up differently in different areas of the world, right?" Weaver says. "So you're gonna have some areas with droughts and some areas with floods and some areas with hurricanes and some areas with tornadoes. And some areas with something totally unexpected that you've never seen before and is gonna potentially show up as a global pandemic. It's gonna look so many different ways. Some that look a certain way locally, and some that look pretty similarly across everywhere. But they're caused by similar injustices, similar systems."

Weaver points to increased police militarization around the world as an example of those harmful systems at work. They point out how the heavily militarized Israeli police forces have been, for years now, training other police forces from multiple countries in these more militarized tactics and technologies. This policing is, Weaver describes, "a form of military occupation against Black, brown, and Indigenous communities." While police forces around the world may look different on the ground, when you look at them as a whole, you can see how connected they are—not only in tactics or equipment used but also in their overall goals for control over Indigenous communities and communities of color.

Weaver also points out technologies like ShotSpotter—a surveillance product that uses artificial intelligence to analyze input from microphones placed throughout target areas to detect gunshots in order to expedite police response to where guns are suspected to have been fired. Studies have shown ShotSpotter to be largely ineffective in deterring or detecting gun crime (Schuba 2021). What ShotSpotter does seem to be effective at is increasing the amount of surveillance technology in communities of color, and sending more police officers out looking for crime that more often than not doesn't exist.

But the resistance to these systems is also both local and connected: "Like, right now in Detroit there's a big fight against ShotSpotter," Weaver says. "There's also a fight against ShotSpotter in Seattle. There's also a fight against ShotSpotter in Cleveland. Cuz these oppressive technologies get shared across their similar municipalities or whatever corporate equivalent is in a different geography."

The collective points out that just as universal systems of oppression may have different actors and outcomes around the country and around the world, universal practices of liberation must take different approaches in order to meet those different situations and the different needs of different communities.

"How are we going to make an intervention? What do we need to learn from each other? And how do we customize it to our community's weather systems and needs and cultures?" Weaver asks.

Taylor and Crump point out that this work will take creativity, if it's to defeat the varied approaches that systems of oppression take. But people are inherently more creative than the systems that try to exploit them. And that creativity doesn't require special technology or education or access.

"You just reminded me of Grace's quote," Weaver says to them, referencing Grace Lee Boggs. "'A people exercising their creativity in the face of devastation is one of the greatest contributions to humankind.'"

## Art as the Keeper of Community

Before we wrote books, we sang songs, we painted on walls, we told stories by the fire. We wove our histories into fabrics and our dreams into baskets. We sculpted our gods out of clay.

Art is deeply human. And in communities of color, our art is what has endured above all else. As white supremacy and colonization toppled our buildings, deposed our leaders, banned our languages, even stole our bodies, we still kept our art alive.

The threads, the brushstrokes, the sung notes of our art, kept us connected to our ancestors and to one another.

In this revolutionary work, we cannot neglect our healing, our connection, or our joy. Whether it's art programs to empower youth and teach restorative practices, oral history programs to protect the knowledge of our elders, or ceremonial dances and songs that welcome new life to our communities. Art is what makes our communities, communities.

And yet it is in majority Black and brown schools that arts funding is more likely to be cut under budget constraints. Private art schools are often priced out of reach of BIPOC families, and least likely to offer financial aid.

BIPOC students who are able to attend art schools or have art education in their public schools are almost guaranteed to be taught primarily Eurocentric art. They will often encounter racist instructors who refuse to see the value of BIPOC artists or art traditions. And they will usually be trained with the assumption that they will be making art for white consumption.

Even when BIPOC-centered arts education is available, economic hardship and uncertainty make many BIPOC families less likely to steer their children in artistic directions.

This hesitancy isn't necessarily wrongheaded. Art is incredibly underpaid as a career in the United States, and many artists need additional sources of income or the support of financially comfortable families in order to be able to provide for their basic needs. For BIPOC artists, who are more likely to be underpaid for their art, less likely to receive grants, less likely to land more secure industry jobs, and less likely to have family wealth to fall back on—the life of an artist can truly be out of reach for many.

Still, when we think of this revolution, and what we want to see on the other side of it, I'm positive that for many of us, vibrant, beautiful, joyous art—art made by us and for us—is surely a part of that vision.

In fact, whatever vision of that great future we hold in our mind's eye was surely painted by art itself in some way. Art will create and sustain that vision for us, even in our darkest days of the battle against oppression. Art is the keeper of the future we are trying to build.

## INYE WOKOMA AND ELISHEBA JOHNSON

The first time I visited Wa Na Wari was to assist with the wedding of two dear friends and members of our Black arts and movement-work community. It was going to be a very small, private, spiritual ceremony, and they told me they couldn't think of a better place for it than Wa Na Wari.

The first thing I noticed about Wa Na Wari as I approached the modest gray craftsman home was its stairs. At first glance, the house doesn't stand out from the rest of the block. Yes, there's a small sign out front letting you know you're at Wa Na Wari, but it's easy to overlook. The house style is typical of homes built in the Seattle area in the early 1900s.

But as you move closer to the house, you notice the wooden stairs leading to the front door. The stairs have a beautiful triangle pattern carved into them. They are, to me, reminiscent of West African mud-cloth patterns. And in the center of each stair riser, lines from the Langston Hughes poem "Mother to Son" have been engraved in bold capital letters:

WELL, SON, I'LL TELL YOU:
LIFE FOR ME AIN'T BEEN NO CRYSTAL STAIR.
SO BOY, DON'T YOU TURN BACK.
FOR I'SE STILL GOIN', HONEY,
I'SE STILL CLIMBIN'.

As I climbed the stairs and stood on the little front porch, I noticed a Black woman sitting on a small cushioned bench. I thought she might be helping with the wedding as well, but she appeared to just be utilizing the space to read a book on the beautiful late spring day. To the left of the front door, BLACK LEGACIES MATTER is proudly displayed in large black lettering.

My partner and I entered the house and were immediately enveloped in the warmth of it. Yellow walls were covered in art by local Black artists. A large wooden table in the front room showed evidence of the community arts projects it had hosted. The beautiful large, dark wood beams framing each room spoke to the permanence of the space. I looked around and saw how this house, in its current life as Wa Na Wari, had become a home for an entire community.

In order to understand Wa Na Wari—a Black arts and community space that is part of the revitalization of a historically Black neighborhood in Seattle—we have to look back more than seventy years ago, to the beginning. It all started with a house. Well, six houses, to be more accurate.

Frank and Goldyne Green came to Seattle after World War II in search of opportunity. There was a small but growing Black population in the area, who had been drawn to the region by the promise of new jobs in industries that had grown massively during the war. It was a time when many who had long been excluded from well-paying jobs (like Black people, people of color, and women) were able to enter the industrial workforce in numbers previously unseen in US history. Frank used his military pension and what pay he was able to save from work he found on the docks to buy a home in the Central District, one of only a few neighborhoods where Black people were allowed to live in the heavily redlined city.

As the years passed, the Greens became one of the foundational families of the Central District. (Today, Frank Green's portrait is prominently featured in a large mural in the district's commercial area, honoring his local legacy.) Over time, the Greens bought more homes in Seattle's Black neighborhoods: four in the Central District, one in the Mount Baker neighborhood, and one in South Seattle.

Many who work for racial or economic justice may feel wary at the mention of how many homes the Greens owned. Landlords and property developers have often been active participants in the oppression and exploitation of people of color—whether it's displacing communities of color for development projects or forcing communities of color into substandard living conditions or simply taking advantage of the economic discrimination and marginalization that keeps many people of color from being able to buy their own homes. Many of us have little love for landlords. But the Greens did not buy these homes in order to hoard land or amass personal wealth at the expense of renters. These homes were for family.

The Greens' grandson, Inye Wokoma, explains: "My grandparents' ethos around family was such that they purchased and had homes specifically for family to live in, and created an opportunity for there to be an internal economy within the family for family members working on the properties, both in repair and general maintenance."

Communal economies may seem strange or unusual to those more used to Western capitalism, but they are widely practiced in communities of color. It is often through the pooling of resources and the creation of alternate economies that we have been able to survive in a white supremacist society that has largely shut us out of mainstream wealth channels. What the Greens built with their homes is a beautiful example of one of these communal economies. The system that circled around these homes supported the wider family. Family members had affordable, stable housing that allowed them to establish themselves or weather personal or economic hardship. The rents they paid supported maintenance on the homes and family businesses.

Wokoma lived in these homes through various periods of his childhood, with both his mom and his grandmother. He grew up surrounded by family and their artistic pursuits. "I have long memories of my cousins making music in the bedrooms," he recalls with a smile. "Having little mini-studios, making music from the bedroom, and other kids break dancing and doing dance routines for talent shows and whatnot in the backyards or in the living rooms."

The homes the Greens owned were always filled with Black music and Black art. Community was always welcome in these homes, and they often served as community meeting and performance spaces. Small Black-owned spaces—especially in places like Seattle, where the relatively small Black population was often unwelcome in larger venues—have long been part of the beating heart of our communities.

It has meant so much to Inye Wokoma and his partner, Elisheba Johnson, to be able to bring art and Black community back to the Central District. But it was almost all lost—the homes, the legacy, the community—and Wokoma and Johnson are still fighting every day to hang on to it.

Homeownership, or lack thereof, is one of the driving factors behind the racial wealth gap in the United States. The ability of whites to own and pass down property generation after generation, to have that property accrue value, and to be able to borrow against that value, has given white people a multigenerational wealth advantage that Black communities have had much less access to due to racial hiring and wage gaps, redlining, predatory lending, and other systemic factors.

The National Association of Realtors reported in their *Snapshot of Race and Home Buying in America* that, as of 2020, 72 percent of white households owned their own home, versus 62 percent for Asian households, 51 percent for Hispanic households, and 43 percent for Black households—a percentage that was lower in 2020 than it was in 2010. They also found that Black applicants are twice as likely to be rejected for a mortgage than white applicants (Snowden and Evangelou 2022).

But homeownership doesn't guarantee an escape from economic racism. Even when Black people are able to buy their own homes, they don't benefit to the same degree that white people do. Black-owned homes are regularly undervalued in comparison to white-owned homes; Black people are often targeted by predatory lenders and end up paying higher mortgage payments than white people for homes of the same value; and Black families are still made more economically vulnerable due to systemic racism in ways that can make it harder for them to hold on to their homes or successfully pass them on to future generations. As Black homeowners age and eventually pass away, Black families are especially vulnerable.

"People are already in these states of vulnerability across different areas of their lives," Wokoma explains. "Then . . . having to take on the responsibility of inheriting a house that needs a lot of work because of the long history of economic marginalization—to use the nice cushy words for economic oppression—people sell. Also people sell because they see that as an opportunity to have probably more cash than they've ever seen at one time in their lives, not realizing that it's also giving away probably the most valuable thing that they own collectively."

As Frank Green aged and then passed away, it became harder for the family to keep the homes. They started selling off property to cover expenses, even though doing so threatened the economic and social security of the family. They felt they had no choice.

"The selling of the homes represented the dissolution of that economic framework," Wokoma says, "and in addition to everything else, the social framework, the familial frameworks. And it also made my grandmother that much more vulnerable."

Goldyne Green was diagnosed with Alzheimer's and eventually needed full-time care. That care was expensive, and like with many Black families, economic and medical racism increased their vulnerability. The family found themselves in an economic crisis.

By 2016, the family was faced with the very real prospect of having to sell all of the homes and put Goldyne Green into a nursing home. In search of a solution to save what they could and allow Goldyne to spend her last days in her own home, the family turned to Wokoma. He spent about three years working out a solution to save some of the family property and keep his grandmother out of a nursing home. "The last piece that made it all sort of come together was the creation of Wa Na Wari," Wokoma tells me.

Inye Wokoma and Elisheba Johnson run Wa Na Wari. Johnson steps in to introduce Wa Na Wari, as she's the one who usually does so for visitors to the house. She's an artist, arts administrator, and curator, and has long worked to create gathering and arts spaces for the Black community in the area. And Wokoma is a journalist, filmmaker, visual artist, and community organizer. Johnson serves as Wa Na Wari's curator, and Wokoma is the land steward.

The house we are in is the second house Frank and Goldyne Green bought. Johnson points next door and explains that it is the first house the Greens bought. These first two homes they have been working to save with Wa Na Wari.

Wa Na Wari was born from conversations between Wokoma, Johnson, and fellow Central District artists Jill Freidberg and Rachel Kessler. The group wondered if there was a way they could address the displacement of communities of color that was affecting not only Wokoma's family but also Black families throughout the Central

District—a way that would be sustainable and rooted in collective benefit instead of capitalist profit and exploitation.

"We wanted to see what it would look like or be like if we rented Inye's grandmother's home and gave it back to the Black community as an arts and cultural center," Johnson explains.

This was not just about saving a Black family's home. This was about preserving all that Black homes and Black spaces mean for our communities.

"Black homes have always been community spaces and organizing spaces," Johnson says. "We're actually not doing anything different. The house functions as it has always functioned. Because Inye's aunt, Aunt Bertie—Frank's sister—who lived in that house for forty years, and passed away in that house, always had the door open. . . . There was always food cooked. The neighbor kids could come in—they had a place to stay. So we're actually just continuing a lineage of how that house has been in the community. Creating a space for Black folks who have been disenfranchised from that community for a long time, and creating a space for them to feel welcome again."

In order for Black homes to continue to be safe spaces, and the economic and cultural drivers they are in Black communities, they have to stay Black homes.

"The thing that's most important about Wa Na Wari is the invisible thing that you don't see, which is that the rent is paid, right?" Johnson says with a laugh.

Wokoma and his siblings are working together to purchase the home, which has been in probate since his grandmother passed. They plan to place it in an organization they started, the Frank and Goldyne Green Cultural Land Conservancy. They will then lease the home from the Conservancy, much as they are now while it's in probate, as the family maintains ownership of the home, ultimately guaranteeing a home for Wa Na Wari.

It can be hard to explain what exactly Wa Na Wari does. Not because the work is vague or hard to quantify but because they do so much, and it can seem so widely varied. But when you take a step back, you can see that it's all a part of their core mission of preserving the Central District's Black community.

Wa Na Wari is, first and foremost, about Black art and culture. And their arts programs are geared around not only celebrating and centering Black art and artists but also ensuring the future of art in Seattle's Black community. Central to this are ventures like their Seattle Black Spatial Histories Institute and their artist residency program.

The Spatial Histories Institute teaches Black community members how to gather, archive, and preserve oral histories. Wokoma tells me, "We work with Black professional oral historians from around the country that come in and do the training, and then the cohort members go out into the community and collect stories, do the archiving process, and then create ways of bringing those stories back into the community."

Their artist residency program provides a stipend and space in Wa Na Wari for local Black visual artists to stay and create work. The work is then showcased at Wa Na Wari for two months. The team at Wa Na Wari embraces resident artists like they're family, providing more than just space and funds to create art. The community support, too, can be vital for creation. The team hopes to turn all of the Green family homes that they can save into permanent artist live-work spaces. From there, their organization can establish a model of living, working, and community that can be adapted by others to not only help Black homeowners stay in their homes but also sustain a vibrant community.

This informs their activism work with their Central Area Cultural EcoSystem, 21st Century program—or CASE 21. This community organizing program is aimed at empowering Black homeowners in the Central District and throughout the county. The team educates homeowners about land-use policies and advocates for changes to these policies to enable more homeowners to build what they call "micro-cultural spaces" on their properties. "These spaces would be scalable for neighborhood life, responsive to the needs and norms of Black communal life, and would provide economic opportunities for Black homeowners and new opportunities for displaced cultural workers alike" (Wa Na Wari, n.d.).

Wa Na Wari has shown in many ways what it means to be "responsive to the needs and norms of Black communal life." In the early years of the pandemic, Wa Na Wari was a lifeline to the local Black community and other communities of color. Art is not separate from us. Art is a part of communities of color and in just about everything we do. So it makes sense that a community arts space like Wa Na Wari would quickly become about so much more than art.

In 2020, while we were all trying to keep our distance and yet still stay connected, I was suddenly seeing friends selling flowers online. These were not people I had ever seen show a particular interest in flowers or the floral trade. But there they were, selling bouquets of flowers every week, offering to drop them off at your door. "Support Hmong farmers," they said.

It turns out the flowers came from Wa Na Wari. A group of Hmong farmers had long sold their flowers at storefronts around the city. But during the pandemic lockdown, their sales spaces disappeared. They reached out to Wa Na Wari and asked if they could use the house as a drop-off place for their flowers, so that community members could pick them up and deliver them to buyers.

"We laugh sometimes because we don't always even know what's going on," Johnson tells me. "Like, somehow produce started showing up every other Saturday. And we're like, 'Okay, we have all this produce now.' Which is good."

It turns out that the produce came from Haki Farmers, a Black farm collective in Olympia who'd heard about Wa Na Wari through the Hmong farmers. They started sending produce to be redistributed to the community. It's likely Haki Farmers knew Wa Na Wari would be able to distribute the produce because they were already hosting a community meals program that was giving out 225 African- and Indigenous-inspired meals a week. Wa Na Wari also helps local residents feed themselves by hosting urban farming classes, taught by Black and Indigenous farmers.

Wa Na Wari's food programs are just as vital to building and maintaining community as its arts programs are. Johnson tells me that when elders can't make it to food pickup days, other members in the community have begun volunteering to bring food to them. "There's just this way that we are able to keep community or be a part of community that makes me feel really whole and happy," she says with a smile.

Wa Na Wari is part of a wider movement throughout the Central District to combat the gentrification that has devastated what used to be a vibrant Black community. Black-owned restaurants, shops, and venues have been opening up in recent years. Residents who long ago were pushed out of the neighborhood are coming back. Some for an event or a weekend, and some for good.

"So now we have neighbors who are moving back to this community, who are telling us it's because—yes, it's cuz of all the restaurants and shops, but also because the arts and culture is coming back," Johnson says. "And they don't have to leave their neighborhood to see artists like them and to be able to create in their community."

Wa Na Wari has been transformational, not only for the Central District but for Johnson and Wokoma as well.

"Honestly it's just really empowering. It's like a sanctuary," Johnson tells me. "It's the only time in my career that I've curated exclusively Black people. And so I'm able to have these unique conversations—one-on-one, artist-to-artist, Black person to Black person—that I'm really cherishing. And that makes me more whole. It's not just the work. The work is also changing me, and the shows themselves are constantly building upon who I am as a person. But I think the more and more people that become a part of our community, the more I realize that the work is kind of—it's spirit work."

Wokoma talks about his mother, an artist in her own right, who encouraged his love of art. Her ability to create art as a Black single mother was made possible in part by the stability and security of being able to live in one of Frank and Goldyne's homes. Homes that are providing opportunities for Black art today.

"Her ability to do those things had everything to do with the environment that was created around her," Wokoma tells me. "And then, my ability to think more expansively about what my life might possibly be about has everything to do, one, with that environment, but also seeing her move inside of that environment in specific ways. So I think when we talk about the connection between Black homes, property ownership, and community building, we talk about culture and the arts . . . You can't disentangle them."

# White Supremacy in the Art World

While many people in arts spaces like to think that art exists beyond the base bigotries and oppressions of society, art is actually a field uniquely insulated from racial progress and protective of its racial privilege.

A 2022 article in *Humanities and Social Sciences Communications* found that populations of color are vastly underrepresented in the art world. BIPOC artists make up only 22 percent of people working in contemporary art, 22 percent of people working in high fashion, and 19 percent of people working in box office film. Meanwhile, white men are overrepresented in all categories (Topaz et al. 2022).

It's not just representation that is lacking. Pay for BIPOC artists who are able to make their careers in art is often lacking as well. A survey of arts administrators in Los Angeles County found that BIPOC administrators made an average of 35 percent less than white administrators (Dafoe 2021). A study by Australian researcher Jeremy K. Nguyen showed that even in emerging digital arts sectors, racial bias still works against BIPOC artists. Analyzing 18,883 sales of CryptoPunk NFTs, Nguyen found that CryptoPunks with lighter skin tones consistently sold at significantly higher prices than CryptoPunks with deeper skin tones, even when controlling for rarity and market conditions (Nguyen 2022).

Perhaps the most shocking numbers, though, come from museums. In 2019, researchers at Williams College took a look at racial representation in art gallery collections. It's easy to predict that there would be a bias favoring white male artists in museum collections, but I wasn't prepared for what the study showed.

Looking at the collections of eighteen major art museums in

the United States, researchers found that over 85 percent of the art was by white artists, and 87 percent was by men. Art by Asian artists made up 9 percent, Hispanic and Latino artists made up 2.8 percent, and Black artists made up 1.2 percent with all other non-white groups making up less than 1 percent. Perhaps the least represented artists were women of color, making up just 1 percent of art in museum collections as a whole (Bishara 2019).

It's a cruel irony that while museums don't want to spend their money to purchase the art of named artists of color, they will fight for decades to keep our ancestors' stolen remains, historical treasures, and sacred artifacts. Many museums across the United States—and throughout most of North America and Europe—contain hundreds, if not thousands, of stolen or unethically procured artifacts of cultural importance to BIPOC communities.

The Nigerian government, for example, has been fighting for years for the return of historical and sacred artifacts that were stolen by British colonizers. Many of these artifacts now reside in US museum collections (Associated Press 2022).

The University of Pennsylvania Museum of Archaeology and Anthropology came under fire after it was made public that it had kept the remains of children killed in the 1985 MOVE bombing hidden away in a box after claiming they were lost. A professor at the university even used the bones of these children murdered by the state in a class lecture (Kassutto 2021).

Lest you think the horrific case of the mishandling and exploitation of the remains of murdered Black children was an anomaly, it is clearly not. A leaked 2022 report commissioned by Harvard found that they had the remains of seven thousand Native people and nineteen (likely enslaved) Africans in their museum collections (Brockell 2022).

Our art isn't valued by white museums, but our artifacts are. Our humanity isn't valued by white museums, but our bones are. It is in these exclusionary, extractive, and violent environments that our artists are trying to create the art so vital to our communities. Art that can strengthen, inspire, and educate us, art that has helped keep us alive, can wither and die within white institutions.

This reality underscores the need to look at equity in the arts from a racial justice perspective.

It's not just about access denied. It's also about the active harm being caused by institutions that suck up such a large portion of the resources allocated to the arts, and use those resources to steal from us and exploit us.

## FAVIANNA RODRIGUEZ

As human beings, we are defined by culture. By song, by image, by the stories we tell around the fire. And white supremacy did a lot to extinguish our cultures. Through genocide, of course. Extinguishing cultures in terms of how we took care of the land. So much was extracted and violated, and yet so much culture over and over again has been the place where we resist."

Favianna Rodriguez is a Latine artist of Peruvian and Afro-Peruvian descent. She's the founder of the Center for Cultural Power, an organization that distributes millions of dollars to artists and arts organizations, and to the creation of arts infrastructure.

Rodriguez's journey began in the Bay Area—Oakland, specifically—where she still lives and works today. She grew up around the mass incarceration and police violence of the "war on drugs," the mass deportation of the Latine community targeted for political gain, and the widespread and systemic state violence that defined a lot of the '80s and '90s on the West Coast. But she also grew up in the birth of West Coast hip-hop and was surrounded by people from

BIPOC liberation movements, like the Black Panthers and the Chicano Movement. "My mentors were Amiri Baraka, Elizabeth 'Betita' Martinez, Emory Douglas, Kathleen Cleaver," she says. "They were all very present there."

From the Chicano Movement, Rodriguez learned that there are three types of power in the world: money power, people power, and Earth power.

"And I feel like what I've been able to develop in my life is the concept of cultural power," Rodriguez adds. She argues that cultural power is one of our most important forces, shaping and influencing other forms of power, and motivating and educating our movements. And yet it's the least supported aspect of our movement work.

She explains that it's easy to see the impact that money and people power has on our society. Corporations and politicians have power that can often be seen and felt, and is invested in maintaining current systems they benefit from. But cultural power can affect all other types of power, and can move and adapt much more quickly than the others.

As an example, Rodriguez points to the huge part that visual artists, musicians, painters, poets, and writers played in the Civil Rights Movement. The arts have been integral to all BIPOC resistance movements in our history. And yet the story of that has been largely erased from our history books. Some of that erasure is due to the fact that patriarchy has often been in control of our narratives, even our resistance narratives.

"Organizing culture when I was growing up was very male. And it was very much about fight, struggle. And I feel like what I learned, especially from women—Black women, Latinx women—is that we also need to imagine what is possible. And it has to feel good," Rodriguez says. "So now when I talk about culture, it's not just about our 'No'; it's also about our 'Yes.' What does our 'Yes' look like?"

Art helps us define that "Yes," helps us focus not only on what we're fighting against but also on what we're fighting for: our history, our culture, our community, our beauty, our future.

Part of the erasure of art in our resistance work is also due to the fact that past generations of BIPOC artists, as well as the arts organizations that were so vital to our movements, were not supported in ways that allowed them to effectively pass on the legacy of their work to future generations.

"A lot of the collectives that were happening—the Black Arts Movement, the Chicano Arts Movement—they didn't have institutions. They didn't build cultural wealth. Which is why in Oakland, for example, so many great things happened, and yet there's nothing to show for it. Because we got pushed out. We didn't own our buildings."

Where past generations of artist-activists may have been more likely to focus on getting into existing buildings that were controlled primarily by white men, later generations of artist-activists have learned from their example how limited that approach is. The buildings were erected to protect white supremacy in the arts, and even if you were to get inside, you'd never have the freedom to create the art you need.

"My mentors were really fighting to get into the room," Rodriguez says. "They were fighting for recognition. And we are fighting for the ownership and the full control of our culture."

Rodriguez has made building and supporting BIPOC arts spaces her life's work, while remaining dedicated to the creation of her own art too, which keeps her connected to the artists she aims to serve.

There are a lot of barriers that BIPOC artists encounter in their work. Rodriguez sees this with the artists she knows and in her own experience as an artist. BIPOC artists are unappreciated and under-resourced in both the "mainstream" arts world and the arts funding world, as well as in our movement spaces.

"It's not like we're demanding cultural equity," Rodriguez asserts. "We're asking for safer schools. We're asking for less guns. But culture isn't a part of our demands. I think less than 5 percent of all art philanthropic dollars are going to communities of color or BIPOC-led organizations. It's a cultural apartheid problem, and yet it's very invisible."

This cultural apartheid starts even before a BIPOC artist knows they want to be an artist. Underfunded schools, which BIPOC are more likely to be in than white students, often cut arts programs first in order to meet tight budgets. When students of color do have arts programs in their schools, rarely are they taught about art from their communities or other communities of color. Rodriguez herself found that when she applied to art schools in high school, her lack of art classes contributed to rejections from all of the schools. She ended up dropping out of school in order to find her own way in the arts world.

"These young people who are creative, we need to support them from, like . . . eighth grade. Because then, I feel like if we were able to do that, by the time they're graduating, we are gonna have so much more of an abundance of creative folks."

For Rodriguez, art is about survival.

"Art is a way of resistance," she says. "It's a way to sustain our cultures, and it's a way for us to express ourselves and to make a mark on the world. And the more we do it . . . we are building that muscle—that's very, very valuable. It's not just a hobby. It's not just 'Oh, let me relax and do something fun' but more like 'Let me build my critical analysis tool and practice expression that is beyond the vocal and the rational, but moves into the emotional landscape.'"

Embracing and supporting the art that comes from our communities can look different from how art is supported in the white-led mainstream. Yes, it's important to collect art and to support shows and performances of our artists. But we must also pay special attention to art forms that are indigenous to our communities, like traditional dance, fabric arts, hip-hop, even graffiti art. These art forms, which are often neglected by traditional arts spaces, are part of our histories and our stories. And story is one of the most important aspects of our art. Stories inspire and motivate, but they also heal.

"I think people underestimate how important it is for us to be embodied in our transformation," Rodriguez tells me. "For example, I'm the first generation that can talk about, publicly, how my mom had to give up her firstborn to adoption. My grandmother, who was Afro-Peruvian, was the maid in the house of my grandfather! I'm able to release these things and to witness them by the creation of art. . . . I feel like the word 'art' is important, but even more important than that is storytelling. Because that's what art is doing—it is helping us to continue the story. And by us saying the story, releasing it, we make it not only available to other people, to tune in to it and feel it, but we [also] don't hold it so much. And I think that's so important in our healing."

Rodriguez believes in the power of art in our communities and our movements. She believes in the artists themselves, too. It's easy for people to consume art and benefit from art without considering the artists who create it.

These artists—who are often the heart and inspiration of our movements, and the keepers of the flames of our culture—should not die penniless and unappreciated. Yet they often do.

"We need to support artists, and especially BIPOC femme artists, who are doing such revolutionary things. In the sense that we're not just talking about representation. We're talking about healing. We're talking about the next generation, about saving Mother Earth. We need support. We need people to stand with us to protect our culture. It feels like culture is seen as soft and politics is seen as hard. And that needs to shift, because culture is what keeps us alive. It's the heart space—it's what keeps us going. I have seen so many of my mentors and past generations dying without the recognition they deserved. I don't want to see that anymore."

The more we support artists, and the more we create spaces for BIPOC to create art, the more we can change the world. Art is an amazing educational tool for informing people about social issues. Art can clearly communicate complicated social and cultural ideas in ways that transcend language barriers and reach across educational levels. Art can work its way past the guards of the most repressive regimes. Art can be uniquely accessible for both the artist and the audience. With a pencil or pen, with chalk, with your body, with your voice, you can create art that tells an important story about the world you live in, and the world you want to live in.

"One person can change culture," Rodriguez tells me. "It is possible to change culture through one story. Which means that we need an abundance of stories. I always tell people: 'Don't be afraid to tell your story. We need your story. Your story might be that thing that pivots us.'"

## Art as a Weapon

When I think of revolution, I think of poetry.

I think of Simin Behbahani saying:

*My heart is greener than green,*
*flowers sprout from the mud and water of my being.*
*Don't let me stand, if you are the enemies of Spring.*

I think of Audre Lorde beginning her excoriation of Jesse Helms with:

*I am a Black woman*
*writing my way to the future*

For most of my younger life, I didn't like poetry. I didn't actively dislike poetry, I just didn't *get it.* It felt to me like a way of making words more complicated or obtuse than they needed to be, just to be fancy. I felt like there were better ways to tell someone you loved them, or to say you were heartbroken, or to describe a sunny day. I didn't understand why people couldn't just say what they were gonna say.

Then, around middle school, I came across the work of Black queer poets. And suddenly the power of poetry became more clear. These poets were saying what *couldn't* be said, in a way that the soul could hear. Then I started reading more poetry of BIPOC existence and resistance, and almost every poem hit me in my core. As a young queer Black woman, I suddenly had a collection of lines in my memory that could speak to my entire state of being. This felt like the opposite of the poetry my teachers had made us study in high school. This wasn't about taking a simple concept and adding so many flounces and filigree that it would become unrecognizable. This was about loading an entire battle onto an arrowhead and aiming straight for the heart.

For so many of us, the story of our struggle is told in a poem, sung in a song, painted in a mural.

Art itself is a powerful protest, and many artists are some of our most dedicated movement workers.

In June 2020, during the global uprising for Black lives, Seattle activists held protests day after day in the Capitol Hill neighborhood of the city, right outside of a police precinct.

Every day for a week police officers pepper sprayed, fired flash grenades at, and brutally arrested peaceful protestors. I remember watching a livestream from one of the protestors, their phone camera trained on a protester at the front of the group who was standing with her hands in the air, as she was hit in the chest point-blank with a flash grenade. She dropped to the ground unconscious. Volunteer medics said that her heart stopped and she had to be resuscitated.

Many businesses in the area shut down during the protests and police violence. But others kept their doors open to aid the community fighting for justice outside of their buildings.

One of the artists I'd met through our Artist Relief Fund had a community art space in the neighborhood. She converted her studio into a sanctuary for protestors; many were younger artists she'd worked with and mentored in the past. She provided food and water, basic first aid, and a place of safety from the increasing brutality of the officers in the street.

After four or five nights of this work, she called my partner in tears. She was exhausted and heartbroken, seeing so many young people coming in bruised and bloody. But after one person stepped in for the evening, taking her place so that she could rest, she was back at it the next night, caring for protestors.

After about a week, and after more than twelve thousand complaints were filed by community members and Capitol Hill residents about the police handling of the protests, the Seattle Police Department made the surprising decision to abandon the precinct, temporarily ceding the area to protestors.

For three weeks, the area around the police station became known as the CHOP (Capitol Hill Occupied Protest). Fox News sent in correspondents like they were sending reporters into a war zone. Panic about the lawlessness and violence of the area spread throughout conservative media. Many of my friends who lived anywhere within ninety miles of the city were getting calls from their out-of-state family members, concerned for their safety. Surely antifa was there and had taken over. Nobody in Washington State was safe.

Soon white nationalists started rolling into the area, heavily armed, itching for a fight. They could be seen walking around in camo, carrying guns and US flags.

I visited the CHOP a few times at the invitation of some of the artists who had been staying there. I did not find the war zone that conservative news outlets were describing. I instead found art. Art was everywhere. The external walls of every building were covered in murals, posters, and messages. Just about every available surface carried a message of resistance. The messages were filled with rage, with hope, with demands, with despair, with joy. Live music could be heard throughout the area as musicians sang about struggle and hope from makeshift platforms. There were stations for people to create their own art. In the center of the CHOP, artists were busy painting a large Black Lives Matter mural down the middle of a street. There was a book exchange, where people could pick up free copies of revolutionary and anti-racist volumes donated by community members and local bookstores. A grassy area beyond the soccer field had been turned into a community garden, and people showed CHOP community members how to grow their own food.

This place was not utopia by any stretch of the imagination. Even as I felt completely safe, every moment that I was there, I could also see the potential volatility in the mix of people now crowded into a few small city blocks. Any collective of traumatized people trying to work actively in its trauma, while under threat from authorities, is going to be especially complicated, and many people who had very good reasons to want to be in a space free from the violence of state intervention were now trying to hold space together.

There were multiple incidences of gun violence around the perimeter of the occupied zone at night, resulting in two deaths. Although those incidents weren't definitively tied to the CHOP, they were used to bolster the insistence by conservatives and moderates that the CHOP was dangerous anarchy that had descended into violent chaos.

But that's not what I witnessed, or what many of my peers who were a part of the occupation experienced. We saw people jump in at the first sign of conflict, defusing situations with restorative practices. We saw people exercise great care for community members in mental health crisis or emotional distress. We saw complicated discussions on violence, on retribution, on patriarchy, in revolutionary spaces. We saw debates on power and privilege.

People would point at the color and beauty all around them and remind one another why they were there and what they were fighting for.

After three weeks, the city retook control of the area with minor fanfare. They tore down the structures that had been built, they painted over the murals, they dug up the community gardens and replaced them with grass. All they left behind was the Black Lives Matter mural on the street. The impassioned work of BIPOC artists in the middle of an uprising, reduced to a cardboard sign in the window of a gentrifier's home. Today, all the shops have re-opened and Capitol Hill is once again the trendy majority white neighborhood it has been since Black people were priced out of it decades earlier.

But in areas on the buildings where the paint is sheer, in the alleys where their rollers missed, the art is still there, peeking through. Reminding us that for three weeks every surface on every building proudly declared that Black lives matter.

## RAFAEL SHIMUNOV

Rafael Shimunov would describe himself as an activist, not an art-ist. He's an activist with incredible artistic talent, and an activist who uses that talent in his work.

"I come from another perspective," Shimunov tells me. "It's this utilitarian plot, where it's like, political is art. You try to start from what you want to get done, versus like, 'I'm gonna make what I make meaningful.' For me, it's always been really utilitarian. Just because it's, like, a shortcut on people's senses. You can write something really brilliant, you can say something really brilliant, but when you create something with sound, with visuals—it grabs people differently."

Shimunov has been a jack-of-all-trades in the activist world for de-cades now. He has worked on prison abolition, electoral activism with the Working Families Party, he's worked with Jewish anti-racist and pro-Palestinian groups like IfNotNow and Jews for Racial & Economic Justice, and he works with the Center for Constitutional Rights.

He's currently organizing against Amazon's unjust business, labor, and environmental practices with a coalition of Amazon workers, neighborhoods, small businesses, and local democracies concerned about and affected by Amazon's practices.

Shimunov also organizes Art V War, self-described as "a tactical faction of shrouded artists" who are "creating extraordinary art against war." With Art V War, he uses art and visual media to draw attention to systemic violence.

Shimunov first began to understand art as a practical tool when he was in school. As a student with ADHD at a school with little administrative support for neurodiversity, he struggled to keep up with assignments. But one teacher allowed him to use art to learn and also to communicate his ideas.

"Rather than writing an essay in Latin, I would create visuals and things," Shimunov remembers, "and that got me into this practice of understanding that not only are we learning things differently, but different people react to things differently. And there are people who react when there's a powerful visual, in a way that shortcuts through their biases, through their barriers."

Shimunov did not consider himself political in his youth, and he grew up in a family that didn't consider itself political. But as a Jewish refugee from Soviet-dominated Uzbekistan, his entire existence in the United States was political in ways he wouldn't understand until adulthood.

He was always reminded by his parents that they were "guests" in the United States and that it was important to not rock the boat. He was told to focus on making money instead, to be able to move out of the projects in Queens, where he grew up.

Heeding his parents' advice, he put his artistic skills to work at an ad agency. It was while working in ad agencies that Shimunov was introduced to activism work. The agency he worked for donated a small percentage of its time and skills to nonprofits, free of charge. Turned off by his experiences with traditional advertising, Shimunov jumped at the chance to work with these clients. His coworkers, who preferred to work with paying clients, gave him their nonprofit projects as well.

These nonprofits were large, with advertising budgets that would dwarf the entire operating budgets of some of the organizations Shimunov works with today. And it was not necessarily these larger organizations that he was interested in.

In his advertising work for these organizations, Shimunov was introduced to the small organizations they sometimes worked with and provided grants to. He applied to one of those smaller organizations, and the rest is history.

Shimunov has used every tool at his disposal in his work. He has been in frontline protests, has worked behind prison walls, has infiltrated and sabotaged white supremacist groups. But time and time again he has turned to his artistic skills—to infiltrate institutions, to disrupt oppressive groups, and even to battle his own state governor. And when he shares stories of some of his use of art, I'm reminded that art is not just about symbolism or inspiration—it can also be a part of direct action.

In the few years before the 2022 election, there was a widespread campaign on New York City public transportation encouraging people to wear a mask and showing how to wear one properly in order to protect the community from COVID. The cheerful yellow and black posters showed simple drawings of subway riders wearing a mask in different ways, many incorrect. "Nope," "Not quite," "Try again," the poster said after each illustration of incorrect mask wearing. "That's the one!" the poster exclaimed next to the drawing of a subway rider wearing the mask over their nose and mouth. "Stop the spread. Wear a mask," it said at the bottom.

The goal of the posters was to encourage riders on the crowded subways to wear a mask for collective safety, in a way that wasn't too negative or preachy. But by 2022, the horrors of how brutally COVID-19 had hit New York City were no longer of political significance. Governor Kathy Hochul was running for reelection and was being challenged for that seat by Lee Zeldin—a right-wing congressman who was promising to end all COVID-19 mandates (Zeldin for New York, n.d.). In trying to appeal to more right-wing voters and undercut her opponent at a time when many were complaining of "COVID fatigue" (not fatigue from having COVID but fatigue over COVID concerns and safety practices), Hochul replaced the MTA posters with a new version.

"She turned that campaign on its face and actually mocked the campaign with a new campaign, using the same MTA budget that was supposed to be for COVID prevention," Shimunov says, his voice betraying the outrage he still carries.

The posters utilized the same simple yellow and black illustration style, and featured drawings of people wearing masks various ways, and then finally a drawing of someone not wearing a mask at all. Under each drawing, the wording simply said, "Yes." Except for under a drawing of a person wearing a mask just over their nose. Under that drawing it said, "You do you." At the bottom of the poster, instead of "Stop the spread. Wear a mask," it said, "Let's respect each other's choices."

To Shimunov and many others, these new posters were an insult to all of the work New Yorkers had put in to keep one another safe, and it made light of the continued need to try to prevent COVID infections in such a crowded city. Shimunov and Art V War sprung into action. If the Hochul administration could use the masking posters for their own political purposes, they would do the same with Hochul's posters.

"We made a guide using the same 'You do you' concept, to show people how to protect people who are beating the fare, how to beat the fare, how to open the door and keep the door open for others, how to distract the police when someone does it." Shimunov smiles.

They also used their posters to point out the absurdity of the "You do you" concept itself when it comes to issues of public health and safety. "It was summertime, so we turned it around on pools." Shimunov laughs. "So, you know, next time you come to a New York City pool, feel free to vomit, pee, and poop in these pools. You do you."

The graphics went viral, and when Art V War made them downloadable for people to print out on their own, others started putting them up around the subways.

The backlash to the "You do you" campaign, and the posters that were suddenly all over social media and on subways in response to the campaign, made headlines. As soon as the election was over and Hochul had secured her reelection, Shimunov says, the "You do you" posters that Hochul's administration had put up disappeared.

Activist art often faces down oppressive governments and systems. But sometimes it has to go head-to-head against "mainstream" art itself.

In 2018, US Customs and Border Protection officers deployed smoke grenades and tear gas against hundreds of Central American asylum seekers trying to cross the border into California. Photographs hit the news cycles showing the chaos and violence as people who were seeking nothing more than safety were instead attacked with toxic chemicals.

It was soon made public that the weapons used against the asylum seekers were manufactured by Safariland, a Florida-based company that has supplied weapons for use against protestors in Ferguson, Missouri, Standing Rock, the Gaza Strip, and more (Greenberger 2019). Safariland is owned by Warren B. Kanders, who was vice-chairman of the Whitney Museum of American Art's board of trustees. When this connection was revealed, many artists, staff, and community members were outraged. The group Decolonize This Place organized protests outside of the museum. Artists who were slated to participate in the Whitney Biennial demanded that their art be pulled if Kanders remained on the board.

It was said that it would be impossible to remove Kanders from the Whitney's board. He was too well known in the art world and had been on the board for fifteen years. He had also given over ten million dollars to the museum. The Whitney stood in support of their relationship with Kanders. And the hypocrisy of them doing so, especially in light of having recently been applauded for their exhibition of Indigenous Latine practices, motivated Shimunov to action.

While Decolonize This Place held protests outside, Shimunov looked to bring his protest inside.

He printed out photos of mothers and children choking on the tear gas that Kanders's business had made and sold to officers. "And all I did was take the photograph and stylize it in a way, and add oil paint to it as a layer," Shimunov shares. "And add this really gaudy frame around it."

He and two associates then scoped out the museum and found a spot on the fourth floor that was out of view of security cameras and rarely patrolled by staff. "It was just this vulnerable spot," Shimunov remembers. "And it was a beautiful big clear open wall."

Shimunov and his associates entered the museum and quickly hung the two pieces, along with a description matching the font used in the gallery. "The Whitney Museum of Art's Vice Chairman owns weapons manufacturers that supply Trump's attacks on families and children seeking asylum," it read. It then encouraged people to sign a petition calling on the museum to acknowledge that Mr. Kanders's "war and oppression profiteering is diametrically opposed to the values of the Whitney Museum," among other demands.

The petition gained over ten thousand signatures. In the months that followed, Decolonize This Place continued their protests and more artists demanded their work be pulled from the museum. Finally, in 2019, the impossible happened: Kanders resigned.

"The targeted campaign of attacks against me and my company that has been waged these past several months has threatened to undermine the important work of the Whitney," Kanders said in his announcement.

Our connection to art makes it a particularly potent form of protest. In looking back at his protest art at the Whitney, Shimunov reflects on how this protest was treated when it was on the walls of the Whitney versus what he had experienced in past protests. If he had walked into the museum holding up a sign in protest, he'd have likely been swiftly escorted out. Protest over.

But once it was discovered that his pieces on the wall didn't belong there, security wasn't sure what to do with them. "It was really remarkable," Shimunov says. "No one took [them] down. Even when the security found out, they didn't know what to do. They didn't want to damage [them]. Like, this was fake. But it had the right frames, and it had the right label. So it's art, and it's hanging in a museum."

Now in his mid-forties and a father of a teen daughter, Shimunov has shifted away from some of the more direct action of his younger years. You're less likely to find him wheatpasting or spray-painting protest messages in the dead of night or running from cops. "I can no longer, like, hang from a ceiling somewhere outside or from a light post," Shimunov confesses. "Or not sleep, or spend a night in jail, without affecting my family in a terrible way."

This doesn't mean that Shimunov's best years are behind him. Far from it.

It's true that he may not be able to stay on the front lines of protest actions like he used to. "But others can, and they do," he says. "And now I can support. Do the bailing out. Do the legal counseling. Do the creative collab. Tell them all the mistakes I made so they can avoid them. It's great. It's, like, almost illegal how fun it is. It feels illegal."

## BE A REVOLUTION

On Sunday, September 15, 1963, white supremacists bombed the 16th Street Baptist Church in Birmingham, Alabama, killing four Black children: Addie Mae Collins, Cynthia Wesley, Carole Robertson, and Carol Denise McNair.

When she heard about the murders, Nina Simone's first instinct was to grab a gun. She later said that her husband stopped her, saying, "Nina, you can't kill anyone. You are a musician. Do what you do" (Fields 2021).

"Mississippi Goddam" is perhaps the most powerful song I've ever heard in my life. Few pieces of art have affected me in so many ways at once. It is a song that I've turned to in my darkest times in this work. When I've needed an outlet for my rage or despair, when

I've needed to remember the strength that is our history and our legacy.

Written in under an hour, Nina Simone's song responding to the bombing at the church, as well as to the murders of Emmett Till and Medgar Evers, put a voice to the rage and heartbreak that, to many Black Americans, felt unspeakable.

> Oh, but this whole country is full of lies
> You're all gonna die and die like flies
> I don't trust you anymore
> You keep on saying, "Go slow."

You can hear her desperation and weariness as she tries to understand the continued apathy of whiteness toward the continued brutality against Black people.

> Why don't you see it?
> Why don't you feel it?
> I don't know,
> I don't know.

It's not just the words themselves. It's the background instruments conjuring the sounds of a Black church. It's Simone's crisp and clear and commanding voice. It's the smile you can hear in her voice as she says, "This is a show tune, but the show hasn't been written for it yet." It all combines to create a song so much greater than the sum of its parts, something that is, unfortunately, always speaking to a pain that is fresh and new.

Over the years, Simone would change the lyrics to reference different cities and states as the Black community found itself outraged and mourning more Black people brutalized and killed by violent white supremacy.

"An artist's duty, as far as I'm concerned, is to reflect the times," Simone explained of her work. "That to me is my duty" (Fields, 2021).

352 ➤ IJEOMA OLUO

Every activist I know in the struggle for liberation has a piece of
art that is their "Mississippi Goddam." The piece of art that can speak
for them when their own words fail.

Every person trying to survive these violent systems of oppression
has the song, the poem, the painting, that has reflected their pain,
their joy, their rage, their fear, when nothing else could.

Many of us can point to the art that has opened our eyes to issues
we weren't previously aware of, that has given us perspectives we
didn't previously have.

Many of us can point to the art that has helped us find the strength
to go on when we felt hopeless.

Perhaps the art that will do that for you or for your children or
for the person who will save your life, perhaps that art hasn't been
created yet.

If we want to ensure that it will be, we have to start treating art
and artists as indispensable parts of our struggle for freedom.

Here are some places you can start:

➤ **Support BIPOC-owned art spaces.** A lot of times when we think
about supporting BIPOC artists, we think of creating space and
opportunity for them within white arts structures, and the largest
white-led institutions swallow up 60 percent of all funding. But
these large institutions have no incentive to truly diversify their
mission, as the white-centered mission they've had continues to
pay them well. Their entire structure is built around whiteness,
and that's not something easily changed. Meanwhile, institutions
that make conscious efforts to serve communities of color are
neglected by funders, receiving a paltry 4 percent of arts funding
(Cunniffe 2018). Favianna Rodriguez stresses that we have to invest in institutions that are invested in us, instead of hoping that
larger institutions will change. "People don't realize just how powerful culture is, and how much vested interest there is in these
institutions to not change," she says. "We have to build alternatives. There are alternatives now, but over the next ten, twenty

years they're going to be very powerful institutions." Yet they'll only be powerful institutions if we support them. If we fund them, visit them, and spread the word about them.

➤ **Don't support arts institutions that don't support BIPOC artists.** As we saw earlier, many larger museums buy art almost exclusively from white artists. Many theaters almost exclusively debut plays by white playwrights, or directed by white directors. Why are we still giving them the majority of our arts spending?

➤ **Support racially informed and culturally competent arts education in K–12 schools.** This helps all students of all races and ethnicities, but especially students of color. A robust arts education is vital for all students, no matter what field they may want to go into in the future, but it's an education that our children of color are often denied.

➤ **Support BIPOC community-led arts education.** Yes, it's important to have robust and diverse arts education in schools, but it's also vital that we support the educators who have been working in our communities to keep our artistic traditions alive and who are often the standard-bearers of our artistic practices.

➤ **Support living wages for all arts workers.** Pretty much every artistic field (with the exception of fields like architecture and design) pay dismal wages for arts workers—if any wages at all. Arts workers deserve living wages, insurance, benefits, and protections that most other workers expect or are fighting for. And yet people often scoff at the idea of a musician who plays local gigs getting affordable dental coverage or sick pay. Arts workers are workers, not hobbyists. They deserve pay for their labor.

➤ **Buy art made by BIPOC artists.** Become a collector of BIPOC art by buying directly from BIPOC artists or BIPOC-owned galleries. A large part of what makes our house a home is the beautiful art, made by BIPOC artists, that hangs on just about every wall. We purchased a lot of it locally, and some of it in our travels, at widely varying prices. Some are large paintings we paid thousands of dollars for; others are small prints we paid twenty dollars for. But we were never in search of a "good deal," expecting BIPOC artists to charge less than their white peers. We bought what we love because we want to see it every day, at prices the artists thought were fair. And in return, not only do we have great beauty to gaze at every day; we also have a reminder of the vibrant communities we are lucky to be a part of.

➤ **Hire BIPOC artists.** Hire BIPOC artists for your design work, hire BIPOC photographers for your events, hire BIPOC entertainers for your parties. A lot of the gig work that helps artists get by goes to white artists first, and that makes a career in the arts much less sustainable for BIPOC artists. For our wedding, my partner and I tried to hire as many BIPOC artists as possible. We chose a Native-owned venue. My dress and his suit were made by BIPOC designers. Our photographer was Black, as were our wedding planner and floral designer. Our videographers were BIPOC, our DJs were Black, and so were our host and our caterer. All were artists and creatives from our community, and it made that hefty wedding bill feel a lot lighter knowing that those checks were supporting local BIPOC artists.

➤ **Pay arts activists.** That beautiful piece of graphic art you've been sharing on social media to show how down with the cause you are? There's a good chance a BIPOC artist made that. They deserve credit, and if you have a few bucks to put on their Venmo or Patreon, you really should. Wherever you engage with and benefit from protest art, it's important to remember the artist who made that, and the likely unpaid labor they put into it. Send them some dollars to let them know that you appreciate what they do.

➤ **Protect BIPOC artists and their art.** Why would the white art world pay for our art when they can so often steal it with little recourse? BIPOC art is stolen by individuals and corporations every day. And often the people stealing it are able to make money off of that art, or build an audience from it, to a de-gree that the original artist hasn't been able to. Always check the sources of your art, especially art that references BIPOC culture or struggle, or seems "influenced" by communities of color, and yet is being used by white individuals or corporations. Was credit given clearly? Did the original artist give permission? Know this before you give any reward or patronage to the entity that may have stolen it.

➤ **Demand that museums return stolen artifacts and remains to BIPOC communities, and pay restitution to the communities they have stolen from.** This one seems pretty simple. Millions of stolen artifacts and stolen human remains are in US museums to-day. These museums have not only robbed communities already devastated by white supremacy and colonialism; they have also made billions of dollars of profit from the thefts. It all needs to go back—all of it—and those who were stolen from need to be compensated.

➤ **Mentor young artists.** When I asked Rafael Shimunov what advice he'd give people who want to improve equity and access around art, he wanted his advice to go to seasoned artists and activists who use art: "Put out the word that you want to mentor. Put the word out that you want to show people the mistakes you made," he says with a laugh. "Or the things that you found successful. I used to feel powerful as an individual to go outside at night and put something up. And then have people talk about it the next day. Changing hearts and minds. But now when you see people—dozens of the people that you've worked with who are younger or newer to it—when you see them going out and doing things, and they're all doing it at the same time, and it's all multiplying . . . It's the most rewarding feeling ever. It's just such an amazing reward."

## A LIFE'S WORK

OFTEN WHEN PEOPLE THINK about movement work, they think of something they would only be able to do for a limited time, or under limited circumstances. You're either an ACTIVIST or you aren't part of the movement at all.

In many people's minds, movement workers can't have a job that isn't clearly a part of the movement, can't have kids or a family to care for, can't have vibrant social lives or hobbies that don't involve movement work.

"From when I was fourteen until I was about twenty-six, that was really my only understanding of organizing," Richie Reseda admits. "The only way that the world was gonna get fixed was if everybody took time out of their personal lives to go out and fix public problems. I'm not saying that's not true anymore; I'm just saying that was my only frame at the time. I had this idea that eventually there would be this revolution in which everybody's mind would be changed, and then we would change systems, and then we would all live in liberation. And I thought my job as a young organizer was to help us get closer to that moment, with every moment of my being."

People tell me all of the time that they wish they could "do something" about systemic racism, but they can't just quit their job and dedicate their lives to it. And there really is a common belief that this is what it takes. In order to be a part of a movement, you have to dedicate every part of your life to direct action, and if you're dedicated to it, you must stay dedicated to that same work forever.

This is a very limiting understanding of activism and movement work. Yes, there are certain types of movement work that look exactly how many expect them to look—the type of work that's often in the spotlight. Yes, some movement workers spend many of their days in protests, handing out fliers, wheatpasting posters on walls, shouting down police officers. And this is very important work that will always have a place in the struggle for liberation.

But as you have read in the stories shared in this book, the world of movement work is so much larger than the direct action that makes headlines.

In these pages you've seen people representative of much of the movement-work community I've known for decades. They're dedicated, longtime movement workers, and many of them do work that the majority of people have never heard of, and they've lived diverse lives—with families, friends, and careers they love.

Movement work has many beautiful rewards, and it's vital to our society. But it's in no way easy. Many people who start out in this work full of fire, swearing they'll keep up the fight forever, burn out quickly.

So what keeps some people in this work for a lifetime? In these conversations, and in my years of relationships with movement workers, I've noticed that while there is wide diversity in the work they do, there are some similarities in their paths through this work.

## Ages and Stages

Almost every seasoned movement worker I spoke with is doing different work from what they started out doing. Some are doing different jobs within the same movement; some are in different movements entirely.

The passage of time and the simple reality of aging can bring about some of these changes for a lot of people, especially those who got involved in this work in their teens or early twenties.

As we saw in the stories shared by Richie Reseda, Tarana Burke, and Chris Smalls, younger, newer movement workers often start with on-the-ground tasks and direct action. This work can be particularly well suited to younger people, who are likely to have more energy, may be more socially inclined, and in this day and age are more tech savvy.

Younger movement workers may feel they have less to lose from more direct, and often riskier, action and a lot more to gain, as they're looking at a longer future with these oppressive systems.

Younger workers are also likely to have less organizational experience than some (but not all) older movement workers. Many of them spend a lot of their early activist work doing the important job of learning from those who already spent a fair amount of time on the front lines.

Of the more seasoned movement workers I talked with, like Rafael Shimunov and Leah Lakshmi Piepzna-Samarasinha, several shared stories of their days spent running from cops, handing out fliers, or occupying buildings in protest.

But the risks and disadvantages of frontline work increase as we age. Many of us can't run from the cops like we used to. Hell, even canvassing around my neighborhood would be a much bigger ask of me and my knees now that I'm in my forties and well settled into my writer's bod than when I was in my twenties. We might have jobs that won't allow us a few days off to occupy a building. We may not be able to spend a night in jail if we have kids at home to take care of. As our responsibilities increase with age, the particular risks of direct action increases and can become untenable.

Now, in no way are these hard-and-fast rules. Plenty of people stay dedicated to this sort of work their entire lives. And it's not uncommon for lifelong movement workers who moved to more behind-the-scenes work in their late twenties or thirties to come back to direct action once they retire or their kids have moved out of the house.

Another factor that often shifts us into other movement work is that as we learn more, we can do more. Young movement workers may graduate into organizational strategy and leadership as they gain experience. That transition is vital for the health and longevity of our movements and has been a deliberate strategy of many organizations, as shown in Tarana Burke's stories of growing up with 21st Century Youth Leadership Movement and Mahnker Dahnweih's work with Freedom, Inc.

In addition, as we gain other life experiences, those experiences may pull us into other areas of movement work. And some of us may discover that the work we started out doing doesn't really align with our values like we once thought it did.

Nikkita Oliver first started their movement work at the Christian college they were attending. "I went to Seattle Pacific University thinking that I was going to be a missionary. Like, how colonial can you get?" Oliver remembers with a little laugh. But these goals started to shift during college, as Oliver interacted with more people from different backgrounds and with different beliefs.

After college, they started to really question the work they had started out doing. "When I graduated, I was working for a small Christian community development nonprofit that was doing work in the areas of education, economics, and health. And I started to see the limitations of that work when it was so deeply connected to an expectation that people would be proselytized to."

Oliver was also coming out of the closet with their own sexuality and gender identity, while the organization that Oliver worked for was putting up posters on the walls in defense of "traditional marriage," even though a lot of the young people coming into the space were queer and trans like Oliver.

Oliver left that space in search of others that would better fit who they are, and what they wanted to see in the world. What they found was work that has them still making revolutionary change almost fifteen years later.

## Ability and Privilege

Ability and privilege are two important factors in what movement work a person chooses to do. And these factors are likely to change over time.

For some, disability and access—or lack thereof—will steer work in a particular direction. I want to be clear here: disability itself is not often a limiting factor in the work, but ableism in society and in a lot of movements can be limiting for people with disabilities.

Many disabled activists are involved in direct actions, and many of the leaders of our movements are disabled. But for some, direct actions may be too risky. People who need sure access to medications or medical equipment may decide that a protest where protestors are likely to be arrested is too great a risk. Disabled people may also be at increased risk for police brutality at protests. Movement spaces, too, are not always made accessible, or are so ableist in nature as to not be safe for disabled movement workers to spend time in them.

But the lived experience of disability has unique value—value that disabled activists often utilize to the benefit of their work. Disabled movement workers I've talked with frequently shared how much better at organizing and leading they are than many non-disabled people. They're more inclined to find multiple ways to communicate with people, are used to looking for the people who are less likely to be invited into a room, and often have a more intersectional lens, which leads to a more whole revolutionary framework.

Others have learned how to integrate movement work into everything they do, because they've had to advocate for themselves in just about every space they're in. Disabled BIPOC movement workers often feel their entire existence is political and part of movement work, simply because they constantly have to battle oppressive systems just to live their lives.

For some people, this is a lifelong reality, but others will move in and out of disability or chronic illness throughout their lives. The more inclusive and disability-centered our movement work is, the more likely it is we'll be able to find a place in this important work.

Privilege and access can change over time, too. When either decreases, we're usually made aware of that pretty quickly, as we encounter new barriers or hardships because of it. But when our privilege, in particular, increases, it's very easy to be unaware of it. And that can damage our movement work. It's vital to notice changes and look for ways in which this may influence the work you're trying to do.

If you aren't sure how to go about this, here are some good questions to return to periodically:

- Do you have reliable transportation when you didn't before?

- Do you have reliable income or stable housing?

- Do you have the money for a lawyer?

- Do you have money for childcare?

- Do you have flexible work hours?

- Do you have more institutional power (work, church, government, community) than you once had?

- Do you have more connections than you once had?

- Do you have access to and the ability to pay for medical or mental health care?

- Has your formal education level changed in a way that may cause others to prioritize your viewpoints over others?

- Have you moved into a movement space that values a particular aspect of your identity (like race, skin tone, gender, sexuality, ability) over others in the room?

These are just some examples, but all of these questions can have an impact on what movement work you are able to do, and what movement work you should do.

## Navigating Privilege in Movement Spaces

One of the most common questions I'm asked by people of privilege who are trying to support the fight against systemic oppression is: "Where do I start?" My answer for many years now has been very straightforward—especially if you're outside of the particular group you want to support: "Give money if you have it, and give time if you don't."

This may seem overly simplistic, but the truth is that most BIPOC-led movement work is severely underfunded. If you have money to give to the people who are already out there doing great work, please give it and give it as directly as possible. The more funds that can go directly into the hands of people working and living in our communities, the better.

In the "Resources" section of this book, you'll find a lot of different organizations worthy of your financial support, but if you're looking to become more directly involved, it's vital that you try to be aware of your privilege as well as be careful to not allow that privilege to derail the work being done—especially if you're a white person entering this work.

Matt Remle has worked in environmental justice for decades, and in that time, he's seen the damage that can be caused when someone with unchecked privilege enters a BIPOC movement space.

For racially privileged individuals coming into racial justice and environmental justice work, Remle wants them to understand that the work they'll be entering into has been in progress for many years, even for multiple generations, and they shouldn't come into this work expecting to lead. Remle says, "Folks can be involved in supporting some of these strategies. They're not gonna lead it, but they can support. Our communities—we know what we're doing. We know what we're talking about. We know what works. Folks can support the work that we're doing but can't lead it."

For me personally, it's important to understand what my privileges mean in the different rooms that I'm in, and how those privileges have changed over time.

At protests, I'm often simply a Black woman in the crowd, and therefore very vulnerable to police violence. People with racial privilege in spaces around me should be aware of that, and should be using their privilege to protect those of us more at risk.

Standing at a podium, I'm someone with a lot of privilege while I'm there. All attention is on me, and many will take what I say to heart, and possibly use my words to represent organizations, movements, even my entire race. I have to be aware of the responsibility and the risks of this privilege. I have to be aware of how my words may have an impact on others who may never have their time at the podium and whose lived experiences I may not have the right to speak for.

With my Black peers, I can have more privilege due to my status as a writer and a speaker, and due to my lighter skin tone (especially if white people are present, because they really do tend to show a preference to people with any visual proximity to whiteness). But as a queer woman, I can have less privilege in male- and/or straight-dominated spaces.

As someone who now has class privilege, I have to be aware that I'm not in the same financial place that I was in for most of my life. And while I can empathize and clearly remember what decades of financial struggle feels like, that empathy should only serve as a reminder that I'm no longer qualified to be centered in conversations around economic justice, and that the work I do around that should primarily be to amplify and support those who are doing the day-to-day work.

These are just a few of the numerous privileges many of us have that we need to be aware of if we don't want to cause harm. But when people are activated by emotion over injustice, they often want to dive in headfirst without doing this important work.

After the 2016 presidential election, when Trump was voted into office, the political action organization Rafael Shimunov was working with at that time found itself flooded with volunteers. "We never had so many volunteers," Shimunov remembers. "They're literally breaking down our door, saying, 'How do I help?' It was so overwhelming. They came with their own talents, but they also came with their problems."

One volunteer, who had a lot of experience with technology and social media, wanted to drive more traffic to the organization's Instagram account. She decided to take matters into her own hands—but without first taking the time to assess her privilege.

"Basically, behind our backs, she designed a bot to auto-'like' any group that says, 'racial justice' or whatever."

The volunteer designed this bot in hopes of increasing engagement, which was her expertise. But organizing work was *not* her expertise, and putting forth such changes without consulting her team put the organization at risk.

"I was like, 'Okay, so what's gonna happen when a racist group on IG says "social justice"?'" Shimunov asked, pointing out that these sorts of bots could have their organization automatically liking racist and violent content.

Shimunov took the time to have a conversation with the volunteer around the problems that her rash actions could have caused, and luckily, she was open to having that discussion and learning from her mistakes.

"I'm glad we had that conversation," he says. "She, like, shifted and is an incredible asset to the movement and now part of it. But it could have gone sour, and it has gone sour in other ways."

## Mental Health and Well-Being

The number one reason why I see people transition into new roles in their movement work, and the number one reason why many movement workers are able to do this work for decades, is care for their own health and happiness. This is especially true for BIPOC in racial justice work.

We're trying to heal our society and our community, when we ourselves are often in most need of healing. And as we're all trying to do this work together—all traumatized in our own ways and all too busy doing this work to address our trauma—the personal difficulties of this work are compounded.

When Talila Lewis and I sat down to talk, Lewis was in a space where it was obvious that something needed to change.

"Ignoring the traumas we are enduring is not healing them, and it's not allowing our body, minds, spirits, hearts, to be at peace. In my case, I had stopped experiencing almost any amount of joy. For years. I stopped living. If you look at pictures, videos, webinars of me—I didn't wear any color. I wore the same outfit. And there's nothing wrong with that innately. But there is for me, because that is not my natural state. I'm very naturally flamboyant, colorful, out of the box." Lewis says, "Yeah, there was a lot of guilt. There was a lot of survivor's guilt for all of these years. I'm only just identifying it."

The urgency of this work can make us feel like we don't have time, or even the right, to care for ourselves. And this adds to messages that have long been sent by white supremacy, that we aren't worthy of care. It can make us feel like it's wrong to seek and feel joy or comfort.

Richie Reseda remembers his earlier thinking around movement work was very binary. "It was very 'oppressed' and 'not oppressed,'" he says. "I didn't understand healing justice. I didn't understand all this stuff about self-care. I didn't care about none of that. I ran myself into the ground every single day."

It took years, and the caring influences of his friends who wanted Reseda to be healthy and happy, to get him to appreciate how important healing was for his work.

As a writer who spends most of her days focused on issues of race and racism, I've often struggled with the guilt of the relative privilege that my work affords. And that guilt has made me reluctant to prioritize my own well-being.

Yes, I've spent the majority of my days for years now documenting violent white supremacy. Yes, this has brought cops to my door. This has brought bomb threats, rape threats, and more.

But I can afford to pay my bills and even take vacations. So many others doing this work cannot. And I'm not being kicked out of my home for this work, or taken off to jail—at least not yet.

It wasn't until 2022, when it got to the point that I couldn't write anymore—because my constant anxiety was preventing my brain from being able to focus enough to type a single sentence—that I started looking for a therapist in earnest.

I no longer feel guilty for the time and money I've spent to prioritize the therapy that is partially responsible for the book you're reading right now. But I'm also keenly aware that it is itself a privilege that many movement workers don't have.

Therapy is expensive and it takes a lot of time and energy. Further, finding a mental health practitioner who can understand our particular traumas is very difficult in a very white-dominated field. It took me months to find a Black queer therapist, and I was the last opening they had.

But even if we're able to get that help and care for our mental health, many of us still find that we need to transition into new phases of movement work as we grow and change.

The work we were doing before may no longer be appropriate for the skills, privileges, responsibilities, or interests we now have. The healing that we need to work on may require that we move in a different direction. It's important to listen to the different signals our bodies and minds send when it's time for us to move into different areas of work.

If you're BIPOC doing this work, remember that this work should serve you, as it serves your community. You're part of the community you're fighting for. Where can this work intersect with your joys and passions? Where can it utilize your skill set? Where can it grow skills that you want to acquire?

If the work harms you, it can't help others, because you're an important part of this work. You're an important part of the future that we're trying to build.

Finally, it's vital to our mental and physical health, and our ability to do effective long-term work, that we stay connected to others.

When I asked movement workers for what advice they'd give people who are new to this work, maintaining connections was one of the top recommendations.

Connection is often the first thing lost when we enter an unhealthy place in our movement work, and many of the people I spoke with had lost connection at some point in their journeys and had to work hard to restore it.

If we're doing this work for our communities, it's vital that we stay connected and accountable to our communities in order to stay relevant to the issues the community is facing and to not cause further harm.

It's often very clear what we're fighting against, the systems of oppression that are having an impact on our lives every day. But that isn't in itself motivating or guiding. Our communities are what we're fighting for, and it's our connection to community that will keep us going, and going in the right direction. I try to remember that if all my community gets from me is my struggle, they're not getting the best of me. They deserve my joy, and I deserve theirs.

It's also vital that we maintain relationships with people who know us outside of movement work, who can remind us that we're whole people with hobbies, quirks, and senses of humor. People we can be vulnerable with and people who can help us stay true to ourselves.

I've never met anyone who has been able to stay in this work for the long haul and done it on their own, without the support of community or family, at least not without causing a lot of damage to themselves and often to the movements they work in. Nobody should feel like the lone hero out in the world doing this work. We need one another—to keep us well, to keep us going, and to keep us accountable. So be intentional in cultivating and maintaining loving and supportive relationships. Give them the time and energy they need. Treat your relationships like the essential component to our collective survival that they are.

Many of the movement workers I spoke with talked about the people in their lives whom they can't imagine doing this work without.

For Mannie Thomas, his daughter is a constant reminder of the connections he needs to maintain. "I look at my daughter, and I'm like, 'This is what this is about,'" Thomas says. "The way that she can just be happy doing nothing. The way that her world is just, like, Mommy . . . Daddy. It reminds me of the connections that I'm supposed to have with my folks and my tribe, my people that I love and are closest to me. And the remembrance that shared energy brings joy and healing."

I don't know where I'll be ten years from now, as a writer or as a movement worker. I used to think I needed a clear road map to the years ahead, but so little about this work is predictable. This used to be very anxiety producing for me. (I'm a Capricorn in just about every sense of the word.) But as I've moved through various areas of this work over the years, I've embraced this unpredictability. The unpredictability of movement work is not uncertainty—it's actually the opposite. It's the certainty that no matter where you are in life, if you love people and care about injustice in the world, there will always be a place for you in this work.

I hope this book—my little piece of this work that you're reading right now—will help you find your place in this work, or get you on the path to finding it. I'm so grateful that this work has taken me to this space right here and now, where I have been able to share the amazing stories of all of these beautiful people with you, and I'm so excited to see where all of us go from here.

HERE ARE THE PEOPLE profiled in this book and ways that you can find and support their work, as well as some additional resources they have recommended to readers.

## Punishment, Accountability, and Abolition

### PEOPLE

Mahnker Dahnweih (she/her)—co-executive director of Freedom, Inc.; executive director of Freedom Action Now

Ian Head (he/him)—abolitionist; senior legal worker at Center for Constitutional Rights; co-editor of *The Jailhouse Lawyer's Handbook*; DJ; djianhead.bandcamp.com; social: @djianhead

Talila A. Lewis (no pronouns)—abolitionist; community lawyer; educator; organizer; movement strategist; co-founder and former director of HEARD; www.talilalewis.com; Instagram and Twitter: @talilalewis

Richie Reseda (he/him)—music and content producer; abolitionist; founder of Question Culture; www.questionculture.com; social: @richiereseda, @question.culture

Mannie Thomas (he/him)—co-executive director of Success Stories; social impact advisor for Inspire Justice; advisory board member of TPW; Instagram and TikTok: @prisonfeminism

## ORGANIZATIONS AND RESOURCES

Center for Constitutional Rights—ccrjustice.org

Detroit Justice Center—detroitjustice.org

Freedom, Inc.—freedom-inc.org; Instagram: @freedominc; Facebook: www.facebook.com/aboutfreedominc/

HEARD—behearddc.org; Instagram and Twitter: @behearddc

Inspire Justice—weinspirejustice.com

*The Jailhouse Lawyer's Handbook*—www.jailhouselaw.org

National Bail Out—www.nationalbailout.org

People's Paper Co-op—peoplespaperco-op.com

The Revolution Must Be Accessible! guide by HEARD—ASL: bit.ly /accessrevolutionASL; English: bit.ly/accessrevolution2; Spanish: bit.ly /revolucionacceso

Success Stories—www.successstoriesprogram.org; Instagram and TikTok: @prisonfeminism

Survived and Punished—www.survivedandpunished.org

Transform Harm—transformharm.org

## Gender Justice, Bodily Autonomy, and Race

### PEOPLE

Tarana J. Burke (she/her)—mother; author; founder of the Me Too movement; www.taranaburke.com; Instagram: @taranajaneen; Twitter: @taranaburke

Theryn Kigvamasud'vashti (she/her)—anti-violence activist and organizer; poet; adjunct professor at Seattle Central College; Twitter: @blackgothmommy; TikTok: @peanutbutterchocolatecake; Instagram: @evemariekmv

J. Mase III (he/him)—author; speaker; co-director of *The Black Trans Prayer Book*; jmaseiii.com; social: @jmaseiii

Emmett Schelling (he/him)—executive director of Transgender Education Network of Texas (TENT); www.transtexas.org; Twitter and Instagram: @transtexas

Norma Timbang (she/they/siya)—sole proprietor of New Transitions Consulting; lecturer at University of Washington School of Social Work

## ORGANIZATIONS AND RESOURCES

API Chaya—www.apichaya.org; Instagram and Twitter: @apichayasea; Facebook: www.facebook.com/apichayaseattle/

Black Feminist Future—blackfeministfuture.org

The Black Trans Prayer Book—theblacktransprayerbook.org

Black Women Radicals—www.blackwomenradicals.com

Call In Your People—www.callinyourpeople.org

Collective Justice NW—www.collectivejusticenw.org

Courage of Care—courageofcare.org

Deeds Not Words—deedsnotwords.com; Instagram: @deedsnotwords; Twitter: @deedsactionfund; Facebook: www.facebook.com/deedsnotwords/

House of Tulip—houseoftulip.org; Twitter and Instagram: @houseoftulipno; Facebook: www.facebook.com/houseoftulip/

Me Too movement Resource Library—metoomvmt.org/explore-healing/resource-library/

Native Women's Wilderness—www.nativewomenswilderness.org

SisterSong—www.sistersong.net; Instagram and Twitter: @sistersong_woc

Stop AAPI Hate—stopaapihate.org

Survived and Punished—survivedandpunished.org

Transgender Education Network of Texas (TENT)—www.transtexas.org; Twitter and Instagram: @transtexas; Facebook: www.facebook.com/transtexas/

Trans Justice Funding Project—www.transjusticefundingproject.org; Twitter and Instagram: @transjusticefp; Facebook: www.facebook.com/transjusticefundingproject/

## Hierarchies of Body and Mind: Disability and Race

### PEOPLE

Talila A. Lewis (no pronouns)—abolitionist; community lawyer; educator; organizer; movement strategist; co-founder and former director of HEARD; www.talilalewis.com; Instagram and Twitter: @talilalewis

Leah Lakshmi Piepzna-Samarasinha (she/they)—writer; disability and transformative justice movement worker; brownstargirl.org; Twitter: @thellpsx; Instagram: @leahlakshmiwrites; Facebook: www.facebook.com/leahlps/

Dr. Sami Schalk (she/her)—associate professor of Gender and Women's Studies at University of Wisconsin-Madison; Twitter: @drsamischalk; Instagram: @fierceblackfemme

Vilissa Thompson, LMSW (she/her)—founder and CEO of Ramp Your Voice!; social worker; speaker; writer; activist; rampyourvoice.com; Twitter and Instagram: @vilissathompson

Jennifer "Jen" White-Johnson (she/her)—disabled art activist and design educator; jenwhitejohnson.com; Instagram and Twitter: @jtknoxroxs

Britney R. Wilson (she/her)—associate professor of law and director of the Civil Rights and Disability Justice Clinic at New York Law School

Alice Wong (she/her)—founder of the Disability Visibility Project; author of *Year of the Tiger: An Activist's Life*; disabilityvisibilityproject.com; Twitter: @disvisibility; Instagram: @disability_visibility

## ORGANIZATIONS AND RESOURCES

Autistic Women & Nonbinary Network (AWN)—awnnetwork.org

Black Disabled Creatives—blackdisabledcreatives.com

Black Emotional and Mental Health Collective (BEAM)—beam.community

Critical Design Lab—www.mapping-access.com

Disability Visibility Project (DVP)—disabilityvisibilityproject.com

Disabled and Here—affecttheverb.com

The Disabled List—www.disabledlist.org

HEARD—behearddc.org

Living Altars—living-altars.com

National Alliance of Melanin Disabled (NAMD) Advocates—social: @namdadvocates

Sins Invalid—www.sinsinvalid.org

Society of Disabled Oracles—societyofdisabledoracles.com

## Race, Labor, and Business

### PEOPLE

Laura Clise (she/her)—founder and CEO of Intentionalist; Linkedin: www.linkedin.com/in/lauraclise/; Twitter and Instagram: @lauraclise

Richie Reseda (he/him)—music and content producer; abolitionist; founder of Question Culture; www.questionculture.com; social: @richiereseda, @question.culture

Christian Smalls (he/him)—president and co-founder of Amazon Labor Union; www.amazonlaborunion.org; Twitter: @shut_downAmazon; Instagram: @chris.smalls_

Tevita Uhatafe (he/him)—first vice president of Tarrant County Central Labor Council, AFL-CIO; vice president of Asian Pacific American Labor Alliance (APALA), AFL-CIO; madeintheusafilm.squarespace.com; Twitter: @tuhatafe; Mastodon: @tevitauhatafe@union.place

DarNesha Weary (she/her)—founder and CEO of Black Coffee Northwest and Grounded; Linkedin: www.linkedin.com/in/darnesha-weary-0b9635102/; Instagram and Twitter: @mrsweary; Facebook: www.facebook.com/darneshaw/

### ORGANIZATIONS AND RESOURCES

A. Philip Randolph Institute—www.apri.org; Facebook: www.facebook.com/a.philiprandolphinstitute/

Asian Pacific American Labor Alliance (APALA), AFL-CIO—www.apalanet.org

Black Coffee Northwest—www.blackcoffeenw.com; Instagram: @blackcoffeenw

For Everyone Collective—foreveryonecollective.com; social: @foreveryone.collective

Intentionalist—intentionalist.com; Twitter and Instagram: @intentionalist_

Labor Action Tracker—striketracker.ilr.cornell.edu

Labor Notes—www.labornotes.org

Question Culture—www.questionculture.com; social: @question.culture

## Race, the Environment, and Environmental Justice

### PEOPLE

Aja Barber (she/her)—sustainable fashion stylist and consultant; author of *Consumed: The Need for Collective Change: Colonialism, Climate Change, and Consumerism*; www.ajabarber.com; social: @ajabarber

Jill Mangaliman (she/they)—chairperson of GABRIELA Seattle; national secretariat of BAYAN-USA; Instagram: @gabrielaseattle

Matt Remle (he/him)—Indigenous movement worker; co-founder of Mazaska Talks; Instagram: @wakiyan7

Céline Semaan (she/they)—co-founder and executive director of Slow Factory; Instagram and Twitter: @celinecelines, @theslowfactory

### ORGANIZATIONS AND RESOURCES

GABRIELA Seattle—gabrielausa.org; social: @gabrielaseattle

Got Green—www.gotgreenseattle.org; social: @gotgreenseattle

Last Real Indians—lastrealindians.com

Mazaska Talks—mazaskatalks.org

Slow Factory—slowfactory.earth

Stop the Money Pipeline—stopthemoneypipeline.com

## Race, Education, and the Pedagogy of Our Oppressors

### PEOPLE

Feminista Jones (she/her)—author; educator; public speaker; www.feministajones.com

Saara Kamal (she/her)—Linkedin: www.linkedin.com/in/saaramkamal/

Nikkita Oliver (they/them)—artist; cultural worker; writer; organizer; former executive director of Creative Justice; co-executive director of the Detroit Justice Center; Instagram and Twitter: @nikkitaoliver

Jennifer "Jen" White-Johnson (she/her)—disabled art activist and design educator; jenwhitejohnson.com; Instagram and Twitter: @jtknoxroxs

## ORGANIZATIONS AND RESOURCES

Creative Justice—www.creativejusticenw.org

Educators for Anti-racism—www.edantiracism.com

Puget Sound Educational Service District, Educators of Color Leadership Community—www.diverseeducatorpathways.psesd.org/eclc

Sankofa Summer School—www.sankofasummerschool.com

Technology Access Foundation, Martinez Fellowship—techaccess.org/martinezfellows/

## Arts, Race, and the Creative Forces of Revolution

### PEOPLE

Favianna Rodriguez (she/her)—artist and activist; www.favianna.com; Instagram: @favianna1, @culturestrike

Rafael Shimunov (he/him)—artist; organizer; www.shmnv.com; Twitter: @rafaelshimunov; Instagram: @rafternoon

### ORGANIZATIONS AND RESOURCES

Art V War—Twitter and Instagram: @artvwar

Black Disabled Creatives—blackdisabledcreatives.com

The Center for Cultural Power—www.culturalpower.org; social: @culturestrike

Complex Movements—www.complexmovements.com; social: @cmplxmvmnts

Constellations Culture Change Fund and Initiative—www.constellationsfund.org

Sins Invalid—www.sinsinvalid.org

Wa Na Wari—www.wanawari.org; Facebook and Instagram: @wanawariseattle

## ACKNOWLEDGMENTS

T HIS BOOK WOULD NOT exist without the generosity of the movement workers who were willing to talk with me and share their stories and expertise. I know that time is a valuable resource, and trust is even more valuable, so to be given both is a rare gift that I will forever appreciate. Thank you to Richie Reseda, Mannie Thomas, Talila Lewis, Ian Head, Mahnker Dahnweih, Tarana Burke, Norma Timbang, Theryn Kigvamasud'vashti, Emmett Schelling, J. Mase III, Dr. Sami Schalk, Alice Wong, Vilissa Thompson, Britney R. Wilson, Leah Lakshmi Piepzna-Samarasinha, Chris Smalls, Tevita Uhatafe, Laura Clise, DarNesha Weary, Jill Mangaliman, Céline Semaan, Aja Barber, Matt Remle, Zharina Angeles Luna, Saara Kamal, Jennifer White-Johnson, Feminista Jones, Nikkita Oliver, Complex Movements, Inye Wokoma, Elisheba Johnson, Favianna Rodriguez, Rafael Shimunov, and maya finoh.

This book is, at its heart, about community. You can see in its stories what the love of community can do. It's, naturally, not a stretch to call this entire book a community project. I'm so blessed with community that was willing to sit down and talk with me, make introductions for me, and offer advice and other valuable support. And I'm so grateful to those I did not know before this project started, and who decided to trust me with their words.

My business manager, Ebony Arunga, has been with me through two books now, and she has kept our little ship afloat through some very rough waters. I'm so lucky to have you as a teammate. I also want to thank my research assistant, Tina Catania, for her amazing and thorough work yet again, and Amirah M., for her wonderful transcriptions of hundreds of hours of interviews. This book does not get done any time this decade without all of your work.

This is quite the project to embark upon with a new editor, but Rakesh Satyal took on this book with the perfect mixture of enthusiasm and calm that it needed. Thank you for helping me turn a mountain of ideas into something beautiful. Your guidance and expertise has made every page of this book better.

I've said before that I have absolutely the best literary agent in the business and, dammit, I'll say it again: Lauren Abramo is the best literary agent in the business. There is nobody in this industry I trust more. Thank you for your years of fierce advocacy, guidance, and friendship. You are absolutely never getting rid of me.

These past few years have been some of the most amazing of my life. They have also been some of the most brutal and traumatizing years of my life. I want to thank Dr. G for helping me to navigate it all and begin to work and write from a place of healing.

My sons, Malcolm and Marcus, have survived yet another round of book deadlines with me, and I'm pretty sure they still like me! How lucky am I? Kiddos: You remain my Reason Why for just about every good thing I do in this world, this book included. All I'm trying to do is create a world that is worthy of your beautiful hearts. Thank you for being who you are.

Gabriel: What can I say that I haven't said fifty times a day for the last five years? You are the most partnering partner who ever partnered. You were my first reader for every single page, the first person I turned to for advice, and my number one supporter throughout this entire process. And somehow, through it all, we've managed to smile and laugh every day. I love you to the ends of the universe, and I can't believe how lucky I am to be married to such an amazing person.

# WORKS CITED

Ahtone, Tristan, Lorena Allam, Leilani Rania Ganser, Kalen Goodluck, Brittany Guyot, and Anna V. Smith. 2020. "The Anti-Indigenous Handbook." Texas Observer. September 25, 2020. https://www.texasobserver.org/the-anti-indigenous-handbook/.

American Library Association. n.d. Unite Against Book Bans website. Accessed April 6, 2023. https://uniteagainstbookbans .org/.

American University. 2021. "Who Is Most Affected by the School to Prison Pipeline." School of Education online magazine. February 24, 2021. https://soeonline.american.edu/blog /school-to-prison-pipeline/.

Associated Press. 2022. "US Museums Return African Bronzes Stolen in 19th Century." NBC Washington. October 11, 2022. https://www.nbcwashington.com/news/local/us-museums -return-african-bronzes-stolen-in-19th-century-2/3179785/? _osource=SocialFlowTwt_DCBrand.

Atwater, Will. 2022. "Warren County Commemorates 40 Years of Environmental Justice Struggle." *North Carolina Health News*, September 21, 2022. https://www.northcarolinahealthnews .org/2022/09/21/warren-county-commemorates-40-years-of -environmental-justice-struggle/.

Behbahani, Simin. 1999. "It's Time to Mow the Flowers." In *A Cup of Sin: Selected Poems*. New York: Syracuse Univ. Press, 61.

Bellamy, Claretta. 2022. "Black Women Are Underserved When It Comes to Birth Control Access. The Roe Decision Could Make That Worse." NBC News. June 30, 2022. https://www .nbcnews.com/news/nbcblk/black-women-are-underserved -comes-birth-control-access-roe-decision-ma-rcna35924.

Bishara, Hakim. 2019. "Artists in 18 Major US Museums Are 85% White and 87% Male, Study Says." *Hyperallergic*, June 3, 2019. https://hyperallergic.com/501999/artists-in-18-major -us-museums-are-85-white-and-87-male-study-says/.

Blumenstein, Lindsey. 2009. "Domestic Violence Within Law Enforcement Families: The Link Between Traditional Police Subculture and Domestic Violence Among Police." Master's thesis, University of South Florida. https://digitalcommons .usf.edu/cgi/viewcontent.cgi?article=2861&context=etd.

Brockell, Gillian. 2022. "Harvard Has Remains of 7,000 Native Americans and Enslaved People, Leaked Report Says." *Washington Post*, June 2, 2022. https:www.washingtonpost .com/history/2022/06/02/harvard-human-remains -indigenous-enslaved/.

Buchholz, Katharina. 2023. "How Much Do U.S. Cities Spend on Policing?" Statista. February 6, 2023. https://www.statista.com /chart/10593/how-much-do-us-cities-spend-on-policing/.

Connelly, Eileen A. J. 2020. "Overlooked No More: Brad Lomax, a Bridge Between Civil Rights Movements." *New York Times*, July 8, 2020. https://www.nytimes.com/2020/07/08/obituaries /brad-lomax-overlooked.html.

Creative Justice. n.d. "Our Story: Mission." Accessed January 2023. https://www.creativejusticenw.org/cj-mission-vision.

Crowe, Becky, and Christine Drew. 2021. "Orange Is the New Asylum: Incarceration of Individuals with Disabilities."

*Behavior Analysis in Practice* 14: 387–95. https://doi.org /10.1007/s40617-020-00533-9.

Cunniffe, Eileen. 2018. "Why Do Art Funding Racial Disparities Remain So Stark?" *Nonprofit Quarterly*, June 26, 2018. https:// nonprofitquarterly.org/why-do-art-funding-racial-disparities -remain-so-stark/.

Dafoe, Taylor. 2021. "Arts Workers of Color in Los Angeles Earn 35 Percent Less in Wages Than Their White Colleagues, a New Study Finds." Artnet. May 18, 2021. https://news.artnet.com /art-world/bipoc-arts-workers-1970177.

Davis, Angela Y., Gina Dent, Erica R. Meiners, and Beth E. Richie. 2022. *Abolition. Feminism. Now.* Chicago: Haymarket Books.

Desai, Aditi. 2023. "Opinion: Why Environmentalists Should Oppose 'Cop City' and Defend the Atlanta Forest." State of the Planet (Columbia Climate School). February 24, 2023. https://news.climate.columbia.edu/2023/02/24/opinion-why -environmentalists-should-oppose-cop-city-and-defend-the -atlanta-forest/.

Disability Visibility Project. n.d. "About." Accessed January 17, 2023. https://disabilityvisibilityproject.com/about/.

Egan, Timothy. 1996. "Mail-Order Marriage, Immigrant Dreams and Death." *New York Times*, May 26, 1996. https://www .nytimes.com/1996/05/26/world/mail-order-marriage -immigrant-dreams-and-death.html?smid=url-share.

Elias, Marilyn. 2013. "The School-to-Prison Pipeline." *Learning for Justice*, Spring 2013. https://www.learningforjustice.org /magazine/spring-2013/the-school-to-prison-pipeline.

Fears, Darryl, and Brady Dennis. 2021. "'This Is Environmental Racism': How a Protest in a North Carolina Farming Town Sparked a National Movement." *Washington Post*, April 6, 2021. https://www.washingtonpost.com/climate-environment /interactive/2021/environmental-justice-race/.

Feinberg, Doug. 2022. "WNBA Players Say Life in Russia Was Lucrative but Lonely." CBC Sports. April 16, 2022. https://www.cbc.ca/sports/basketball/wnba-players-say-life-in-russia-was-lucrative-but-lonely-1.6421789.

Fernandez, Manny, and Mitch Smith. 2015. "Houston Voters Reject Broad Anti-discrimination Ordinance." *New York Times*, November 3, 2015. https://www.nytimes.com/2015/11/04/us/houston-voters-repeal-anti-bias-measure.html.

Fields, Liz. 2021. "The Story Behind Nina Simone's Protest Song, 'Mississippi Goddam.'" PBS: *American Masters*. January 14, 2021. https://www.pbs.org/wnet/americanmasters/the-story-behind-nina-simones-protest-song-mississippi-goddam/16651/.

Fleck, Anna. 2022. "Indigenous Communities Protect 80% of All Biodiversity." Statista. July 19, 2022. https://www.statista.com/chart/27805/indigenous-communities-protect-biodiversity/.

Greenberger, Alex. 2019. "After Months of Protests, Warren B. Kanders Resigns from Whitney Board." ARTnews. July 25, 2019. https://www.artnews.com/art-news/news/warren-kanders-resigns-whitney-13036/.

Harriet Tubman Collective. 2017. "Disability Solidarity: Completing the 'Vision for Black Lives.'" *Harvard Kennedy School Journal of African American Public Policy* (Spring 2017): 69–72. https://ccpep.org/wp-content/uploads/2021/04/Disability-Solidarity.pdf.

Hatch, Marcel. 1999. "Makah Tribal Whalers Deserve the Support of Global Environmentalists." Freedom Socialist Party. January 1999. https://socialism.com/fs-article/makah-tribal-whalers-deserve-the-support-of-global-environmentalists/.

Herskind, Micah. 2022. "Cop City and the Prison Industrial Complex in Atlanta." *Mainline*, February 7, 2022. https://www.mainlinezine.com/cop-city-and-the-prison-industrial-complex-in-atlanta/.

Ingraham, Christopher. 2020. "U.S. Spends Twice as Much on Law and Order as It Does on Cash Welfare, Data Show." *Washington Post*, June 4, 2020. https://www.washingtonpost.com/business /2020/06/04/us-spends-twice-much-law-order-it-does-social -welfare-data-show/.

Kaba, Mariame. 2021. *We Do This 'Til We Free Us: Abolitionist Organizing and Transforming Justice.* Chicago: Haymarket Books.

Kashwan, Prakash. 2020. "American Environmentalism's Racist Roots Have Shaped Global Thinking About Conservation." *The Conversation*, September 2, 2020. https://theconversation .com/american-environmentalisms-racist-roots-have-shaped -global-thinking-about-conservation-143783.

Kassutto, Maya. 2021. "Remains of Children Killed in MOVE Bombing Sat in a Box at Penn Museum for Decades." Billy Penn at WHYY. April 21, 2021. https://billypenn.com/2021/04/21 /move-bombing-penn-museum-bones-remains-princeton-africa /?utm_source=dlvr.it&utm_medium=twitter.

Kelly, Kevin D. 2022. "Florida's 'Stop WOKE' Act and Its Potential Impact on DEI Training." Locke Lord. May 2022. https://www .lockelord.com/newsandevents/publications/2022/05/floridas -controversial-stop-woke.

Kelly, Kim. 2022. *Fight Like Hell: The Untold History of American Labor.* New York: One Signal Publishers/Atria.

Kiernan, Tom. 2021. "2021 Most Endangered Rivers List Highlights Need for Environmental Justice." American Rivers. April 13, 2021. https://www.americanrivers.org/2021/04/2021 -most-endangered-rivers-list-highlights-need-for-environmental -justice/.

Klugman, Joshua. 2020. "Do 40% of Police Families Experience Domestic Violence?" Joshua Klugman Temple University website. July 20, 2020. https://sites.temple.edu/klugman

/2020/07/20/do-40-of-police-families-experience-domestic
-violence/.

Last Real Indians. 2020. "Makah Whaling and the Anti-treaty
Mobilization by Chuck Tanner." February 18, 2020. https://
lastrealindians.com/news/2020/2/11/makah-whaling-and
-the-anti-treaty-mobilization.

Lehrer-Small, Asher. 2023. "National Study Reveals 1 in 4 Teachers
Altering Lesson Plans Due to Anti–Critical Race Theory Laws."
The 74. January 25, 2023. https://www.the74million.org/article
/national-study-reveals-1-in-4-teachers-altering-lesson-plans
-due-to-anti-critical-race-theory-laws/.

Levine, Phillip, and Dubravka Ritter. 2022. "The Racial Wealth Gap,
Financial Aid, and College Access." Brookings. September 27,
2022. https://www.brookings.edu/blog/up-front/2022/09/27
/the-racial-wealth-gap-financial-aid-and-college-access/.

Loomis, Erik. 2018. *A History of America in Ten Strikes*. New
York: The New Press.

McGaughy, Lauren. 2019. "Texas Leads the Nation in Transgender
Murders. After the Latest Attack, the Dallas Trans Community
Asks Why." *Dallas Morning News*, September 30, 2019. https://
www.dallasnews.com/news/2019/09/30/texas-leads-nation
-transgender-murders-according-national-lgbtq-organization/.

Mervosh, Sarah. 2023. "Florida Will Review Social Studies
Textbooks for 'Prohibited Topics.'" *New York Times*,
March 16, 2023. https://www.nytimes.com/2023/03/16/us
/florida-textbooks-african-american-history.html.

Milkman, Ruth. 2022. "The Amazon Labor Union's Historic
Breakthrough." *Dissent*, April 8, 2022. https://www.dissent
magazine.org/online_articles/the-amazon-labor-unions-historic
-breakthrough?campaign_id=129&emc=edit_jbo_20220423
&instance_id=59312&nl=jamelle-bouie&regi_id=165306273

&segment_id=90089&te=1&user_id=dc0c210fcd06d01de5efd0
a7d3c7003e.

Morris, Monique W. 2018. *Pushout: The Criminalization of Black Girls in Schools*. New York: The New Press.

Nellis, Ashley. 2021. *The Color of Justice: Racial and Ethnic Disparity in State Prisons*. Washington, DC: Sentencing Project. https://www.sentencingproject.org/reports/the-color -of-justice-racial-and-ethnic-disparity-in-state-prisons-the -sentencing-project/.

Nguyen, Jeremy K. 2022. "Racial Discrimination in Non-fungible Token (NFT) Prices? CryptoPunk Sales and Skin Tone." *Economics Letters* 218, no. 5: 110727. https://www.sciencedirect .com/science/article/abs/pii/S016517652200252X.

Office of Legacy Management. n.d. "Environmental Justice History." Department of Energy. Accessed March 2, 2023. https://www.energy.gov/lm/environmental-justice-history.

Owens, Jayanti. 2022. "Double Jeopardy: Teacher Biases, Racialized Organizations, and the Production of Racial/Ethnic Disparities in School Discipline." *American Sociological Review* 87, no. 6: 1007–48. https://journals.sagepub.com/doi/10.1177/0003 1224221135810.

Peisner, David. 2023. "Little Turtle's War." *Bitter Southerner*, January 20, 2023. https://bittersoutherner.com/feature/2023 /little-turtles-war-cop-city-atlanta.

Perry, Andre M., Molly Kinder, Laura Stateler, and Carl Romer. 2021. "Amazon's Union Battle in Bessemer, Alabama Is About Dignity, Racial Justice, and the Future of the American Worker." Brookings. March 16, 2021. https://www.brookings.edu/blog/ the-avenue/2021/03/16/the-amazon-union-battle-in-bessemer- is-about-dignity-racial-justice-and-the-future-of-the-american- worker/.

Pevar, Stephen. 2014. "Why Are These Indian Children Being Torn Away from Their Homes?" ACLU: News & Commentary. July 23, 2014. https://www.aclu.org/news/racial-justice/why -are-these-indian-children-being-torn-away-their-homes.

Plachta, Ari. 2022. "Gavin Newsom said he would give land back to Native Americans in California. Has he?" *The Sacramento Bee*, August 19, 2022. https://www.sacbee.com/news/politics -government/article264454331.html.

Project Prevention. n.d. "Frequently Asked Questions—Children Requiring a Caring Community." Accessed December 12, 2022. https://www.projectprevention.org/faq/.

Ramadan, Lulu, Ash Ngu, and Maya Miller. 2021. "The Smoke Comes Every Year. Sugar Companies Say the Air Is Safe." ProPublica. July 8, 2021. https://projects.propublica.org/ black-snow/.

Resendes, West. 2020. "Police in Schools Continue to Target Black, Brown, and Indigenous Students with Disabilities. The Trump Administration Has Data That's Likely to Prove It." ACLU: News & Commentary. July 9, 2020. https://www.aclu. org/news/criminal-law-reform/police-in-schools-continue-to- target-black-brown-and-indigenous-students-with-disabilities- the-trump-administration-has-data-thats-likely-to-prove-it.

Robinson, Britany. 2021. "A Whale of a Controversy." *Sierra*, May 11, 2021. https://www.sierraclub.org/sierra/whale -controversy.

Sainato, Michael. 2020. "'I'm Not a Robot': Amazon Workers Condemn Unsafe, Grueling Conditions at Warehouse." *The Guardian*, February 5, 2020. https://www.theguardian.com /technology/2020/feb/05/amazon-workers-protest-unsafe -grueling-conditions-warehouse.

Schuba, Tom. 2021. "86% of Alerts from City's Gunshot Detection System Led to 'Dead-End Deployments,' Researchers Find."

*Chicago Sun-Times*, May 3, 2021. https://chicago.suntimes.com /crime/2021/5/3/22416397/chicago-gunshot-detection-system -dead-end-deployments-macarthur-justice-center.

Schwartz, Sarah. 2023. "Map: Where Critical Race Theory Is Under Attack." Education Week. March 23, 2023. https://www.edweek .org/policy-politics/map-where-critical-race-theory-is-under -attack/2021/06.

Silliman, Jael, Marlene Gerber Fried, Loretta Ross, and Elena R. Gutiérrez. 2016. *Undivided Rights: Women of Color Organize for Reproductive Justice.* Chicago: Haymarket Books.

Snowden, Brandi, and Nadia Evangelou. 2022. "Racial Disparities in Homeownership Rates." National Association of Realtors. March 3, 2022. https://www.nar.realtor/blogs/economists -outlook/racial-disparities-in-homeownership-rates.

Teach.com. 2022. "How to Support Teachers of Color." April 21, 2022. https://teach.com/resources/how-to-support-teachers -of-color/.

Technology Access Foundation. n.d. "Martinez Fellowship." Accessed December 2012. https://techaccess.org/martinez fellows/.

Thomas, Michael. n.d. "Environmental Nonprofits Receive Less than 2% of Charitable Donations." Carbon Switch. Accessed March 3, 2023. https://carbonswitch.com/analysis-of -environmental-giving/.

Topaz, Chad M., Jude Higdon, Avriel Epps-Darling, Ethan Siau, Harper Kerkhoff, Shivani Mendiratta, and Eric Young. 2022. "Race- and Gender-Based Under-Representation of Creative Contributors: Art, Fashion, Film, and Music." *Humanities and Social Sciences Communications* 9, no. 221. https://doi.org/10 .1057/s41599-022-01239-9.

UNCF. n.d. "K-12 Disparity Facts and Statistics." Accessed May 13, 2023. https://uncf.org/pages/k-12-disparity-facts-and-stats.

Vega, Cecilia M. 2003. "Sterilization Offer to Addicts Reopens Ethics Issue." *New York Times*, January 6, 2003. https://www.nytimes.com/2003/01/06/nyregion/sterilization-offer-to-addicts-reopens-ethics-issue.html.

Vera Institute of Justice. 2020. "What Policing Costs: A Look at Spending in America's Biggest Cities." June 2020. https://www.vera.org/publications/what-policing-costs-in-americas-biggest-cities.

Wa Na Wari. n.d. "CASE 21." Accessed May 1, 2023. https://www.wanawari.org/cace21.

Weil, Elizabeth, and Mauricio Rodriguez Pons. 2021. "Postcard from Thermal: Surviving the Climate Gap in Eastern Coachella Valley." ProPublica. August 17, 2021. https://www.propublica.org/article/postcard-from-thermal-surviving-the-climate-gap-in-eastern-coachella-valley.

Wildeman, Christopher, Frank R. Edwards, and Sara Wakefield. 2020. "The Cumulative Prevalence of Termination of Parental Rights for U.S. Children, 2000–2016. *Child Maltreatment* 25, no. 1: 32–42. https://journals.sagepub.com/doi/10.1177/1077559519848499.

Wilkinson, Eric. 2021. "Makah Tribe Wins Legal Battle in Seattle over Whale Hunting Rights." King 5 Television. September 24, 2021. https://www.king5.com/article/tech/science/environment/makah-tribe-wins-legal-battle-over-gray-whale-hunting/281-bdebcb11-ac82-4f5a-92aa-b4be84aa6ad2.

Wilson, Valerie, and William Darity Jr. 2022. "Understanding Black-White Disparities in Labor Market Outcomes Requires Models that Account for Persistent Discrimination and Unequal Bargaining Power." Economic Policy Institute. March 25, 2022. https://www.epi.org/unequalpower/publications/understanding-black-white-disparities-in-labor-market-outcomes/.

Women of Color Network. 2006. "Facts & Stats Collection: Domestic Violence, Communities of Color." June 2006. https://womenofcolornetwork.org/docs/factsheets/fs_domestic-violence.pdf.

Yeung, Bernice. 2018. *In a Day's Work: The Fight to End Sexual Violence Against America's Most Vulnerable Workers*. New York: The New Press.

Youth.gov. n.d. "Child Welfare." Accessed May 20, 2023. https://youth.gov/youth-topics/lgbtq-youth/child-welfare.

Zeldin for New York. n.d. "Defending Your Freedoms." Accessed May 2, 2023. https://zeldinfornewyork.com/freedoms/.